STAR OF INDIA

STAR OF INDIA

The Spicy Adventures of Curry

Jo Monroe

WILEY

Published in 2005 by	John Wiley & Sons, Ltd, The Atrium, Southern Gate Chichester, West Sussex, PO19 8SQ, England Phone (+44) 1243 779777
Copyright © 2004	Jo Monroe

Email (for orders and customer service enquiries): cs-books@wiley.co.uk
Visit our Home Page on www.wiley.co.uk or www.wiley.com

This publication is designed to provide accurate and authoritative information in regard to the subject matter covered. It is sold on the understanding that the Publisher is not engaged in rendering professional services. If professional advice or other expert assistance is required, the services of a competent professional should be sought.

Jo Monroe has asserted her right under the Copyright, Designs and Patents Act 1988, to be identified as the author of this work.

Other Wiley Editorial Offices

John Wiley & Sons, Inc. 111 River Street, Hoboken, NJ 07030, USA

Jossey-Bass, 989 Market Street, San Francisco, CA 94103-1741, USA

Wiley-VCH Verlag GmbH, Pappellaee 3, D-69469 Weinheim, Germany

John Wiley & Sons Australia, Ltd, 33 Park Road, Milton, Queensland, 4064, Australia

John Wiley & Sons (Asia) Pte Ltd, 2 Clementi Loop #02-01, Jin Xing Distripark, Singapore 129809

John Wiley & Sons Canada Ltd, 22 Worcester Road, Etobicoke, Ontario, Canada, M9W 1L1

Wiley also publishes its books in a variety of electronic formats. Some content that appears in print may not be available in electronic books.

British Library Cataloguing in Publication Data
A catalogue record for this book is available from the British Library

ISBN 0-470-09187-8

Typeset in 11/14 Photina by Mathematical Composition Setters Ltd, Salisbury, Wiltshire
Printed and bound in Great Britain by T.J. International Ltd, Padstow, Cornwall

This book is printed on acid-free paper responsibly manufactured from sustainable forestry in which at least two trees are planted for each one used for paper production.

10 9 8 7 6 5 4 3 2 1

For Elsie and Gordon Thomas

Contents

Author's Note

*T*here are two important words I use in this book which are poor but convenient labels, and as they get used on practically every page I would like to explain my use of them at the outset. The first troublesome word is in fact 'curry' which, as we shall see, is a disputed and inadequate catch-all for a vast and varied cuisine. In this book it is used to describe either an individual meal, an entire cuisine or a cultural phenomenon. I hope it is clear in each case which meaning is intended.

The other word is 'India' and its derivatives. Before British rule, India did not exist as a nation state: it was a collection of provinces and states that had both alliances and divisions. After British rule it became three countries – India, Pakistan and, later, Bangladesh. Consequently, at times I have found it easier to refer to the cuisine of the entire subcontinent as 'Indian'. I have felt encouraged to do so because so many of the Bangladeshi and Pakistani chefs who opened the early curry houses in Britain also chose the label 'Indian' for their food, even though the dishes they prepared were specialities of their homelands.

Introduction

*W*hen the Cinnamon Club opened in London's Old Westminster Library in 2001 it was hailed as the most expensive Indian restaurant in the world. Its menu featured the best of Indian cookery combined with unprecedented levels of service, a sophisticated wine list and a demure yet refined ambience that attracted cabinet ministers, lobbyists and political correspondents. It was one of a new breed of upmarket Indian restaurants in London that benefited from the Brits' famous love of curry while simultaneously trying to turn their understanding of Indian food on its head. The Cinnamon Club was both the scion of the traditional curry house and also its destroyer.

The press were duly invited to experience this new dining experience, but after sampling its exquisite food, the food critic for the *Telegraph* walked up to the proprietor and said: 'You know, Iqbal, we English just don't want all this fancy stuff from curry.'

This off-the-cuff remark highlights the almost pathological affection Brits have for curry: we love it, we are comforted and challenged by it and somehow, for some reason, we also feel a sense of ownership over it. There was a point in the 1980s or 90s when we recognised that the flocked-wallpaper-and-vindaloo experience of the local curry house was as British as a bulldog or a day at the Henley Regatta. It had become a tradition, one we would defend from the forces of change. It had become a phenomenon worthy of research and record.

There can't be a better example of how curry became fused with British identity than a song written to support the England football team, called 'Vindaloo'. I remember being in Paris in the summer of 1998 during the World Cup and watching the England v. Tunisia match on a TV in the corner of a bar. Unfortunately, the rioting after the match proved more memorable than the game.

The scenes on the TV from outside the stadium in Marseilles were shameful: cafés were ransacked, windows were broken and cars were kicked in as regiments of thugs squared off. At one point, I remember, the cameras focused on one particular group of England supporters who taunted Tunisian fans with a most unusual battle cry: 'Vindaloo, vindaloo, vindaloo!' I didn't think much of it until the Parisian barman asked me what the fans were saying.

'It's a type of curry,' I said.

'Like Indian food?'

'Yes.'

'But why,' he asked reasonably, 'would they be saying that?' This book is my belated attempt to give him an answer.

I realised that it wasn't enough to tell him that a novelty single had been released with the aim of creating a new anthem for the terraces: I wanted to explain to him why 'Vindaloo' was, bizarrely, an *entirely apt* chant for English football thugs. My answer needed to explain how curry had gone from being a fabled, exotic dish associated with spice

2

traders and the British Empire to being synonymous with yobbery. 'Vindaloo' was a reminder that England, and Britain, had been both welcoming of immigrants and transformed by them. But while it was a celebration of Britain's multiculturalism it was also a taunt to less tolerant nations chanted by men who had no idea that the song's authors were, in all probability, gently taking the piss out of them for being nationalistic. The more I thought about it, the more I wanted to understand how curry had come to be so much more than a meal to the British.

Over the course of researching the bizarre path curry took from being the food of an Imperial colony to conquering the Imperial palate, I have found that if you look very, very closely at any curry put before you, you can see more than just the ingredients used to make your meal: you can see history. Every chicken tikka masala is more than a mix of poultry, spices, vegetables and cream – it can also be a teacher, imparting knowledge of the ancient trade in spice, Columbus's transatlantic expeditions, the days of Empire, the ingenuity of immigrants and the myths we Brits tell ourselves about what it means to be British.

Of course every meal tells a story: the history of fish and chips, for example, involves such unrelated yet awesome tales as the discovery of the Americas, the depletion of North Sea cod stocks and the potent alchemy of salt and vinegar. But, by my reckoning, the history of curry is more mind-blowing than any other meal you've ever tasted (even more mind-blowing, perhaps, than the 'bucket of vindaloo' of the football chant). The ingredients in your average takeaway are about as weird and beautiful as life gets, and the journey curry took to reach our tables is an epic ripe for the Kirk Douglas treatment. Some spices, like star anise, are so refined and complex they could be evidence of a deity; indeed, many are featured in ancient Hindu Vedas and used in worship. Others, like saffron, have a beauty more delicate than the love of your life while some breathe the fire of the Furies. When you start to consider how some spices were discovered, curry becomes even more remarkable: for instance, how did anyone come up with the idea of opening up nutmegs and separating the red aril fronds inside – mace – from the nut? And then think about how spices are prepared: roasted, ground and blended, surely by the hands of magicians.

While curry in its natural habitat is momentous enough to warrant a biography, its journey to every corner of the world – conquering seas, hearts and indigenous cuisines along the way – makes it the most remarkable food on the planet. I wanted to find out how curry got from the kitchens of India to every high street in Britain. And why Britain? Why didn't India's other colonial conquerors like France, Portugal and the Netherlands end up with a similar curry culture? Why did the Brits, a nation famed for a love of bland food, end up with chicken tikka masala being hailed as their favourite dish? And when I found out that chicken tikka masala *isn't* actually Britain's favourite dish – it isn't even close – I needed to know why we hold on to that myth with such tenacity: why do we like the idea of curry being *ours* so much?

As I started my research more questions materialised that demanded answers. Questions like how you got hold of cardamom in Glasgow in the 1880s. What was it like to be the only Asian family in a small village in the 1960s? Why are so many restaurants always empty and yet never go out of business? How did Indian cuisine – as vast and varied as the country of its origin – end up in restaurant after restaurant as regimented and branded as McDonalds without a master plan or billion-dollar marketing deal? And, crucially, where did that wallpaper come from? I had to find out.

PEPPER

Without a doubt, pepper is the world's most widely used spice and is therefore in possession of a fiery history to match its taste. Black peppercorns are the dried berries of a climbing evergreen vine that is indigenous to southern India; they are picked unripe and left to dry in the sun. The same vine also produces white peppercorns: these are produced from the ripe, scarlet berries which are soaked to remove the skins and reveal the seeds which are then bleached by the sun. White pepper is

milder than black pepper, and green pepper – produced from immature berries and freeze-dried or pickled while fresh – is milder still. (Pink peppercorns come from a different species.) Of the many varieties of pepper, the most prized varieties of Piper nigrum are the Telicherry and the Malabar, both from southern India.

The Roman historian Pliny the Elder was not much impressed by pepper. He wrote in his Natural History: 'Some foods attract by their sweetness, some by their appearance, but neither the pod [a reference to long pepper, a related species] nor the berry of pepper has anything to be said for it. We only want it for its bite – and we will go to India to get it ... we value it in terms of gold and silver.' There are even records to show that the Caesars stored peppercorns in their treasuries and were often been carried by sailors and traders as an international form of currency. As well as being used as cash, peppercorns were also used as one of the lightest measures in the Indian system of weights.

Whoever controlled the ancient pepper trade commanded the earth, and it is because of this that pepper is often described as the 'spice that changed the world'. The lust for pepper drove Europe into the so-called Age of Discovery in which Columbus set sail for the East and found what we now call America. It wasn't until Columbus's famous journey that Europe discovered the chilli, which was transported to India where it flourished – both in the soil and in the cuisine. Before the fifteenth century the heat we associate with Indian food came mostly from black peppercorns with a little help from mustard seeds. Pepper is usually ground but is sometimes infused in oil to release a more subtle flavour.

In Medieval Europe black pepper was also used to preserve meat when animals were slaughtered at the onset of winter –

(there was not enough feed to maintain summer levels of livestock so beasts were slaughtered en masse). In addition to its culinary and preservative uses, pepper is thought to have several medicinal properties and is an important balancing agent in an Ayurvedic diet. It is said to aid coughs and colds, control hiccups and mitigate flatulence. It is also thought to stimulate the muse in artists!

It is now so widely used a general seasoning — even roadside truck stops and greasy spoons put pepper on the table — that most modern diners are unaware of pepper's epic history. This is a shame, as it is one of the most remarkable things in everyone's home.

CHAPTER ONE

The Lust for Spice

An Ancient Trade

*T*he story of curry, like curry itself, starts with spice.

For millennia spices have had a hold on man matched only by gold and beauty. Spices, and man's quest for them, have changed fortunes, lives and history – without the lure of spice Columbus would not have discovered America, Britain would not have acquired an Empire and your local high street would be missing a curry house or two. To fully appreciate the true brilliance of curry and its journey, you must first understand the power and consequence of spice.

Throughout the ancient world spices from India were prized for their flavour, aroma and therapeutic properties. They were used not just in cooking, but in perfumes and medicines and for embalming the dead. Some were even used as currency and as an early form of traveller's cheque: therefore, whoever controlled the spice trade also commanded power, influence and money. And whoever presented their guests with a meal seasoned with the flavours of the East was, in consequence, considered a great and generous person. For thousands of years, the host who prepared what we now call curry was considered closer to the gods than other mortals because spice has magical, as well as culinary, powers.

Regardless of any proven chemical power a spice may possess – with an ability to affect our mood, appetite or wellbeing – I came to realise that the magical property of spice really comes from the legends, some rooted in truth, others in fancy, which have wrapped themselves around the facts like a pepper vine on a nutmeg tree.

Take cinnamon, for example. To the modern palate it is a mild spice with a slightly sweet aroma and a dry, tart taste. To the ancients, however, the quills that we buy without much thought in the supermarket were so legendary that it was as if they were made by the gods. Here, the Greek historian Herodotus recalls a most fanciful tale told to him by a fifth-century BCE Persian spice trader:

Where the wood grows, and what country produces it, they cannot tell. Only some, following probability, relate that it comes from the country in which Dionysus was brought up. Great birds, they say, bring the sticks that we Greeks, taking the word from the Phoenicians, call cinnamon, and carry them up into the air to make their nests. These are fastened with mud to a sheer face of rock, where no foot of man is able to climb. So the Arabians, to get the cinnamon, use the following artifice. They cut all the oxen and asses and beasts of burden that die in their land into large pieces, which they carry with them into those regions, and place near the nests. Then they withdraw to a distance, and the old birds, swooping down, seize the pieces of meat and fly with them up to their nests, which, not being able to support the weight, break off and fall to the ground. Then the Arabians return and collect the cinnamon, which is afterwards carried from Arabia into other countries.[1]

Surprisingly, Herodotus – presumably a wise and learned man – didn't turn around and say 'You're pulling my leg, mate' (in fact, he goes on to recall an even more perverse story about a putrid aromatic harvested from billy goats' beards). This begs the question of why our forefathers were willing to believe such preposterous stories. In a time when tales of the Olympian gods had Zeus morphing himself into a swan or turning Orion into a constellation, a tall story from a travelling salesman about giant birds and ox limbs might not have seemed impossible. What is truly surprising, however, is that Herodotus's story still had some currency a thousand years later.

There are a number of factors that seem to have contributed to the fertile ground in which spice myths flourished for so long. The first thing to consider is that such stories allowed traders to keep prices high: if they convinced gullible customers that they could actually taste the danger imbued into every cinnamon quill, then they could charge a premium for being daring. And as very, very few people ever travelled further than the next village – even the aristocracy were unlikely to leave the villas and walled cities they secluded themselves in – very few were ever able to gather enough evidence to contradict the salesman's pitch.

Some historians have also proposed that the lack of international travellers secured the appeal of spice for another reason: instead of bragging about visiting some remote part of Cambodia or trekking across an obscure African plain as today's jet-setters do, world tours

[1] Herodotus, *Histories*, Book III.

were taken in the kitchen and the host who put something on his guests' plates that they had never tasted before was deemed as adventurous and worldly as Arctic holidaymakers are today. In addition, it was the very culture of excess and overindulgence by the aristocracy that kept the spice traders in business: conditions caused by opulence – gout, indigestion, flatulence, hangovers – could all be treated by a variety of different spices (the Romans, for instance, believed that putting saffron in their pillows would mitigate the morning-after effects of too much wine).

A more practical reason why spices held on to their mystery for such a long time was that they travelled far more easily than they could be transplanted. Unlike many herbs and vegetables that needed to be used fresh and were therefore grown locally, spices were unwilling accomplices that would not grow in the gardens of Athens and Rome as imported green-leafed herbs had done. Without the right soil and the correct amount of monsoon rain, spices simply refused to grow: it was as if they'd formed a union and agreed they couldn't possibly lower their standards to European levels. Spices, it turned out, were soil snobs and members of a climate clique; it was this uppity nature that kept the spice trade in business. As we will see shortly, many attempts were made to cut out the middlemen and grow pepper, turmeric, fenugreek and the like in Europe before the advent of the heated glasshouse, but none were successful. Luckily for ancient traders this meant they could carry on importing and exporting for generations, as dried spices could usually remain happily in transit for many months before there was any appreciable loss of quality.

Perhaps the most obvious reason why spices retained their magic was, of course, the flavours they released. As you feel the heat of pepper on your tongue, or the sharpness of fenugreek in your nostrils, you somehow know that the spice is *doing* something to you. You can *feel* spice as well as taste it. Spices might not quite be opium, but the affects they have on both stomach and heart have encouraged us to feel their exoticism. They do not fill you up like grains or meat, but they certainly fill your senses. Even though today we understand the chemistry of spice (so, of course, did the ancient Indians: they called it Ayurveda, of which there is more in the next chapter), that physical response – the ability to overpower and assault our senses – is still surely part of the appeal of curry. It's not surprising then that history is dotted with fragments of information about our ancestors' obsession with spices, and meals that benefited from their inclusion.

The earliest written record of such a meal – that we know of – comes from Babylonian stone tablets dated *c.* 1700 BCE and engraved in a cuneiform script with a recipe for meat in a spicy sauce served with bread. However, the earliest archaeological evidence we currently have for a curry-like mix of spices being consumed comes from excavations in the ancient cities of Harpatta and Mohenjo-Daro along the Indus valley in modern Pakistan. There, millstones have been found with traces of mustard seed, cumin, saffron, fennel and tamarind still on them. As these spices are still used in many modern curries, I've found it impossible not to wonder how closely the food might have resembled the menus of high street takeaways – but as no recipes survive, this is just idle speculation ...

The Judaeo–Christian Bible is another ancient source of tales about the spell spice cast over our forefathers, and some of them are the most famous stories ever told. The Queen of Sheba paid tribute to Solomon with the spices of Arabia while elsewhere Joseph, of technicolour dreamcoat fame, was sold to a passing spice merchant by his brothers. And then, in the New Testament, there is the story about three wise men who travelled from the East to offer the infant Jesus frankincense and myrrh, which were as prized as the gold they also gave him. Other religions give spice an even greater role: an Assyrian creation myth declares that, before the gods created the earth, they drank a wine made from sesame seeds to give them strength.

It's clear from the ancient European, Arabic and Chinese sources I've come across that peoples all over the world were fascinated by Indian cooking. A Chinese observer wrote that 'The Indian people are very dainty in their diet – they have a hundred ways of cooking their food, varying it every day.' Much later, that variety didn't much impress the fourteenth-century Arab diplomat Ibn Batûtâ. Here he describes a meal served to him in one of the royal courts of the southern state of Kerala:

> A beautiful slave girl, dressed in silk, places before the king the bowls containing the individual dishes. With a large bronze ladle she places a ladleful of rice on the platter, pours the ghee over it and adds preserved peppercorns, green ginger, preserved lemons and mangoes. The diner then takes a mouthful of rice and then a little of these conserves. When the helping of rice is all eaten, she ladles out some more and serves a dish of chicken, again eaten with the rice. When that is done she helps rice again, and offers some other poultry dish, again eaten with rice. When all kinds of poultry have been served, she brings fish, which is also eaten with rice. Rice is their only food: I once spent eleven months at that court without any bread. I had three years in southern India, the Maldives and Ceylon, eating nothing but rice. I had to help it down with water.[2]

This would appear to be a fairly early account of a Balti meal – so much for those who claim Balti was invented in Birmingham in the 1980s! It also makes it plain that breads like chapati, paratha and naan are most

[2] Ibn Batûtâ, *Travels*, Vol 3.

definitely a north Indian tradition. This isn't, however, the earliest account of such a meal. Around 300 BCE, nearly 1,800 years before Ibn Batûtâ spent time in India, an ambassador of the Syrian ruler Seleucus called Megastethenes travelled through the kingdom of Chandragupta (now northern India) and recorded his observations in a series of books called *Indika*, which have since been lost. However, fragments remain, through the second-century writer Athenaeus who quotes Megastethenes in his *Deiponosophistai*, a fascinating survey of classical food and dining habits. 'At dinner the table that is placed before each person is like a pot-stand, and a golden bowl is set on it. In the bowl they first put all the rice – boiled just the same way that we might boil cracked wheat – and then many different relishes are prepared according to Indian recipes.' This, surely, must be the earliest record of a European eating a curry.

What each of these anecdotes tells me is that for centuries and across continents, Indian food was different from meals partaken in different parts of the world. No other cuisine produced such a variety of dishes for one meal, nor could the cooking of any other regions produce such a variety and depth of flavour. This, understandably, is a direct corollary of the Indian soil's effortless and enthusiastic production of spices.

The desirability of Indian spices meant that there was profit in trading them. Some of the oldest surviving written records from antiquity are traders' tallies indicating that spices (and man's quest to find them) were the spur for much early exploration and commerce. Spice, to put it succinctly, brought continents into contact for the first time since the earliest humans left Africa, went wandering, got separated and got lost.

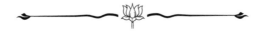

The Consequence of Spice

The ancient lust for spices had all kinds of unexpected consequences. For instance, the need to cross the Indian Ocean led to a greater understanding of what are now called 'trade winds'. In 100BCE the ancient Greek mariner Hippalus wrote a study of the effects of the monsoon on ocean crossings and noted that at certain times of the year the journey to the Indies was shorter by several weeks. Accordingly, there were advances in navigation, map making and astronomy as traders tried to save time and, more importantly, improve their chances of making a successful crossing. It should be remembered that sea travel in ancient times was without lifeboats, GPS and satellite phones: men risked their lives to make their fortune from spices. And there were indeed fortunes to be made.

Throughout ancient texts there are snippets of information that reveal the extent and sophistication of the spice trade, not to mention its profits. The second-century traveller and writer Pausanias records that this rich trade wasn't just all one way. 'Those who sail to India say that the natives give other merchandise in exchange for Greek cargoes, knowing nothing about coinage, and that they have plenty of gold and of bronze.' The problem with testimony like this, however, is that the information has passed through several hands before it reached Pausanias's quill, rather like the spices themselves. Just as his information may have become inflated over distance, so were the prices of pepper, turmeric, fenugreek and ginger. Between harvest and consumption, a single peppercorn may have been traded tens if not hundreds of times – and with each transaction a little bit of commission was added and the price inevitably rose. By the time shoppers in the forums and agoras of Rome and Athens were sampling the merchandise, they were paying hundreds of times what the growers in India had been paid. The psychology of this inflation of both myth and of price was that customers believed they were buying something precious. Something that, frankly, was worth what the traders were charging. This wasn't an accident.

For millennia the Persians were the guardians of the spice trade and as such they controlled the prices, and hence ensured their wealth. Theirs was a fortune of geography; sandwiched between the spice-growing lands of the East and the eager consumers of the Mediterranean, Persia was able to control the flow of spices from East to West. And that meant that when prices fell, the Persian traders simply stockpiled merchandise until demand, and prices, rose again. Naturally, many Europeans took a dislike to the Persians and some tried to find their own way to the growers in the East. But whether attempts were made to cross the mountains to the north or the seas to the south, the Persians had every route covered and a band of thugs were sure to intercept any illicit booty.

Consequently, the Persian control of the spice trade endured for millennia. Although we cannot know when their dominance of the trade started, we can be very precise about when it ended. The Persian stranglehold on the world economy was finally broken on 21 May 1498, as it happened, not long after dawn. At this very moment Vasco da Gama, the Portuguese explorer, sailed a small fleet of three ships (he'd left Portugal with twenty) into the Indian port of Calicut on the Malabar coast and in doing so made the first direct sea voyage from Europe to the East. He had sailed south around the Cape of Good Hope and survived, partly because he'd had a luckier wind and a slightly more benevolent sea than those who had tried before him, but mostly because Persian pirates hadn't intercepted him. They had never imagined Europeans would want spices so badly that they'd rather sail right round Africa than deal with a middleman.

The Age of Discovery

Da Gama's arrival, you could argue, was one of the most important events in world history. From that moment on, Europe's isolation from, and ignorance of, Asian wisdom, culture and – crucially – booty ended forever. With mighty ships and powerful weaponry, and an iron willingness to deploy them both, it was only after da Gama that Europe began the colonisation of Asia that would endure for centuries. And with those new empires would come developments that would transform our world: an entirely new merchant class emerged and forms of commercial credit that changed banking structures across the globe were devised. At this time insurance was also invented in the coffee shops of London – one of them was called Lloyd's – as patrons placed bets on which ships would successfully return to port. Perhaps the most significant shift in world affairs that was created by the renewed quest for spice was a new age of exploration, and ultimately exploitation that would rewrite maps and change our ancestors' vision of the world.

And the reason for this exploration, financial revolution and colonisation? Religion and spices. Legend has it that da Gama's men ran ashore in India proclaiming 'for Christ and spices'. As it happened, the people of Calicut were already familiar with Christian missionaries as Syrian proselytes had arrived centuries before to start conversions. And the reason the Syrians had sought out Calicut in the 1200s was the same reason that da Gama had searched for it at the end of the fifteenth century: pepper. This spice, above all others, was so coveted that it drove men to perform awesome feats of bravery, as well as spectacular acts of cruelty. Knowledge of these deeds has helped me see curry in a different light.

Calicut, in south-western Kerala, is still the gateway to one of the most important pepper-growing regions in the world. Here the relationship between landscape, climate and fortune is still forcefully apparent. This spot was the Holy Grail of fifteenth-century explorers: its discovery and settlement opened up the area to trade and wealth for those who came and those who stayed. In the towns around Calicut the evidence that peppercorns were once as valuable as gold is as obvious as the heat.

According to romantic travel guides, Iddicki is a couple of days journey inland from Calicut. Reached by mountain ghats that roll in and out of mist and cross the path of passionate waterfalls and herds of wild elephant, Iddicki is said to have the quality of El Dorado: isolated, magical and promising riches. The Portuguese traders actually called it El Negrado after its most famous crop. These highlands produce the most sought-after pepper in the world. Iddicki peppercorns are dark and heavy, almost sumptuous, and they exude a flavour and strength that makes every meal fit for a king. Or kings: at one time or another the envoys of the Portuguese, French, Dutch and British monarchs all had their sights on Iddicki.

Given its isolation and insubstantial size, you might expect this town to have an insignificant commercial profile, but the West's fascination with Indian food has brought Iddicki wealth beyond expectation. Many houses have washing machines, televisions, computers and stereos, and on roofs all over town satellite dishes cock their metallic ears to the sky – not exactly the necessities of normal rural life. There is also a roaring gold trade, a direct result of the wealth created by the black gold that grows, literally, on every single tree in town.

Iddicki's magical location, defended from weak-hearted invaders by a permanent shroud of mist, no doubt added to the allure of pepper. Journals of the Europeans who went in search of spices at this time are filled with references to legends and myths that nutmeg and pepper trees were protected by everything from semi-divine warriors to ancient curses: Iddicki fits the bill perfectly. Reading these journals breeds an understanding of the awe in which European invaders held spice and gives an indication of how they viewed the dishes that were made with spices – a mix of admiration and trepidation. Eating Indian food was, for some of these adventurers, an act of conquest.

But for da Gama conquest wasn't enough: he wanted to kidnap pepper and take it back to Portugal. He wanted the first curry takeaway. Although he already knew his name would be remembered for ever after his historic voyage, more than anything he wanted to be known as the man who emasculated India of its spices, and ultimately its hold over the West. And the way to do that was to take a pepper vine to Europe – after all, cultivating pepper in Lisbon had to be easier than losing 85 per cent of your fleet each time you made the journey to Asia.

So before he left India he asked the Zamorin of Calicut if he could take a tree or two with him. At first, the legend goes, the Calicut courtesans were outraged: as if they'd let the secret of their wealth be taken away from them! However, the Zamorin remained calm and agreed to let da Gama take two trees, but warned him: 'You can take our pepper, but you will never be able to take our rains.'

It's that divine mix of location and climate – Kerala has two monsoons a year – which has continued to bring Iddicki abundant harvests, trade and fortune. Even though pepper is now grown across the globe, Iddicki pepper is still considered special. Consequently its streets these days are crammed with the evidence of profit: jeeps and sports cars clog up the traffic, and its cafes are full of men and women with mobile phones clamped to their ears. These accoutrements might not be essential purchases, but the profits of pepper have not been squandered on the purchase of satellite dishes and mobiles – now the growers know as much about the price of pepper as the traders in Amsterdam (which is still the centre of the international spice market, thanks to the legacy of the VOC, Vereenigde Oost-Indische Compagnie, or Dutch East India Company). No longer do white men in suits tell these farmers how much their crops are worth: and Iddicki peppercorns have never fetched a higher price.

You may be wondering why pepper was so important a commodity. You may even be wondering what it has to do with curry; after all, you won't find many Indian recipes that call for copious amounts of black pepper. Practically every curry recipe in modern cookery books states the quantity of *chilli* pepper you should use. But the chilli is native to America, and Columbus hadn't crossed the Atlantic by this time. And before Columbus the fire in Indian food came from a mix of black pepper and mustard.

As is well-known, Columbus didn't go in search of a New World, his explorations – like da Gama's – were motivated by pepper. In fact he only got funding for his expedition because his backers fancied they'd make a profit on the cargoes of pepper he promised to return home with. So when Columbus landed in America and insisted that he had found the East, he sought to prove it by finding pepper. Of course he only found chillies, which offered a different kind of heat, but he was so adamant that he *was* in the East and that he *had* found pepper, that he called chillies 'peppers' anyway. On docking in Lisbon he announced that they were just another type of pepper. This confusing misnomer survives to this day, of course. It seems ironic that the man who failed to find India ended up misnaming and exporting back to India the spice now most widely associated with that country's cuisine.

The Brutality of Spice

For me, much of the romance I have come to see in curry is bound up in the spice trade. Understanding the spell that nutmeg, mace, pepper and coriander cast over the whole of Europe, and the epic consequences of their desirability, has bred a sense of awe for the dishes served in my local curry house. It is the journeys of spice hunters like da Gama that make Indian cuisine exotic by reputation as well as by taste.

But the history of the spice trade isn't just populated with romantic adventurers fighting off seasickness and mythical creatures while in search of delicate aromas. The history of spice is stained not just with the yellow of saffron or the orange of turmeric, but with the red of blood. Lots of it. The more I have learnt about the true value of spice, the more amazing curry has become.

Without the quest for spice, Columbus would not have 'discovered' America, the Conquistadores would not have wiped out the Incas and the British government would not have offered boundless riches to the first man who could measure longitude. Spice, basically, changed the world and it became the planet's first global industry. And the country that controlled the spice trade – as Persia had done for profit and glory for millennia – controlled the world. Everyone knew it and in a period of about twenty years, between 1490 and 1510, just about every European nation invested a substantial portion of its wealth in securing a trading route with spice growers. Even Sweden, a nation not famed for its imperial tendencies, and landlocked Austria built fleets and set sail in search of riches and global domination. Almost half of all the ships that journeyed in search of spice were never heard from again.

The winners of the spice race – or what could easily be called the first truly world war – were unquestionably the Dutch, who conquered and colonised some of the most remote, beautiful and aromatic places on earth. But that's where the romance ends. To really appreciate the power of spice, its importance, its hold over reason and its true value – to really understand how phenomenal curry really is – you have to see how far people were prepared to go in order to secure spice wealth.

The VOC was the most ruthless of the European East India Companies: documentary evidence suggests these relative latecomers to the spice business had no scruples whatsoever. Spice not only drove the Dutch to the farthest corners of the known world; it drove them to commit some of the most brutal crimes in history in order to wrest the power of spice away from the Portuguese and Spaniards.

For nearly a hundred years, the Iberian nations had divided up the spice trade between them using familiar business practices like bribery and coercion. For example, the Sultans' palaces on the clove islands of Ternate and Tidore – names that inspired awe and wonder in the sixteenth century – prove testament to the Portuguese and Spanish offerings: Venetian glassware, Chinese vases, daggers inlaid with ivory, ornaments of gold, silver and jewels the size of peaches. The Sultans of Ternate and Tidore were persuaded by these gifts to give a monopoly on cloves to Portugal, then Spain, in exchange for protection from potential invaders. So in addition to the Sultans' palaces, these tiny islands are still encrusted with the remains of Spanish and Portuguese fortresses.

In contrast, the Sultan of the tiny Bandas islands – thought to be the only place on earth where nutmeg was grown – refused to agree to such a monopoly and insisted he be allowed to trade with whichever nation offered the best deal at the time. As a consequence, no forts were built which meant that when the Dutch were looking for a trade to call their own, they fancied that the nutmeg business was theirs for the taking.

Of all the Bandas, the island of Run is possibly the prettiest: it is described as a perfect circle of green hemmed by white sand and surrounded by turquoise sea in which dolphins frolic. The sun is a daily visitor but other guests have difficulty getting there: Run is so small that only the tiniest of boats can come ashore and then only at high tide. Despite its size and remote location, the Dutch wanted Run so badly that they traded their prized colony on the other side of the world so they could dedicate themselves to its capture. That colony was New Amsterdam, now New York, a vibrant port that was the gateway to a new continent. But the island of Manhattan did not grow nutmeg; and so the Dutch wanted Run.

The Bandanese managed to resist Dutch invasion and bribery until the VOC was under the command of its most infamous leader, Jan Pieterszoon Coen. It was during his leadership that his men found a new way to persuade the islanders to let them control the nutmeg trade: genocide. Within fifteen years of capturing the island, the Dutch had reduced the Bandanese population from 15,000 to just 600 under a regime that was said to have employed Japanese mercenaries to torture, decapitate and quarter village elders.

Once the Dutch had muscled in on the world's nutmeg trade, they aimed to boost the spice's value, and in turn the value of their empire, by destroying every nutmeg tree on other islands. Under one of the most brutal rules in history, they executed anyone found growing, trading or stealing nutmeg trees and did not let trees leave Run unless they had been drenched in a sterilising dose of lime.

It was tactics such as these that led to the Dutch domination of the spice trade and made the VOC the most powerful company in the world at that time. Bigger in its day than Microsoft and NewsCorp are today, by 1670 the VOC was the richest corporation in the world paying its shareholders an annual dividend of 40 per cent – despite the enormous cost of paying 50,000 employees, 30,000 fighting men and maintaining 200 ships. Brutality, it would seem, had its rewards.

Across India and Indonesia there are communities bearing the scars – both physical and financial – of these earliest days of empire. Not all of those scars are disfiguring, as the wealth of Iddicki indicates, and some would argue that the European influence was a 'civilising' one. Aside from such patronising attitudes, it is clear that India did get at least a couple of small consolation prizes for its trauma: for all they took away from India, European traders brought a couple of things with them that would change the curry forever – the chilli and the potato.

The Etymology of 'Curry'

Considering that so many European countries tried to conquer and control India – Portugal, Holland and France as well as Britain all had a go – and spent so much time and money there, it has always seemed curious to me that only one of these colonial powers took the curry to its heart. Even though the Portuguese ruled parts of India for over two centuries, you will not find many curry houses in Lisbon. And in Holland, for all the Dutch fury that was invested and squandered in the name of spice, you could walk for many miles before sitting down to a Cobra beer and a couple of poppadums.

I found a possible answer to this riddle while I was looking into the origin of the word 'curry'. It seems the indigenous British diet might not have been as bland as most people assume; indeed some have even suggested that the Brits invented curry. Well, the name at least. Over two hundred years before the incorporation of the British East India Company in 1600, Richard II's palace cooks produced what might well have been the first English recipe book. Of the 200 or so dishes outlined in the 1390 tome *The Forme of Cury* a great number are surprisingly spicy. At the time – contrary to popular conception – cooks employed by the aristocracy used many spices, among them ginger, cinnamon, nutmeg, cloves, galangal, coriander, cumin, cardamom and aniseed, in an enormous variety of dishes. It seems that long before the days of the East India Company and imperial rule – and centuries before Indian dishes were served on British soil – the Brits were making spicy 'cury' for themselves. And what does this word mean? Apparently it is just another word for cooking and is thought to come from the French verb 'cuire', to cook. Perhaps if curry was British all along, this might explain the current love of Indian food?

But this is just one such suggestion for the etymology of the word. A more common belief is that curry is a British colonial corruption of the Tamil word *kari*, which simply means sauce. In the Tamil Nadu province, kari may be used to describe a number of wet dishes, but never a dry one. However, kari is also a corruption of *kari pulia*, which means curry leaves, a herb used in southern Indian cookery, and some argue that this might be the true source of the word we use today.

There are yet more theories. Some believe the word is derived from *karhai*, a wok-like pan made of silver and brass that Indian dishes are prepared in. Or perhaps it came from *khari*, a North Indian yoghurt concoction. Other possibilities are that it came from *curryup*, a Tamil word used when foods are fried until they are blackened, or maybe it has its root in yet another Tamil word, *curryi*, which means uncooked vegetables.

Possibly the most bizarre and entertaining theory I've read on the origin of the word is that it is neither an Indian nor a British word, but an Irish one! In an old edition of the Curry Club magazine, there is a story about an Irish sea captain who had married into a wealthy family but then gambled away their fortune, forcing them to sell some of their stable of racehorses – and eat the rest. This sea captain was heard to say in the coffee houses of London that he had been forced into eating *cuirreach gosht*, which appetisingly translates as racetrack meat! If this is the origin of the word, it doesn't reflect well on what Londoners at that time thought of curried dishes.

Wherever the word comes from, there are even more fevered debates about what the word curry should actually be used to describe. Some find it insulting that such a varied and rich cuisine should have a 'nickname' that (a) is not used in India and (b) discourages diners from exploring the cuisine further. Even those of us who use it as a shorthand accept that it is inadequate. In this book, I use it to describe a phenomenon as much as a meal and, as such, it is meant to revere, not disparage.

GINGER

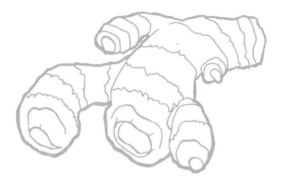

Ginger was one of the first spices used by man. We know this because it can only be propagated by the human hand: it has been cultivated for so long that it has lost the vital property of a wild plant – the ability to reproduce – indicating that it has evolved into its present state after many, many millennia of cultivation. Ginger's close relatives galangal, zerumbet and zedoary still grow in the wild.

There is also a linguistic clue to its prehistoric use: the word for ginger is so similar in many Pacific languages that it is thought ginger must have been carried by the earliest of explorers and planted in each new territory. The theory here is that if different peoples thousands of miles apart independently discovered the same plant it would have had different names on different islands, as happened with most other species. The fact that it was so widely grown is another clue: most species are specific to a much smaller geographical area.

So why was it so important, so long ago? In classical times it was famed by Dioscorides and Pliny for its medicinal qualities as well as its taste. Dioscorides wrote: 'Its effect is warming, digestive, gently laxative, appetising; it helps in cases of cataract, and is an ingredient in antidotes against poison.' It was also considered a cure for impotence. No wonder then, that Pliny tells us a pound of ginger cost six denarii, or three days' wages for the average working man.

We now know that there are medical reasons for the ancients' beliefs – ginger is packed with vitamins and minerals, most notably vitamin C which is known to boost the immune system. This is probably why Chinese sailors always carried some on board ship as it offered protection from scurvy. Presumably, its reputation for conquering nausea also helped those sailors who hadn't yet found their sea legs.

The Latin name for ginger is zingiber, coming from the Sanskrit singabela, which means 'horn-shaped'. This is thought to describe the shape of the ginger root. The root is the most widely used part of the plant as the longer the root is in the ground the stronger and more pungent it becomes. It can also be stored for months without any significant loss of quality, unlike the shoots that are best eaten freshly picked. The roots have a tough brown skin that is removed to reveal a yellowy, orangey (gingery) interior which can be sliced, diced, ground or crushed. The shoots, which are harvested in spring and summer, are milder and fibreless, and are used in pickles, relishes and chutneys. These are particularly prized in Japanese cooking.

In Indian food ginger is often cooked with fish, as it is said to remove fishy smells, or is used as a thickener in sauces. It is also used in tandoori marinades, goes particularly well with spinach, cauliflower, aubergine and potatoes and is an ingredient in many

Indian dishes from both the north and the south. It is also used in desserts and to flavour tea. In some parts of India, it is placed raw on a banana leaf with a little salt and served as a starter, as this is said to stimulate both appetite and salivation.

CHAPTER TWO

Why Spice + Spice = Magic

The Teachings of Ayurveda

Curry isn't just delicious; it's good for you.

The Indians have known about the power of spice for five thousand years and have long understood how the sweetness or bitterness of a meal can affect both mind and body. These Ayurvedic properties of spice, not to mention the magic of home cooking, means that food has long played a central role in Indian health, happiness and family life. In contrast to the West's covetous obsession with spice, India has had a more intimate, nurturing relationship with the magical ingredients of curry. Understanding a little of these properties has greatly enhanced my appreciation of curry.

Ayurveda is an ancient Hindu tradition that, it is said, brings balance and happiness to the mind, body and spirit. Ayurveda (which literally

33

translates as 'life knowledge') has sometimes felt to me to be a bit of a fad or marketing ploy used to sell massages and bath salts. But in India the ancient principles that have now been embraced by the Body Shop lie at the heart of why Indian cuisine developed in the way it did. Ayurveda might be a recent arrival in the West, but in India people have believed for centuries in its teachings that suggest humans have three 'life energies' or *doshas* – vata dosha, pitta dosha and kapha dosha – which must be balanced for wellbeing. This is achieved by eating a diet that feeds each dosha with meals in each of the six taste classifications. Of these six tastes, 'sweet' is thought to be soothing, nourishing, energising and satisfying; 'sour' is said to increase the appetite, aid digestion and stimulate salivation; 'salty' makes the skin glow, increases water intake and maintains flexibility; 'bitter' purifies the blood and firms the skin; 'pungent' boosts circulation and cleans the blood; while 'astringent' aids both digestion and blood purification. These tastes are best created through the knowledgeable and skilful blending of spices, which goes some of the way to explaining the great variety of tastes in every Indian meal.

Many curry eaters with no knowledge of Ayurveda can testify to the potency of spice, particularly chilli. Scientists and nutritionists have observed some of these effects and few would contradict their findings. Chillies of sufficient heat can produce euphoria as well as streaming eyes. They produce feelings of health due to their high vitamin C content (gram for gram they have more than oranges) which boosts the immune system, and few people fail to feel the instant kick they give to the circulation. And that's just one spice! It's no wonder that curry is more than just a meal to many and why spice is an obsession for some. When I started talking to those in the curry business, I began to realise just how deep that passion goes in some people.

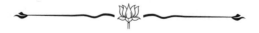

The Subtlety of Spice

Of all the people I've met, the person who has best explained the passion of spice and, in consequence, of Indian food is Meena Pathak of Patak's Foods. 'There is a huge bond with spices. A lot of Indians have it,' explains Meena who has been crazy about spice since childhood. Talking to her is a bit like talking to an astronaut about the universe: new and unexpected worlds come into view. 'Did you know,' she asks me, 'that you can tell which region of India a mustard seed is from just by looking at the shape of the seed?'

Funnily enough, I had no idea.

'The same spice can be grown in two or three different regions, but the potency or essential oil in the seed will vary because of the soil conditions in that area or the climate, and that will affect the taste. Even if you grow the exact same variety of plant, the taste will be very different from region to region.'

This principle will be familiar to wine lovers who choose one vintage over another, or one vineyard over another, based on rainfall or sunshine hours in any given growing season, but I had – ignorantly – never considered that these same factors would affect all other crops too. And just as the fermentation process or type of barrel affects the flavour of wine, so the production of spices affects their flavour.

'There are fifteen different grades of turmeric,' she reveals. 'Each one is just a tinge lighter or darker than the other one to look at, but if you taste it, the difference is huge, and this is due to the processing conditions – how the root of the turmeric plant is boiled and dried.'

Meena's love affair with spices started when she was growing up in Bombay. 'When I fell in love with cooking I started going to the markets to buy my spices and herbs and vegetables, something that the servants normally did. But I used to take twice as long as the servants because I used to be so finicky about the quality as I have always been particular about my ingredients. I think that if you start from good, you get good. This made my mother irate because she thought I was just wasting my time at the market.'

Although she grew up in a huge city, Meena developed an affinity for the land as many children from rural India have done. 'I was very lucky because my father used to work in the army and we travelled around India with him. So I always saw where rice was grown, or the spices, or the tea. And because of my interest in food I actually stopped to see what a tea plant really looked like.'

At the time neither Meena, nor her mother, knew that while she was indulging in her hobby, Meena was also investing in her future. Today she develops recipes at Patak's Foods, a British company which started life as a grocery shop in the 1960s and now sells curry sauces and pickles to over 50 countries. The original shop was opened by Meena's father-in-law and the current business is run by her husband Kirit.

'Today I can be sitting in my office in the factory where we roast and grind the spices, and I can tell if the team on the other side of the building are roasting cumin seeds from India, or cumin seeds from Iran. The aromas are very distinct to me, as are the flavours, which is why we import two different crops to get the different flavours in different recipes.'

Not only do I find Meena's sense of smell extraordinary, but I am also dumbstruck at the complexity of spice preparation. I have never stopped wondering how the ancients discovered that if you boiled and dried this root, or let this plant go to seed, you could get a different taste from it. And to roast spices to different degrees in order to get a variety of aromas, and to blend them to produce an almost infinite range of flavours – spice seems so complex as to be improbable.

The spice that has long intrigued me the most is nutmeg. Not for its astounding history or its culinary uses, but because I just can't imagine how people ever worked out how to get the flavour from it. Nutmegs look rather like peaches when they are harvested, yet the flesh (although it can make good chutneys) is used less often than the hard, dark kernel that you find in shops. I know that if I'd picked the first nutmeg, it would never have occurred to me that I could grate and grind the kernel to create a powdered spice. And I'm damn sure that I would have thrown away the red slimy web that surrounds the kernel, but some curious soul decided to dry the slime and discovered it was transformed by the sun into lacy fronds with their own distinct flavour. You can buy them under the name 'mace'.

Obviously I can't interview the first person who put a nutmeg to its full use, but Meena has a theory as to why Indian cooks turned some of the unlikely produce of their gardens into essential flavours in their kitchens: 'Indians don't like to waste anything!' she jokes.

Meena's passion for spice extends beyond culinary use and she believes ardently in the healing and beneficial properties of spices. 'In India we grew up with things like head massages and what's now called aromatherapy. It was very normal for us. Every other day we used to put coconut oil in our hair and condition our hair that way. And from two weeks old we were given mustard oil massages to strengthen our bones. It was very normal and I think we took so much for granted.'

Many Indian children know, as Meena knows, that fennel can enhance your mood or that chewing green cardamom pods can alleviate feelings of depression. I've come to realise that to get so much from spice, to know how to harvest its flavours and tame its temperament for both physical and mental sustenance, you have to know spice intimately. You have to nurture it. And it has ever been so.

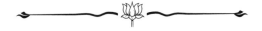

The Passion of Spice

In the twelfth century, a Jewish traveller known as Benjamin of Tudela visited India and recorded the following insight into each farmer's love of his own crop: 'Pepper grows in this country, they plant the pepper vines out in the country but each person knows his own plants.' Eight hundred years later, each man can still tell his pepper from that of his neighbour. The person I have met who can best explain this devotion in the modern day is a London restaurateur called Das Sreedharan. In his restaurants, Das prepares authentic Keralan dishes but is keen to explain that what makes his food authentically Keralan is not the recipes or the ingredients: it's the love.

'Most people think that home cooking is about recreating what mummy cooks at home. But what makes mummy's food special is not just what she cooks,' he explains. 'Where I come from the kitchen is the most mysterious, most elegant, most powerful place for mummy. That is where she commands, where she shares, where she becomes most humorous because, if you notice, outside the kitchen mummy doesn't behave the same way with children. And this is because of the love she creates around the cooking. The people who think that home cooking is about using the same recipes don't understand the depth of the love.'

For Das, that love starts with the farming. 'If you look back 30 years ago, 70 or 75 per cent of all our produce was home grown. When you understand what it takes to grow all those vegetables and those spices, that's when you realise how much love is in the food,' he believes.

'There is tremendous pain in sustaining the growth of a crop and making it beautiful. An aubergine becomes beautiful after a long time,' he says dreamily. 'It's grown from a very small seed and needs a lot of nurturing on a daily basis. Some of the farmers' feelings are tremendous: when the flower comes on the plant they cry because they have waited for that day. Sometimes they have nightmares and they wake up in the night and go and see their plant in case something has happened to it. I have seen it, I have done it,' he insists. 'If a chef is buying something from Sainsbury's you do not have this feeling and so it is not a perfect meal you are making.'

Das grew up in a small village a few hours inland from the spice markets of Cochin. Many of the meals he ate as a child were made of vegetables that he had harvested himself, or which had been picked by his family or other people in his village. When you grow up surrounded by the food you eat, and when your food is at the mercy of the sun, or the rain, or your ability to pick it at the right moment, or the generosity of a neighbour to lend you his tools, it is easy to understand how you develop such an intimate, passionate relationship with food.

A few years ago, Das says, he was on a fishing trip that made him realise exactly what makes a meal special. 'The fishing community on the coast of Kerala is very isolated,' he begins. 'They live separately from the inland and highland community where there is still much financial and religious segregation. In the fishing community there is not the same classification; it has survived as a community because each person understands what it takes to go to sea. In Kerala fishing is an elaborate tradition, but it is also a commitment and a duty.

'The monsoon is the darkest time for the fishing community,' he continues. 'In the monsoon you are legally prohibited from going to sea in rough weather, but to the fishing community fish is everything. It is food, it is the economy, it is the religion and all these things can only be satisfied if you go out to sea. So a father must send a son out to sea, even though it is dangerous, because if you do not fish you do not have a future. A fisherman feels that it is his duty to fish even when there is danger, even though sometimes the children do not come back. That is the pain that goes into fishing,' he reminds me.

'So I went out fishing with these men and I learned what it means to put a fish on the table. I realised that these men have a relationship with the sea in their little boats with their little nets that fishermen in big trawlers with big nets cannot have. With the little boats you cannot just throw the nets over the side and sit back and relax while you wait for the fish to come – you have to go and catch the fish.

'After a morning's fishing,' he remembers, 'the crew stopped to make lunch and they prepared a simple fish curry with just a very few ingredients because you do not take anything you do not need on a boat. It was a very simple meal, but everybody on board that boat agreed it was the best meal they had ever had because for the first time they understood what it means to eat fish. When you understand an ingredient, I realised, it makes the meal special.'

I have been very moved by Das's passion. In a time when so much of our food comes to us in tins and packets – sometimes even ready-arranged on microwaveable plates – I can't help but be persuaded by his arguments. If we understood what it takes to produce ingredients, would we really be happy to have them extensively mechanised by fast food chains and TV dinners? If we had the respect for food that Das talks of, surely we would take greater care with the fruits of farmers' and fishermen's labours?

In India, according to Das, it has only been in the past few years that the younger generation has lost this connection to the land and the sea. This has made me wonder if the cuisine exported round the world by earlier generations of Indian emigrants – the food, by and large, that is the international curry – contained some of the wisdom and reverence that Das speaks of. Could this, in some way, explain why so many people responded to curry? Did we taste the love?

For Das, and for many of the restaurateurs I've interviewed for this book, there certainly was an emotional aspect to cooking for strangers. 'If I am cooking a meal for you, I am responsible for how you feel afterwards. If you have a bad afternoon after eating my lunch, I am sorry,' Das explains. 'This is because I am not just feeding your belly, but I hope I am also feeding our friendship.'

Throughout my journey into the history of curry I have, as you might expect, been treated to some remarkable meals both in people's restaurants and in their houses. I have been made to feel welcome in their homes through the care and time they have put into cooking for me, and in restaurants I have been brought exceptional meals not just because there's a chance I may write about the restaurant more favourably, but because my host has used food to convey his or her enthusiasm for talking to me. Das may sound like he's talking in fairytales, but I can vouch for the truth of his words. And some of the pioneer restaurateurs I've spoken to who opened restaurants in the 1950s and 1960s said they used food to make friends with their clientele in order to build a better life, as well as a better business. Cooking a curry for someone – taking the time to gather such a wide variety of ingredients, having the patience to create meals of such sophisticated complexity – is indeed an act of friendship. There is as much passion in cooking curry as there is in eating it. Or as Das puts it: 'Indian cooking is a taste of *you*. I've come to discover that you are the main ingredient in any meal that you cook. How you're feeling affects the taste. If you're not caring for the person you are cooking for, you will not make such a nice meal.'

The taste of curry, then, is not just determined by the timing of the monsoon rain or the skill of the person who roasts and grinds the spices, it is affected by the mood of the chef. 'You can use the same ingredients, the same utensils, the same procedures,' insists Das, 'but the taste will vary depending on your mood. People can taste the love and that is the magic. That is why you can create Indian food anywhere in the world: you do not have to see the aubergine grow, but you must know what it takes to grow an aubergine, and you must know how your food affects your guest. In India, nobody cooks for today, they cook with love so that tomorrow they will have your friendship.'

Indian Food in India

There are many differences between the European view of Indian cookery and the Indian view. In the West, Indian cookery may be well established, but it is still in many ways a novelty. A non-Indian host who cooks curry for dinner is seen as adventurous, ambitious and possibly even fashionable. Curry still has an otherness and most of us are slightly distant from it. So, generally, we accept that it is either prepared with a jar of one of Meena's pastes, or we buy it from a restaurant. We do not have a tradition of cooking Indian food, although the couple who always order the same dishes at the same time from the same restaurant every Friday could be said to have their own established tradition.

I think what I have observed is a disconnect between the meal that is prepared with respect – for the ingredients, for the traditions, for the diner – and the same meal which is often eaten in haste and with little respect for either the ingredients, the traditions or the chef. As restaurant-goers, I think we are becoming more experimental and knowledgeable and can make informed decisions as to whether we want tandoori, Punjabi, Goan or Bangladeshi cuisine, but I do not see – in many curry fans – the appropriate sense of wonder to accompany the amazing array of choices. This ignorance of what it takes to make a meal is starting to become apparent in India too.

'Back in India home cooking is happening less and less,' observes Das. As you may expect from a man who sees the beauty and pain of a vegetable, Das sees this shift as a loss for his homeland. 'A child doesn't want to go home any more because what is special about home if there isn't home cooking? You can talk to family on the phone so why bother unless there is something there that you cannot get anywhere else? So the food becomes unhealthier and we have disrespect for the soil.'

The connection Das has made is that food doesn't just tie you to the land, but also to your family and your heritage. When you recognise the connection between food and family, it becomes obvious why so many emigrants started restaurants: familiar food can make an unfamiliar place seem like home.

Out of respect for his elders, out of love for his homeland, Das is now in the process of opening a school in Kerala to teach the next generation about food. Many Indian, Bangladeshi and Pakistani chefs are also doing the same as all over the subcontinent, changes in the economy are taking people further and further away from the land. The motivation isn't just to ensure the survival of certain regional cuisines though: it is, of course, much easier to arrange visas and residency for a trained chef with specialist knowledge. Nevertheless, I still find it interesting that in an era when Brits are buying more Indian recipe books than ever before, India is also having to formalise the education of curry making.

'Indian food is changing,' Meena Pathak informs me. 'The economy is changing, more women are working and people do not have the time to cook as they used to. When I was young, a woman might spend all day preparing a meal. These days she is likely to pick something up on the way home from work.'

Amusingly, Patak's Foods now sells its pickles, pastes and sauces in India because there, like most other places, customers don't know how to prepare spices and if they do, they're too busy to make the masalas – the spice blends – themselves. This is just one of the many ways in which Indian cooking is changing within India itself.

'The economy is changing everything,' says Meena. 'Not only are more women working, but more Indians are travelling around the country and people are discovering the huge differences in the regional cuisines. What's happening to Indian cooking at the moment is that the state cuisines are merging. There has been some Western influence too, but mostly there has been fusion from within.'

Meena still travels round India looking for new suppliers and new recipes, so although she grew up in Bombay with a Gujarati chef in the family kitchen, she has an extensive knowledge about food from all over the subcontinent.

'There are very distinctive cuisines within India,' she explains, 'from the north to the south, and from the east to the west.' Generally the food Brits first learned to think of as 'Indian' was in fact Bangladeshi and Punjabi as migrants from these areas were the first to open restaurants in Britain. In the north, food is more commonly served with bread than rice; food from the south is more likely to have coconut, mustard seeds and curry leaves. But when you have Meena's knowledge and palate, even the smallest of differences are detectable. 'You can tell from the way the vegetables are cut or the shape of the meat which region you are eating in,' she says. 'Even chapatis change from place to place.'

Just as regional Indian restaurants are opening in Britain, so they are in India. 'The dining out culture in India has always been very big,' says Meena. 'That and Bollywood were the only forms of entertainment and still are. Whether it's snacking or occasion eating, people in India just eat all the time! So now that people have more money, there is a real interest in fine dining.'

There is also a new business: the takeaway. Frozen and ready meals are still largely unheard of in India. 'You pick up your ready meal from a restaurant you are familiar with,' Meena explains. 'On her way back from work a woman would just pop into a restaurant and pick up a meal.' As it is in Birmingham, so it is also in Bombay.

TURMERIC

Turmeric roots have been used in India for millennia for flavour, worship and dyeing cloth. In China turmeric is used in herbal medicine for controlling blood clotting and haemorrhaging; in India it is considered an effective appetite regulator and is also used boiled in milk to treat sore throats, coughs and chills. It can be used to treat liver complaints and is rubbed on faces to discourage facial hair! Like ginger, turmeric is another domestic plant that requires human intervention for propagation.

Its strength of colour is not matched by its flavour, typically mild and slightly tangy, which may account for its lack of notoriety in Europe in classical times. This lack of pungency means it is now widely used as a substitute for more expensive saffron (indeed it is variously known as 'false saffron', 'safran d'Inde' and 'Arabian saffron'). Its effectiveness as a cloth dye accounts for the Buddhist monks who have long worn 'saffron robes', but it is also considered auspicious by Hindus too. Turmeric is banned from use during mourning as it is considered a spice of celebration used to anoint brides and grooms at Hindu weddings and to colour festival rice. In Malaysia it was traditionally rubbed on the stomachs of women who had just given birth and on umbilical cords to discourage evil spirits. Its reputation for bringing good luck explains the appearance of clumps of turmeric in the middle of paddy fields: with turmeric in the ground you are thought more likely to have a better rice harvest.

Turmeric is one of the foundation spices of any curry powder mix and is used in the majority of Indian dishes to give a slightly sharp taste and a rich hue. Some chefs call turmeric 'the soul of Indian food' because it is so widely used in everything from tandoori pastes to biryanis. In Ayurvedic terms, turmeric helps create pungent and bitter tastes, but the taste of turmeric depends on its preparation.

The roots are peeled before boiling, after which they are left to dry. Only then are they ground into a powder for cooking. The length of time for which the roots are boiled, the drying process and the grinding all affect the flavour, which means there are fifteen recognised categories of taste for turmeric. The root can also be eaten raw but is more popularly pickled in brine to make a relish.

When cooking, turmeric is usually added to oil before the main ingredients so it can infuse the dish with its deep yellow hue and pungent taste. Its slight bitterness can be removed by roasting it before cooking. When added later in the cooking process, its flavour is much subtler and its colour more lemony: it gets darker the longer it's cooked.

Chefs consider turmeric their ally, for not only does it bring luck and flavour, but it can also be mixed with water into a paste to apply to burns. And its antiseptic properties mean that chefs have been known to pack nicks and cuts with turmeric to stop any blood flow so they can carry on cooking!

CHAPTER THREE

The Food of Empire

The Origins of Empire

This is the story of curry, not of the British Empire. However, to understand why chicken tikka masala became known as the Brits' favourite dish, it helps to know a little of how India became a British colony. It all started with – you guessed it – pepper, because by the end of the sixteenth century, the Dutch had sewn up the Indian pepper trade.

In England, the most notable consequence of the Netherlands' new monopoly was the rise in the price of pepper from two shillings and eightpence per pound to eight shillings.[1] This did not much amuse Queen Elizabeth, so she granted a royal charter to a small group of

---

[1] J Brennan, *Curries and Bugles*, Periplus Editions, 2000, p. 6.

merchants, enabling them to form a trading company. The Company's purpose was to secure for the Crown a better price for pepper than the Dutch were demanding – not to found an empire. The East India Company – or to give it its original name, The Governor and Company of Merchants of London Trading into the East Indies – came into being on 31 December 1600.

In the early days the Company was to be operated on a voyage-by-voyage basis, as the risks were so great. However, the first voyage was such a success that the company's future was assured: Captain James Lancaster's maiden shopping trip to the East may have taken three years, but when he returned to England he had pepper worth a million pounds in his hold which he had bought in Sumatra for less than sixpence a pound.

In the early seventeenth century, the British had no great wish for an empire and no huge desire to trade with India. They merely viewed their future colony as a useful stopping off port and a place to exchange cottons and linens before reaching Indonesia. However, a few embassies were established in India after the Dutch made trade in Indonesia more difficult, and the deals brokered by ambassadors usually gave the British trading rights in exchange for some form of naval protection. Similar deals were entered into around India between sundry potentates and various European traders.

As a consequence, the coast of India became lined with ports built and defended by the private European armies of the national East India Companies (most countries had one) who were paid to ensure the safety of their trader-masters. Naturally, with so many trading nations competing for the same trade, there were often scuffles between them.

At this time, what we now know as India was made up of separate territories and states ruled by Mughals and emperors who were, more often than not, in conflict with each other. As generations of infighting between Mughal factions had already diminished their respective power, the Europeans saw their chance to seize control for themselves. The French were particularly greedy for control of India and funded attempts to oust their European rivals. After a particularly bitter French-funded insurrection against the British was dealt with successfully by young Company man Robert Clive – the Clive of India of school history books – the English age of dominance in India could be said to have begun.

Many historians have called the British Empire an 'accidental empire' as India was 'acquired' without any real forethought, or so the legend goes. The British were simply the most organised presence with the most adept political operatives in a country whose traditional power base – the Mughals – was crumbling and imploding. Indeed, the Brits' rule over India has occasionally been described as a gentlemanly gesture, as if they were just helping to run the country until someone else could be found in a rather pleasant, toffish, chappish sort of a way. My suspicion is that empires are not quite so easy to acquire and that it must have involved more blood and scheming than the gentlemanly history books betray.

Certainly one reason why the British fared better than their European rivals in India was that they never tried to impose Christianity on the regions they governed. The Portuguese missionaries' attempts to win new servants for the Lord didn't endear them to the indigenous population (although they did actually remain in India longer than the British: Goa was still a Portuguese colony in the 1960s). The lack of desire to convert 'the natives' paved the path to British supremacy in another way too: instead of good Christian men taking their families to India with them as the Portuguese did, young British officers tended to be single. In turn, this meant that there was more intermarriage between Indians and British than there was with other Europeans, and hence a greater acceptance of cultural differences on both sides. This would serve the EIC well until the opening of the Suez canal in 1869 when the journey time to India was more than halved – making it much more possible for British women to undertake the crossing.

As Mughal after Mughal succumbed to the British, the fortunes of the East India Company flourished. Before too long the British had inveigled their way into everything so that not a single penny of tax or private commercial transaction was carried out without the EIC's knowledge – or without the Company's officers taking their slice of the profit. Even quite lowly officers of the Company were able to amass considerable fortunes, which is why ambitious young men were willing to endure the three months at sea to secure a vast and rapid bounty. It was possible to amass in a matter of years the kind of wealth that it took generations to accumulate back in Britain.

It is impossible to imagine just how rich India made some of the EIC men. They weren't just rich like a lottery winner who buys a few houses and a couple of Ferraris: these men bought seats in Parliament, country estates and power. Unsurprisingly, as their wealth was too conspicuous and too rapidly acquired, Company men were not well liked when they returned to Blighty as people were jealous of their status and suspicious of the methods with which they had acquired their fortunes. In fact they got up so many noses, so successfully, that their wealth proved to be their downfall: annoyed and embarrassed by the Company men's extravagances, the British government resolved to limit their powers. So, in 1818 the process of transferring governance of some 360 Indian provinces from Company to Crown began and the British Empire of India was formed.

The years between the first Viceroy's appointment in 1858 and the outbreak of the First World War in 1914 are generally held to be the 'golden age' of the British Raj. Quite why a period of time when the Brits behaved like stuffy, overbearing, racist snobs is thought of as 'golden' I'm not quite sure, apart from the fact that it inspired some wonderful literature. Although, if you were one of those snobs, life in India during the reign of the Raj does sound like quite a lot of fun.

The Food of the Raj

Social events involved riding, tennis, picnics, gymkhanas, garden parties, shooting parties, masquerade balls and cricket matches. At a time when the rest of the world was getting used to inventions like plastic, tape recorders and aeroplanes, life in the Raj was unashamedly nostalgic. Cheap labour and hot weather ensured the appeal of tailored cotton and silks while America was embracing nylon, and the lack of electricity in rural areas meant those Noel Coward 78s were played on a wind-up gramophone. And despite the fact that aeroplanes could do the journey in days instead of weeks, it was considered unbecoming to arrive in India on anything other than a fine liner from the Peninsular & Oriental Steamship Company. Perhaps the best thing about the lifestyle was the food. Just about every diary date – indeed just about every hour of the day – was accompanied by a designated opportunity to eat. And it is in these meals – prepared by Indians for British patrons – that we find the origins of the modern British curry. Everything from the décor of restaurants to the selection of dishes to the attire of the waiters has its origins in these heady days of Empire.

A British *memsahib* – the mistress of the house – could find herself running a household with as many as thirty staff. To maintain one's status, one really ought to have the full complement of *malis* (gardeners), *ayahs* (maids), *syces* (grooms, for the many horses), *bhistis* (water carriers), *punkah wallahs* (who operated the fans when there was no electric air conditioning) and of course *khansamers*, or cooks. It was with the khansamer that the memsahib had to get on particularly well: while the household staff could show one up with lop-sided topiary or a dirty vestibule, none could do as much damage to their mistresses' reputations as the cooks.

By the end of the nineteenth century most khansamers had become very used to cooking for the British palate. Most domestic cooks were highly trained chefs and were often as skilled in French and British cuisine as they were in dishes from their home provinces. And that's probably because there was an awful lot of cooking to do, as even breakfast had several courses. After years in each other's company, many Indian dishes displayed their British influences and many traditional British dishes were rejuvenated with fresh interpretations from the khansamers.

Not that this stopped the know-it-all Brits from producing guides for recent arrivals about how to get the most out of their khansamer. Many of these Raj cookery guides were written by military men with such condescension that you can easily imagine that they irritated those they employed to feed them – surely a short-sighted attitude. In an 1869 guide, *Wyvern's Indian Cookery Book* by Colonel Kenney-Herbert, not only are there chapters on 'the omelette' and 'macaroni' (presumably because the British in India had never had to cook themselves and therefore could not instruct their khansamers in the British way of omelette preparation), but there is the following piece of advice: 'If you want to put nice dinners upon your table; you must not only be prepared to take a certain amount of trouble, but you must also make a friend of your cook.' However, the Colonel warns, 'In introducing novelties of European construction it is advisable to proceed with caution.'

Such guides were generally written to help the memsahib educate her staff in the proper meals of the day from tea and toast in bed in the morning (ahead of breakfast being served in the dining room) to late suppers and brandies at night. In the grander colonial residences in India, breakfast would have consisted of meat and fish dishes to accompany pots of tea and toast and were not always a successful blend of cuisines. In *The Complete Indian Housekeeper and Cook*, written in 1893, the authors bemoan: 'Breakfasts in India are for the most part horrible meals, being hybrids between the English and French fashions. The ordinary Indian cook has not an idea for breakfast beyond chops, steaks, fried fish and quail; a menu rendered still less inviting by the poor quality of both fish and meat.' In more modest abodes, breakfast was more likely to consist of fresh chapatis served with freshly churned butter and whisky marmalade! On hunt days or other grand expeditions (which always started early to get enough killing in before the thermometer rose too much) servants would often ride ahead to lay out trestles covered with linen and groaning with hams, mixed grills, eggs, fruit and kedgeree before the exhausted Brits arrived in need of sustenance.

While the breakfast dishes may have looked familiar to someone straight off the boat from Southampton, they would have tasted completely different. Scrambled eggs were often spiced with cardamom or chillies, omelettes were fried in ghee with curry powder to add a little flair and bacon sarnies were often served with a large handful of chopped coriander wedged between the meat and the bread. Perhaps the most famous breakfast dish of the Raj is kedgeree which is a perfect example of the fusion of cuisines that went on during these years: originally, it was probably a corruption of a traditional Indian dish of rice and lentils, known as *khichri*, to which the Brits added their beloved smoked kippers that had been shipped out at considerable expense.

Throughout the day, meals were prepared and consumed using this blend of western and eastern traditions. Lunch, or tiffin as it was called, was by all accounts usually a family meal taken at home – rather than at the club – and would have been the most 'British' meal of the day (although the children would have eaten separately in the nursery of course, just in case they troubled papa). Most khansamers would be adept at producing British favourites, although with an Indian twist, to satisfy their masters' midday cravings for home. Shepherd's pie, for example, would be a close approximation of the dish found on many a farmhouse kitchen in the Shires at the time, but in India it would be served with the added benefits of cumin, sesame seeds and ginger and was known as 'eshepherd's pie'. It was a regular dish in many Anglo-Indian households.

A common belief in the Raj was that the heat of the day could be successfully combated with the heat of a meal. Many thought that as chillies made one sweat they therefore helped to keep one cool, and so the spicy additions to English dishes were done with the approval of the diners. Of all the lunchtime fusion foods the most famous is undoubtedly mulligatawny soup. Even its name evokes visions of tea rooms packed with linen-clad toffs faw-fawing about the heat being awful. In her affectionate memoir of growing up as a daughter of the Raj, *Curries and Bugles*, Jennifer Brennan narrates how the soup became a firm lunch favourite.

She writes that the name comes from the Tamil words *molagu* and *tunni*, which literally translate as 'pepper water', a favoured tipple of the brahmin yogis of the Tamil Nadu province. As chillies were cheap it became a dish adopted by the poor who added salted dried fish and a little tamarind juice when funds allowed. Somewhere along the line, this soup was then taken up by the khansamers to the Raj who added chicken and vegetables to the pot. The fact that mulligatawny is still made and packaged in such large quantities by so many food manufacturers is testament to its satisfying taste. Clearly, the British in India had taken to spice with a passion.

Evening meals were generally grand affairs with countless courses, some of which would be British, some Indian and many a mix between the two. Looking at some of the recipes from the days of the Raj I have been struck with the similarities between Indian cooking then and Indian cooking today. This may surprise some as, quite clearly, dishes like 'sardine curry puffs' (an improvised attempt at a Cornish pasty) or 'aloo chops' aren't on any menus I've ever seen in a modern curry house – but the similarities aren't in the ingredients or presentation, they are in the *spirit*. Indian cooking has always been about improvising, about not wasting food and using the cheapest ingredients around. (Indeed many khansamers had an unwritten agreement with their memsahibs that they were given a set amount to spend on food each week, but if they were able to procure goods more cheaply then it was understood that they could pocket the difference!) The use of tinned sardines or the production of steamroller chicken in the 1800s was the equivalent of Indian cooks in Britain today producing curried spaghetti (as happened in the 60s when rice became expensive) or making chicken tikka masala for the British palate. Indian cooking has always been endlessly adaptable to available ingredients and local palates and this characteristic must go some way towards explaining its international success.

This need to respond to the available ingredients and diners' peccadilloes guided the cook's hand. For instance, getting hold of tender meat was difficult and unnecessary if you cooked it correctly (not forgetting, of course, that the reward for skill in the kitchen was pocketing the difference between the price of tender juicy lamb and the price of chewy old sheep). This meant that meat was mostly tenderised extensively before it was stewed for hours. Another technique for disguising the quality of the meat was to braise it. One of the Indian words for braising is *quoorma*, or korma as it appears on menus today. Meat was marinated in spicy sauces and then cooked with ground nuts and cream. Originally this was a dish of the aristocracy from the north. It gradually spread throughout India with various Mughal conquests but is still considered an upper-class dish today.

The evening meal was usually very social and involved either entertaining or being entertained. On the nights when you didn't have an engagement, the ladies and gentlemen of the administration could be found in their clubhouses having a pre-prandial pink gin or two. Many of these clubhouses were decorated to resemble English country manors and as such displayed the most lavish – some would say vulgar – flocked wallpaper. Often imported from Britain at considerable expense, fleur-de-lis patterns and damask prints were a sign of a proprietor who knew how to take care of his patrons.

Recreating the Raj in Britain

Just as Brits in India had tried to recreate a little of home on the fringes of the Empire, when they returned to centre of it they desired to recreate a little of the East. It seems it is part of the human condition to want what you haven't got: just as the Brits craved bangers and mash when they were in India, when they were back in Blighty there was only one thing they wanted – curry. And it is around this time that debates about what was an 'authentic' curry and, presumably, an 'inauthentic' curry began.

Many of the returning 'nabobs' (an unflattering corruption of *nawab*, a term used for provincial rulers in pre-Empire India) insisted that any curry they were served was inferior to either the true dishes of India or anything they could make themselves. Consequently it appears that towards the end of the 1700s, there was a bit of a bragging contest in London about whose curries were either the 'best' or the most 'authentic'. (I'm using authentic in inverted commas, because as I hope I've made clear, even the curries served in India were always adapted to local ingredients and demands: the idea that there was one 'authentic' way to make a curry is like saying there's only one way to pluck a chicken.)

Curries in London at the time were served in a few select hotels and the odd coffee house. Many nabobs also took their khansamers home with them so they could continue to eat their curried offerings, and of course there was a largely unrecorded curry scene for the Indian sailors and servants who had been abandoned once their ships reached London or when their masters decided they had no more use for them.

The history of Asians, and therefore curry, in Britain is a much lengthier one than most people think. Many have assumed that curry arrived sometime after the War and sometime after the pubs shut, but long before the post-war, post-pub curry boom of the late twentieth century, curries prepared by Indians were being eaten at British tables.

In *Asians In Britain: 400 Years of History*, Rozina Visram has compiled a thorough and enlightening account of Asian immigration to the UK. She notes that the earliest record of an Indian in Britain is the baptism of a boy at St Dionis Backchurch in the City of London in 1616 – only sixteen years after the incorporation of the East India Company. His Indian name is not recorded, only his adopted Christian name, Peter. A few of the first British Asians, like Peter, made the journey to London in order to receive training as Protestant missionaries, a few more were students while a fair number were abandoned servants. Scant information survives about the number or nature of Indians in Britain in the seventeenth century, but there are a couple of surviving newspaper classifieds from the London Gazette seeking 'a runaway

Indian boy servant' or 'runaway Bengali boy', presumably placed by nabobs out of concern or anger. The other major source of information comes from the missionaries who would go to the docks in search of heathens to convert. Joseph Salter was one such missionary who recorded the awful plight of many Indians, sometimes making a note of how they tried to make a living: and one, he records, sold curry powder.

By far the greatest proportion of the new immigrant population was made up of sailors known as lascars. British merchant ships and liners used lascars as cheap labour on the return leg to replace seamen lost on the outward journey; this kept costs down. Although they were legally responsible for the lascars' upkeep while on British soil, it was a law that was either unenforceable or just not enforced, which meant many lascars were quickly disowned as soon as the ships docked in order to further save money. Many therefore ended up begging, or in poorhouses – a fate that would long colour people's attitudes towards Indian immigrants.

To feed the lascars, ship owners employed cooks (known as *vandary*) who were also left to fend for themselves once in dock. Not only were Indian cooks' reputations for making meals from whatever was to hand a particularly useful attribute on sea journeys, they also had a formidable reputation for producing excellent food. In *Nabobs In England* James M Holzman records that 'The Company's ships held a position analogous to that of the great transatlantic liners nowadays; their galleys, in particular, set a new standard in marine cookery, and when in port, London Aldermen would not disdain the captain's invitation to dine on board ... Many ships' cooks went on to work in tavern kitchens.' Indeed, some coffee shops even offered a 'P&O menu' to indicate the authenticity and sophistication of their fare.

Rozina Visram's book chronicles the desperate plight of many of the abandoned Indians in London who relied on the charity of the poorhouses. Unfortunately, how the Indians fed themselves is, perhaps unsurprisingly, less well documented than how the nabobs indulged in their curries from the East. What we do know about the Indian community is that in the years of the Napoleonic Wars and between 1808 and 1813, a thousand lascars a year arrived in London and relied on the charity of soup kitchens, some of which served 'curried rice' to the destitute immigrants.

At the other end of the social scale, curries were finding their way on to menus in the West End of London. The earliest surviving record of such a menu comes from the Norris Street Coffee House. *Nabobs in England* records curry's London debut: 'Curry was added to the pleasures of the table. It was a speciality of the Norris Street Coffee House, Haymarket, as early as 1773. Eleven years later it was still sufficiently strange to be credited with undeserved virtues. Sorlie's Perfumery Warehouse, 23 Piccadilly, near Air Street, advertised in the Morning Herald in 1784 that curry "renders the Stomach active in Digestion – the blood naturally free in Circulation – the mind vigorous – and contributes most of any food to an increase in the Human Race".'

The claim that curry boosted the eater's sex drive was made on many occasions, and one can only imagine that in the impending Victorian era, men who ate curry were seen as a bit louche. Heaven knows what the prim Victorians would have made of a woman eating curry! Perhaps it was to counter such attitudes that some of the nabobs made such impassioned treatises on the other benefits of curry. In his snappily titled *Indian Cookery, of Fish Curries, their excellent qualities, easy and speedy preparation with Selim's curry paste*, Captain William White implores the doubtful to partake of their first curry:

'As a savoury and healthful diet, easy of digestion, no dish can be compared with a true Indian Curry, and which, instead of producing the effects that rich stews and greasy-made dishes generally do, has a different tendency, by removing bile and promoting secretions of the body. This is easily accounted for. The compound from which a Curry is made, be it a paste or a powder, is or ought to be, a selection of a variety of seeds and aromatics, highly impregnated with essential oils of different flavours and properties, and some few roots, that also contain valuable stomachic properties. These, when blended together with care as to due proportions, afford a most savoury dish, and at the same time a diet that is highly conducive to health, by its invigorating powers and capacity to keep the body in a salutary state ... Curries are highly digestive, anti-bilious, anti-spasmodic, anti-flatulent, soothing and invigorating to the stomach and bowels, preventing debility in warm weather, and fortifying the constitution against cold in the severest.'

No wonder, then, that curry started to make a bit of a name for itself. In the late 1700s, with only a handful of coffee shops serving curries, one desperate young woman even started what must have been the first curry delivery service. Sarah Shade's life story is one of those windows into the world of the nabob that warrants closer inspection. An exquisite, delicate pamphlet in storage at the British Library chronicles this forerunner of the free delivery services offered by most Indian restaurants today. It seems that Ms Shade was indeed a little shady and didn't have the best of luck, but through cunning and gumption always seemed to muddle through until a solution presented itself. The full title of this crumbling pamphlet is *A narrative of the life of Sarah Shade, by some gentlemen, and published for her benefit* which indicates to me that she had the gift of the gab and could bend men of a certain persuasion to her will.

She had a rollercoaster life. Orphaned young, she was at the mercy of anyone who could do her a favour and at some point in her teens was 'adopted' by an elderly gentleman with whom she travelled to India where she later married an officer, or two. During her time in the East she survived a shipwreck, was so ill she was pronounced dead and then buried alive – forty-eight hours later she woke up and started knocking on her coffin till someone heard! Following the death of her second husband, she returned to London with a reputation for scandal and was cast out on the streets by her late husband's family. The *Narrative* then records that: 'she took a room; and, for about the space of a year and a half, subsisted herself chiefly by making curry for different East India families – a dish for which she is famous.'

If, however, you fancied doing the cooking yourself, there is a record of a certain Mrs Turnbull of 57 Queen's Gardens, Hyde Park to whom you could write and she would send you, by return of post, 100 different recipes for curry. Some were very complex – one required a mix of turmeric, cardamom, coriander, ginger, black pepper, red pepper, caraway seeds and cloves – so Mrs Turnbull had an arrangement with 'Beeces Medical Hall' in Piccadilly who would supply mixes ground to her specification upon request.[2]

Recipes for curries started to appear in cookery books in the middle of the century. The first known printed recipe was written by the Delia Smith of her day, Hannah Glasse, although decorum dictated that she publish her recipes anonymously. In the 1747 book *The Art of Cookery ... By A Lady* she informs her readers how 'To make a Currey the India Way'. It is repeated here with all its printing and spelling curiosities intact:

Take two Fowls or Rabbits, cut them into fmall Pieces, and three or four fmall Onions, peeled and cut very fmall, thirty Pepper Corns, and a large Spoonful of Rice, brown fome Coriander Seeds over the

[2] A Baron, *An Indian Affair*, Channel 4 Books, 2001, p. 138.

Fire in a clean Shovel, and beat them to Powder, take a Tea Spoonful of Salt, and mix all well together with the Meat, put all together in a Sauce-pan or Stew-pan, with a Pint of Water, let it ftew foftly till the Meat is enough, then put in in a Piece of frefh Butter, about as big as a large Walnut, fhake it well together, and when it is fmooth and of a fine Thicknefs difh it up and fend it to Table. If the sauce be too thick, add a little more Water before it is done, and more Salt if it wants it. You are to obferve the Sauce muft be pretty thick.

Britain's First Curry House

For all the wonderful characters that played their part in the history of curry, perhaps the most adventurous figure was a man called Sake Dean Mahomet who has the distinction of being the proprietor of Britain's first ever curry house. An almost mythical character from the eighteenth and nineteenth centuries, records reveal him to be a romantic cross between Sinbad the Sailor and Arthur Daley. In a remarkable life he became the first Indian to publish a book written in English, travelled across northern India with the British army, emigrated to Ireland and became a confidante of George IV, as well as being one of the most flamboyant curry pioneers.

Mahomet was born to servants of the Mughal ruler in Patna in 1858, but by the age of 11 was an orphan. With little choice of employers, Mahomet started working for the East India Company in 1769, a time when the EIC's main source of income was tax collection. The 1760s were among the bloodiest years of the British occupation of India when the Company and its servants plundered Bengal and reduced it to near bankruptcy: for Mahomet serving the EIC was probably a case of survival rather than desire. He found himself in the service of an Anglo-Irish officer, Godfrey Evan Baker, and as Baker's military star ascended, Mahomet's horizons expanded and he travelled with his master across India, and later the Empire. Mahomet's allegiance to Baker and the EIC must have made him seem complicit in the growth of colonialism in the eyes of many of his countrymen, and for this reason his relationship with other Indians seems to have been ambivalent at best, according to his biographer Michael Fisher.[3] This may well have been a factor in his decision to follow Baker home to Ireland when his service ended in 1783.

In Ireland Mahomet remained with the Bakers although it appears he gained some independent wealth, possibly by his marriage to an Irishwoman named Mary Daly. While in Ireland Mahomet wrote, in English, a record of his travels with Baker and achieved some notoriety by promoting it in person. In 1807, at the age of nearly fifty, he uprooted his wife and children to make the move to London. Records do not reveal why he chose to make such a move – after all, neither Indians nor the Irish had good reputations in London: the Irish were credited with ill-health and spreading disease while Asians were viewed with a mixture of pity and fear.

It didn't take Mahomet long to realise that there was an appetite for Indian food in London. It wasn't widely served, but where it was available it was popular, as the demand for Sarah Shade's cooking has revealed. Dean Mahomet wasn't the first person to serve curry in Britain, but the arrival of his Hindostanee Coffee House was nevertheless a landmark.

---

[3] M H Fisher, biographical essay from *The Travels of Dean Mahomet*, University of California Press, 1997.

The term 'coffee house' was a fashionable rather than accurate term which referred to about two thousand small restaurants in London at the beginning of the nineteenth century, most of which didn't sell much coffee. *The Epicure's Almanack, a Calendar of Good Living in London* – a Zagat's restaurant guide of its day – recorded every inn, tavern, coffee house, eating house, hotel, restaurant and any other place of 'alimentary resort', and from it we can see that although curry was available, it was not a fashionable choice. At the time the city was under the spell of French cookery and obsessed with prepared meats such as ham, cured beef and continental sausages.

The period was a boom time for the proprietors of 'alimentary resorts', partly due to improvements in agriculture and trade, which provided cheaper and more reliable supplies. Consequently, restaurateurs went to the expense of printing menus for the first time as they were able to provide the same dishes for months on end (previously, diners had had to endure something of a monologue from the waiting staff, who had to recite an ever-changing list of available dishes). For Dean Mahomet, a man of great enterprise, there seemed to be a gap in the market: not only was there an appetite – even if small – for Indian cuisine, but the cooks and ingredients were in sufficient supply and there was no obvious competition.

The Hindostanee Coffee House opened in late 1809 at 34 George St at the corner of Charles Street, in the exclusive area around Portman Square. London had never seen anything like it. Mahomet had procured, or perhaps made, furniture from bamboo (previously unseen in London) and the Hindostanee was decorated with 'Chinese pictures and other Asiatic embellishments'. The dishes, he promised, were 'in the highest perfection and allowed by the great epicures to be unequalled to any curries ever made in England'. By creating a truly unique ambience, Mahomet must have hoped to attract nabobs missing their lives in India. As an extra enticement, he created an en-suite smoking room where he offered ornate hookah pipes and 'real Chilm tobacco'.

At first it seems that the Hindostanee was a moderate success as the following year records show that Mahomet expanded into 35 George Street where his smoking room became known as The Hookah Club, and counted among its clientele infamous bachelors like Charles Stewart (a veteran of India and one of London's most eligible men at the time) and – according to one source – the Prince of Wales whose passion for all things Eastern was most famously displayed when he had the Pavilion in Brighton built in the style of the Taj Mahal. While notable, Mahomet's Coffee House was not as profitable as he had hoped and in 1811 he needed financial assistance and took on a partner called John Spencer. In March of that year they advertised to their target market of returned EIC officers and their families by taking out an ad in *The Times*:

HINDOSTANEE COFFEE HOUSE, No 34 George St, Portman Square.

MAHOMET, East Indian, informs Nobility and Gentry, he has fitted up the above house, neatly and elegantly, for the entertainment of Indian gentlemen, where they may enjoy the Hoakha, with real Chilm tobacco, and Indian dishes, in the highest perfection, and allowed by the greatest epicures to be unequalled to any curries ever made in England with choice wines, and every accommodation, and now looks up to them for their future patronage and support, and gratefully acknowledges himself indebted for their former favours, and trusts it will merit the highest satisfaction when made known to the public.

Presumably *The Times* charged for advertisements by the sentence! With hindsight, perhaps Mahomet should have invested more heavily in his attempts to generate more custom. In time it became clear that he couldn't compete with his City rival the Jerusalem Coffee House, even though it was nearly two miles to the East near the Cornhill Exchange. The Jerusalem was long established and had already secured the patronage of merchants with a trading connection to the East Indies, which meant not enough of them ventured to the West End to sample Mahomet's unusual establishment. It also seems that his appeal to the aristocracy failed, as those who wanted to eat Indian dishes simply ordered their domestic staff to prepare meals for them at home. In 1812, Dean Mahomet turned from Britain's first Indian proprietor of a curry house into Britain's first Indian bankrupt.

The Hindostanee Coffee House continued in some form under John Spencer until 1833 when it finally closed, possibly in response to the arrival of the Oriental Club which opened not far away in Hanover Square in 1824, and provided a more salubrious environment for Company gentlemen.

Despite the disappointment of the Hindostanee, Dean Mahomet's remarkable talent for reinvention meant that this is not the last we know of him. The man who was the first Indian to publish a book in English, who opened Britain's first true curry house, and who through every stage in his life displayed curiosity, tenacity, compassion and enterprise surfaced a few years later in Brighton where he opened a bath house that brought him both acclaim and fame. Brighton at that time was where Londoners went to take the sea air and recuperate. It was also home to the now Prince Regent at the Pavilion. Mahomet's Indian Vapour Baths and Shampooing Establishment pampered the gentry with an array of treatments using oils and herbs 'brought expressly from India'. Yet again, Mahomet had found a way to capitalise on his Indian-ness and his understanding of the British aristocracy. He enjoyed the favour of the Regent, and when he acceded to the throne to become George IV, Sake Dean Mahomet gained the royal seal and became Official Shampooer to the King! Many, if not all, subsequent proprietors of Indian restaurants have entertaining stories to tell, but none have been quite as romantic or colourful as those of the man who did it first.

Following the demise of the Hindostanee, the curry's progress through the rest of the nineteenth century was slow but steady. Records at the Savoy show that the hotel employed an Indian chef and Queen Victoria's personal chef, Charles Elme Francatelli, included instructions for an 'Indian curry sauce' in his book *The Modern Cook*. In 1861, the *chef de cuisine* at the Oriental Club, Richard Terry, published Britain's very first dedicated Indian cook book. *Indian Cookery* was, he claimed, a collection of recipes 'gathered not only from my knowledge of Cookery, but from Native Cooks'; and curries were also being served at a rival club, The Reform. Further evidence that curry had become a household dish can be found in Mrs Beeton's famous *Book of Household Management* which contained no fewer than fourteen curry recipes. Perhaps it's also revealing of a domestic curry scene that the writer William Makepeace Thackeray included an 'Ode to Curry' in his 1846 poetry collection *Kitchen Melodies*.

Curry Powder

The rise in popularity of curry as a domestic dish in the Victorian era followed on from quite a passionate rivalry between curry powder manufacturers, each of whom claimed theirs was the most authentic, of course, and the tastiest.

Captain White – he of the anti-bilious, anti-flatulent praise of earlier – wrote that he 'condemns the fiery compounds generally in use in

England, called Curry Powders, as most pernicious'. His own paste, however: well, that was a different matter; *his* curry paste saved lives! He claimed that the proprietor of the Jerusalem Coffee House, a Mr Harper, had been ill for many years until he started serving sandwiches made with Captain White's paste as 'a curiosity'. The aromatics administered in the paste had, according to the Captain himself, restored Mr Harper to health. Unsurprisingly then, the paste was soon stocked in jars and sold by 'Messrs Hale and Fleming of the Poultry, and Ball & Son of Bond St'. Captain White clearly took his paste seriously: on one occasion he refused to sell his paste through Ball and Sons as they made 'impositions on the public' by selling an imitation 'made by a scoundrel in the west end of town'!

There were many attempts to create a commercial curry powder that would make curries easier to prepare for the uninitiated. These pre-blended mixtures were designed to be added in prescribed quantities to any stew and required no additional flavouring. Captain White recommended his readers try buying their powder from one of two shops: 'George Batty and Co's, Finsbury Pavement, sells "Indian Curry Powder from an Original recipe as prepared for the celebrated Tippoo Saib", and Cross and Blackwell's of Soho Square sells "Shah Soojah, Genuine Curry Powder".' Elsewhere, however, he can't resist referring to Cross and Blackwell's powder as 'Shah Soojah's ashes'. Yet again he reveals the British nabob as an unpleasant stereotype.

Perhaps Captain White's self-regard was well-founded, however, as the establishment most associated with Indian cookery at the time endorsed his powder above all others. On the labels of Captain White's small stone jars of 'Fish and Chicken Curry and Mulligatawny Paste' was an endorsement from the chef at the Oriental Club which read:

Kitchen Department, Oriental Club,
July 8th, 1851

I have for four years exclusively used your CURRY PASTE AND POWDER and have invariably found that they have given general satisfaction.

G Fidle

Of all the venues where one might hope to find a nabob reliving his heady days in India, then the Oriental was the most glamorous. Opened in 1824 in an imposing mansion on the north-west corner of Hanover Square in London's West End, it was the archetypal hangout for rich and bloated Company men. Here it is described in the 1850 edition of the *Hand-Book of London*:

ORIENTAL CLUB, 18, HANOVER SQUARE, founded 1824, by Sir John Malcolm, and is composed of noblemen and gentlemen who have travelled or resided in Asia, at St. Helena, in Egypt, at the Cape of Good Hope, the Mauritius, or at Constantinople; or whose official situations connect them with the administration of our Eastern government abroad or at home. Entrance money, 20*l.*; annual subscription 8*l.* The Club possesses some good portraits of Clive, Stringer Lawrence, Sir Eyre Coote, Sir David Ochterloney, Sir G. Pollock, Sir W. Nott, Mountstuart Elphinstone, Sir. H. Pottinger, Duke of Wellington, &c.

And in *Cruchley's London in 1865: A Handbook for Strangers* we are told that: 'The ORIENTAL, 18 Hanover Square, comprises 1000 members, – persons connected with our Eastern dependencies or Oriental literature, – who pay an entrance fee of 21*l.*, and an annual subscription of 8*l.*' Despite the members' profiles as India men, the club's early culinary offerings were distinctly British in character – chops, steaks, game, fish and oysters were generally served in the Oriental's lavish coffee room. In fact, it isn't until 1839, fifteen years after it first opened its doors, that there is any record of 'curry' at the club. In the Committee minutes from

12 August of that year, a Mr Williamson of the Bombay Civil Service suggests that a 'native Indian cook' might be employed to instruct the chef in the preparation of authentic curries (many of the Club's chefs had been recruited from Paris where, presumably, they had gained little experience of cooking Indian food). However, his suggestion was rejected by the committee as 'the curries made now by the cook give general satisfaction'.

It seems the Committee's assessment of the chef's fare is a little harsh, for in the 1858 edition of *London at Dinner* the club gets a slightly more enthusiastic review of its food. 'The "Oriental Club", in Hanover Square, is famed for its Eastern condiments and wines; and as the members are unquestionably good livers – (we do not speak of the gastric organs) – they may dine here to their heart's content,' it declares.

Later records show that Captain White soon fell out of favour at the Oriental, and a new chef started buying a Madras mix from Payne's of Leicester Square, while another imported curry powder directly from Madras through importers Parry & Co. Elsewhere in London, Sharwood's had also started an import business and among their offerings were 'Madras Curry Powder, Mulligatawny and Curry Paste, Mango Pickles, Lime and Bamboo in Oil and Vinegar, Hot Chutneys, Ground Cayenne and Nepaul Pepper, Delhi Sauces, Tamarind Fish Preserves and Indian Jams and Jellies which always may be had in perfection.'

One can't help wondering if their customers really knew what to do with their purchases. On the side of a tin of Sharwood's Madras powder 'prepared by P. Vencatachellum, Indian condiment manufacturers' there is a recipe for chicken curry that sounds, frankly, godawful:

Take a chicken weighing about a pound and a half, wash it in water and sprinkle over a large teaspoonful of salt, then cut up two onions and fry them in a chatty or stewpan with a tablespoonful of butter or ghee until they become brown then add the Chicken and two tablespoonfuls of Curry Powder with three wineglasses of cold water or gravy: stir all well together and stew for 20 minutes longer, then add a dessertspoonful of lime juice, which will make a delicious Indian Curry.

NB The same quantity or weight of Mutton, Veal, Pigeons, Partridges, Fish etc., may be substituted for that of chicken.

If that was served in a restaurant in Britain today, you'd want your money back! That's because in the twentieth century our education in, and appreciation of, curry was greatly enhanced by a new generation of Indian restaurants that would change the face of eating in London within a matter of decades.

CINNAMON

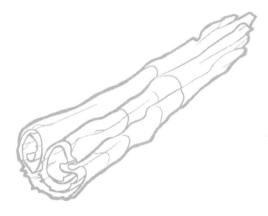

Ancient texts reveal cinnamon was used in Europe with some regularity around the seventh century BCE. As well as Herodotus's fanciful story about its origins (quoted in Chapter One), writers as varied as the poet Sappho and the author of the forty-fifth psalm recorded its use. Perhaps its most lofty endorsement comes from the Jewish God, no less, who in the book of Exodus commands Moses to 'take the choicest of spices' – which included cinnamon – to make a perfume to use in worship.

Cinnamon's Latin name, Cinnamomum zeylanicum, comes from the Dutch name for Sri Lanka, Zeilan, which later became translated as Ceylon. Cinnamon is so named because Sri Lanka is by far the world's biggest cinnamon producer. Cinnamon is harvested from the inner bark of the upper branches of a tropical laurel tree which is native to the country and is now grown in vast plantations. The bark is harvested soon after the monsoon when the tree's oils are at their most aromatic. The outer bark is then scraped away and the thinner, inner bark is left to dry, and as it does it curls naturally into quills.

Sri Lankan cinnamon is a dark buff colour with a hint of red, whereas Keralan cinnamon is much darker, almost mahogany coloured, and comes in smaller, tighter quills. There is also a Chinese variety of cinnamon that is valued more for its medicinal properties than its culinary ones. The ancients were very confused as to its origins, variously thinking it came from Arabia, Eritrea, Ethiopia and Iraq.

It was only in the fourteenth century that Ibn Batûtâ finally accurately recorded its harvest in Ceylon and described 'the whole coast near here is covered with the trunks of cinnamon trees brought down by the rivers. They are collected in mounds on the sea shore. People from Coromandel and Malabar take them away without paying, but they give the sultan cloth and such like in exchange.'[1] Later, in 1579, Thomas Stevens (a Jesuit missionary in Goa, and arguably the first Englishman in India) recorded that while cinnamon grew wild on the Malabar coast, 'the best comes from Ceylon where it is pilled from young trees'.[2]

Cinnamon is used in sweet and savoury dishes to flavour pilau rice, biryanis, stews, teas and desserts. And as one of the principal ingredients in garam masala, cinnamon is more widely used than a reading of recipes would suggest. Most Sri Lankan dishes simmer a quill in every sauce. It is also widely used in

---

[1] Ibn Batûtâ, *Travels*, Vol 3.

[2] M S Randhawa, *A History of Agriculture in India*, Vol 2, 1982, Indian Council of Agricultural Research.

incense, perfume and medicines as it is thought to do everything from cure nausea to soothe colds and clean teeth. In Egypt however, cinnamon had a more exalted use: traces of it have been found in mummies as it was one of the substances used to embalm the bodies of the pharaohs.

Cinnamon is often called cassia, although in fact they are two different spices. The cinnamon tree is smaller than the cassia tree and its quills are generally finer and lighter in colour. Considered to be superior to cassia both in terms of flavour and aroma, cinnamon is therefore more expensive. The leaves of the cassia tree are called tejpat and are also used in cooking.

CHAPTER FOUR

Twentieth-century Tastes

Early Restaurants

*I*t might have been anticipated that the death in 1901 of Queen Victoria, who was believed to have been a great lover of India and its food (although she famously never travelled to see the jewel in her crown) would have signalled a decline in the British interest in all things Indian. And when, in the next decade, the Great War gave Britons another reason to focus attentions a little closer to home, you might anticipate that the Indian love affair would have been nearly over. Yet interest in Indian food in Britain had never been keener.

Part of the reason for this is that by the dawn of the twentieth century there were many thousands of Indians living, studying and working in Britain. In 1892 Dadabhai Naoroj became the first Indian elected to

Parliament, and as many civil service posts in India were only available to those who had trained in Britain, you occasionally found Indian doctors, lawyers and civil servants who had remained in Britain after completing their studies. That said, Indians were still a tiny minority among the professional classes: most Indian immigrants worked as unskilled labourers.

Although there were small lascar communities in the big ports of Glasgow, Liverpool and Portsmouth, the vast majority of Indians lived and worked in London. The relatively high number of Indians in the capital demanded cafés and kitchens to feed them. As with nineteenth century records, details about the food of the aristocracy are much easier to find than information about the restaurants the Indian community itself frequented. In fact the only written documents about turn of the century cafés serving Indian food are the surveillance reports held in the India Office Records archive.

In the early 1900s the British government was so concerned about the rise in Indian nationalism that the India Office set up covert surveillance of premises where Indian student agitators met. Unsurprisingly, these tended to be places where Indian food was served. Perhaps equally unsurprisingly, given the way in which these facts were recorded, almost any description of either the buildings, the food or the clientele is disparaging. Nevertheless, they serve as the only extant record of the restaurants that served the Indian community.

It seems that in 1905 there was an Indian café on Shaftesbury Avenue and another in Red Lion Passage in Holborn serving curries. There is also mention of a Nizam-ud-din who ran the Indian Catering Company at 36 Ledbury Road as well as the Eastern Café near Chancery Lane and, in 1911, there is an account of a KN Das Gupta opening the Coronation Hotel and Restaurant in Gray's Inn Road. 1911 also saw the opening of the Salut e Hind, also in Holborn, and in order to supply these establishments with produce, a man called Nitisen

Dwarkadas is said to have started an import business, according to IOR reports.[3] There were also many more cafés near the docks in the east of London, although not too many records of these survive. Of the few for which we do have details, one was opened in the 1920s by Sylheti sailor Ayub Ali at 76 Commercial Street and called the Shah Jalal; another opened in 1915 in the basement of a barber's shop at 27 Victoria Dock Road. And in the 1920 edition of Ward Lock's annual *Guide to London* there is an ad for 'The Indian Restaurants Ltd' claiming to be 'THE place for curries to suit all tastes'.[4]

Gradually, Indian restaurants made their way into London's West End where the clientele included a small but slowly growing number of indigenous whites. One of the earliest 'curry houses' that regularly served white clients was the Shafi at 18 Gerard Street, which was opened in 1920 by Mohammed Wayseem and Mohammed Rahim serving food from north India. The Shafi proved to be something of a curry university, as many of its employees – almost all ex-seamen – went on to start their own restaurants elsewhere in Britain.

These early restaurants – like so many thousands that would follow in the rest of the century – were mainly run by men from Sylhet. Given that Sylhet is a landlocked region in what is now Bangladesh, it may seem odd that a great number of its sons became seamen. This is because Sylhet relied on river transport in the way that other regions relied on roads. In rural Sylhet, a boat was once necessary to go shopping, go to school or meet with friends and associates. Consequently it was one of the first districts to make use of steamships, which meant that when other districts changed to steam power, Sylheti seamen were in demand to maintain and service the engines. This in turn lured many Sylhetis to Calcutta where they found work on

[3] IOR: POS 5945; IOR: POS 8966; IOR: V/27/262/1, held at the British Library.
[4] R Visram, *Asians In Britain*, Pluto Press, 2002, p. 85, p. 280.

steamships with international routes. A well-developed network of Sylheti boarding houses sprang up in Calcutta, enabling steamship workers to find accommodation and work. The men who ran the boarding houses were known as *bariwallahs* and although many were altruistic, some saw their guests as investments: many were allowed to stay without paying, but only on the condition that when they returned to Calcutta after many months at sea, they agreed to pay a percentage of their earnings to the bariwallah. Some bariwallahs were known to be corrupt, and even insisted on charging rent for the time the sailor was at sea. While this was an incentive for some to earn more money, it was also an incentive for others not to return.

The Veeraswamy

In contrast to the paucity of information we have about restaurants frequented by the Indian community, the details about Veeraswamy's seem as opulent as the restaurant itself. Opened in 1927 by Edward Palmer, a great-grandson of Mughal princess Begum Faiz Bux and English Lieutenant-General William Palmer, Veeraswamy's set a new standard not just for Indian cooking in Britain, but for restaurants in general. Such was its fame and success that it could be argued that it has influenced every single curry house that has opened since.

Palmer was encouraged to invest the necessary funds in the Regent Street premises after a successful stab at providing catering of a certain quality at the British Empire Exhibition of 1924 at Wembley. The Exhibition – a vast complex of buildings, installations and demonstrations from nearly every country in the British Empire which centred on the specially built Wembley Stadium – was designed to elicit British civilian support for the Empire. Reeling from the fallout of the Great War, Britain was missing and mourning a generation of young men and enduring dire financial crises, so unsurprisingly not many could see the point of holding on to an Empire that seemed to be an added drain on energies. It didn't help that the mother country's ability to govern had been impaired by crushing post-war unemployment and world-wide recession: in consequence, there were a number of nationalist movements developing in far-flung places – most notably in India – that made the Empire seem more bother than it was worth.

The Exhibition of 1924, therefore, had quite a task to perform. As its mission statement claimed it was meant to: 'stimulate trade, to strengthen the bonds that bind the Mother Country to her Sister States and Daughter Nations, to bring all into closer touch, the one with the other, to enable all who owe allegiance to the British Flag to meet on common ground, and to learn to know each other. It is a family party, to which every member of the Empire is invited, and at which every part of the Empire is represented.' So, with the aim of bringing India and Britain a little closer together, Edward Palmer ran the Mughal Palace restaurant for the duration of the Exhibition, and in doing so created an appetite among the white population for an Indian restaurant.

Encouraged by friends and acquaintances from India, Palmer set about creating an upmarket venue that soon earned the tag 'The ex-Indian higher serviceman's curry club'. By all accounts, Palmer tried to recreate as best he could the environment of an EIC clubhouse in one of the British cantonments of Raj-era India. It was so unique among London's venues for fine dining that for many years it was simply referred to as 'the Indian restaurant'.

In the 1928 edition of *The Restaurants of London* an account of the recently opened restaurant evocatively describes the décor and ambience of the exotic Veeraswamy's: 'All the waiters are natives clad in spotless white with dark crimson sashes and white turbans. There are three rooms, below ground, ground floor and first floor. All the decoration is Indian, the carpets, the walls, the ceilings and the lights. The Eastern chandeliers have orange-coloured globes, there is much dull gold in the decorations, and the air seems impregnated with shaded sunshine.'[5] There were apparently also tiger skins on the walls and punkah fans operated by punkah wallahs.

As well as contemporary reviews, the other source of information about the original interior of Veeraswamy's is the restaurant itself. Now called The Veeraswamy and occupying only the first floor of the original premises, the venue is still one of the finest Indian restaurants in London. When the present owners Nameeta Panjabi and her husband Ranjit Mathrani, who also own the famous Chelsea restaurant Chutney Mary, renovated the Regent Street premises in the 1990s, they discovered Palmer's original floor plan, which apparently followed ancient Vedic principles about the best way to lay out furniture.

Early reviews also tell us about Palmer's menu. This again is from *Restaurants of London*: 'Nearly everyone likes a properly made curry, and it takes a native cook to make one, the best French chef in the world has never attained to it. There are at least a dozen curries to choose from at the India restaurant, rising in price from one to five shillings and averaging three shillings. Moglai Moorgee Birianni (Mughal Chicken Pillau) is a very special curry and costs five shillings; there is Moorgee Ka Salun Madrassi (Madras Chicken Curry, wings only) at four shillings; Dhall Cha (mutton and Dhall curry); Ginga Ka Salun (prawn curry) both three shillings.' And if that was too avant garde for the new restaurant's adventurous customers, the menu also included 'English rump steak, lamb cutlet and so on'! (As a rough

---

[5] E Hooton-Smith, *The Restaurants of London*, Knopf, 1928.

guide, a shilling in the 20s is the equivalent of about £1.20 in today's currency.)

A decade or so later, a review in the 1937 book *Where to Dine in London* (by the mysterious 'Bon Viveur' – which we now know to be a pseudonym of the future TV cook Fanny Cradock and her husband and writing partner Johnny) reveals that the food at Veeraswamy's was still a novelty for many diners:

> Veeraswamy's India Restaurant, 99 Regent Street (the entrance is in Swallow Street). Gives the lie to those who fondly imagine that curry is the only Indian dish. There is curry, of course, and curry powder plays no part in its composition: it is made entirely with spices. Madras Chicken Curry is the speciality, and it consists of the whole wing of a chicken appropriately treated. Also there are vegetable curries. But this is by no means all. There is Indian Omelette, which is delicately flavoured with spices; Chicken Biriani, steamed in butter with special rice; Grilled Kabab; and some succulent fruit sweets, Mangusteeni, Lichi and Mangoes. There are no less than six different kinds of Indian bread.
>
> Veeraswamy's has coloured panels of Indian scenes on its wall, and there are real Indian punkahs, fans which are worked by the wallahs in hot weather. The waiters, who are all Indians, are attractively got up in white clothes and turbans and red sashes, and the service is an Oriental dream.[6]

Although I'm assuming that a fair proportion of Veeraswamy's customers had worked in India, the odd tell-tale remark in some of the reviews reveal just how unusual the cuisine was: 'the management is to be congratulated on a menu which is unusually clear to the uninitiated,' says one reviewer.

[6] Bon Viveur, *Where to Dine in London*, Geoffrey Bles, 1937.

It would seem that for some old India hands, the desire to recreate for an evening the status they had enjoyed in the East was a bigger draw than the food. Reviewer E Hooton-Smith remarks with a critic's gift for stating the uncomfortable: 'Many of the customers have never been out East and many of them have, and like to eat again a real curry and remember the days when they were important functionaries on salary instead of "retired" on a pension.' Then, with pen duly sharpened, Hooton-Smith adds that after reliving sunnier days in the dining room, 'they go into the London rain and the Indian door-keeper holds his umbrella over their heads as they pass into the full swell of London.'[7] Veeraswamy's, then, was as nostalgic for some as it was adventurous for others.

By the end of the 1930s there were at least two other Indian restaurants serving an affluent white clientele. The Mysore at 6 Glendower Place, South Kensington was reported to be 'frequented by distinguished Indians and by Englishmen who have spent their lives in the East and know a good curry when they taste one'. It seems it was quite possible to get hold of a curried meal in London at the time (made with unfashionable curry powder) but as this review of the Delhi Restaurant, again by 'Bon Viveur', shows, the London palate had matured its appreciation of Indian cookery since the recipes of the nineteenth century.

DELHI, 117 Tottenham Court Road, is a restaurant where genuine Indian curry is served at a reasonable price. Good curry, unfortunately, is the exception rather than the rule in London, and travesties of this noble dish are all too often met with on the menus of inferior restaurants. It is not sufficient to do up a little mutton and rice with curry powder. The real

[7] Hooton-Smith, *The Restaurants of London*.

thing is a much more elaborate affair, and it is essential it should be served with Bombay Duck, Poppadums, fresh chutneys and Lime or Brinjal Pickle. The curry at Delhi is vouched for by no less a person than the Rajah of Sarawak, who is an enthusiastic customer. The coffee is also excellent. There is lunch at 1s 6p and dinner at 2s 6p.[8]

As with Veeraswamy's, there is still a curry house on the site of the original restaurant at 117 Tottenham Court Road, although it has long since changed its name to L'al Qila. According to other reports, the Rajah of Sarawak was not the only visiting dignitary who liked a curry when in London. In fact, the early guests at Veeraswamy's show just how upmarket going out for a curry was in the 20s and 30s. Prince Edward (later Edward VIII), King Gustav of Sweden and Charlie Chaplin are listed as patrons, as was the King of Denmark who has a special – if unwarranted – place in curry's history. His story goes that he visited Veeraswamy's whenever he was in London but was frustrated that he couldn't get a glass of his beloved Carlsberg beer to have with his meal. So, being king, he ordered a minion to arrange a delivery of Denmark's finest to 99 Regent Street, thus beginning the great British tradition of washing down a curry with a glug of beer! This story appears in several articles about the history of curry, but I can reveal that it almost certainly isn't true. It was made up by the man brought in to do the PR for the restaurant's relaunch in 1997 to get publicity[9] – an invention that has been repeated so many times that it has almost become fact.

[8] Bon Viveur, *Where to Dine in London*.

[9] The PR was Iqbal Wahhab, now proprietor of the Cinnamon Club restaurant.

Pre-war Curry

Palmer sold Veeraswamy's in 1935 to the flamboyant MP Sir Charles Stewart who continued to run it as a destination for the well-bred and the well-heeled. Elsewhere in London personal recollections establish that restaurants with more modest clients were starting to appear in the 30s. The centre of curry house activity was just north of Soho around Percy Street where you could find the Durbar, owned by Asuk Mukerjee from Calcutta, and the Bengal India, owned by Jobbul Haque of Urrishi. Nearby in Windmill Street Nogandro Goush from Calcutta opened the Dilkush in 1938; while in Wardour Street you could sample Asif Khan's Punjabi cuisine in the Shalimar; and at 17 Irving Street you'd have found the India and Burma restaurant. Further east, towards the docks, there were yet more including the Oriental Café de Colombo in West India Dock Road. One Indian visitor in 1937 recorded that there were sixteen Indian restaurants in London at that time.[10] Additional information comes from an edition of the *Indian Student* from the same year which carries ads for the Taj-Mahal in West Street, and the Koh-i-noor in Rupert Street serving 'the finest Indian food'.

London's first suburban curry house appears to have been the Oriental Restaurant that opened in the early 1930s at 192 The Broadway in Wimbledon. In addition to these places, where you could eat out, some of the larger restaurants provided outside catering for private functions indicating that curry was considered an upmarket and entertaining choice for hosts who wished to impress.

Of all these early curry pioneers, the men who probably had the greatest influence on the early British restaurant scene were the Bahadur brothers from Delhi, who may well have been responsible for

[10] Visram, *Asians In Britain*.

training an entire generation of restaurateurs. They came to London to study, noticed a gap in the market for Indian food and opened their first establishment, the Koh-i-noor, in Rupert Street sometime before 1934. By the outbreak of the Second World War they had opened Indian restaurants in Brighton, Oxford, and Northampton (all called the Taj Mahal), as well as premises in Cambridge and Manchester (both called the Koh-i-noor) and all mostly staffed by ex-seamen.[11] They had a reputation for being good employers and were often encouraging when any of their staff announced that they wanted to set up a restaurant of their own. As Yousuf Chowdhury records in *The Roots And Tales Of The Bangladeshi Settlers*: 'Nearly all the first generation of Bangladeshis who owned restaurants in the early days learnt their trade from the Bahadur brothers.' In Manchester alone, four pre-war restaurants were opened by Bahadur disciples. They were the Everest Restaurant, the Monzil, the Orient on Oxford Street and the Shalimar. There were probably more, but this highlights how instrumental the Bahadurs were, and indicates why so many restaurants were so similar: they were all run by friends who shared suppliers, staff, recipes and ideas.

There are a few other accounts of pre-Second World War curry houses dotted across the length and breadth of Britain. According to a newspaper report there were 'forty cafés kept by Indians and Maltese in one area' of Cardiff, and in Liverpool Ah Wah's Chinese lodging house employed a Muslim chef and attracted an Indian clientele. I'm assuming that if reports could be found from other dock towns a similar pattern of ethnic cuisine would reveal itself. It is impossible for me to imagine how bizarre a career change it must have been for these men: one month a sailor on the tropical seas of the East, the next a waiter in a provincial town of the 'mother country' where it no doubt always rained, where

---

[11] C & P Grove, *Curry and Spice and All Things Nice*, www.menu2menu.co.uk.

you didn't speak the language and where few of your neighbours had ever seen an Asian before.

Although the wages were poor for restaurant staff, they seemed generous compared to the pay of a lascar (who was typically paid one sixth of a white seaman's pay), and those who shared in a café's profits considered themselves well off. A report in 1944 recorded that a manager of an Indian café made £9 a week plus a percentage of profits, although these rates surely didn't apply to more humble waiters and kitchen staff. Still, it's little wonder then that so many of the Bahadurs' staff went on to open their own restaurants when the wages in other manual jobs typically paid from 17s 6p to £1 a week.

During the war, work in restaurants was appealing for other reasons. World War II hit the Sylheti community in London hard. A great number of Sylhetis fought for the British in the engine rooms of warships as their experience on steamships was still in demand. Due to the design of warships, the engine rooms were generally in the middle and near the bottom, so if a ship was struck and the captain gave the order to abandon ship it took the engine-room seamen longer to escape; by the time they made it to the deck – if they did – the lifeboats were often full. This grief, however, imbued the fledgling restaurant scene with a renewed sense of community.

Little is recorded about the food served in these establishments. What we can deduce from other facts, however, is that very, very few of these pioneers had any experience of cooking domestically, let alone professionally, before their arrival in Britain. In India, food preparation had been a largely female role, and so it was only when these male sailors found themselves living communally in lodging houses in Britain that they taught themselves, and each other, to cook the food of home. Outside of the Veeraswamys and Mysores at the top end of the scale, the curries elsewhere would have been simple, limited both by the skills of the chefs and the availability and price of ingredients.

The one-sauce-fits-all style of cooking was developed to accommodate both shortcomings: not only did it allow unskilled cooks to produce a wide variety of dishes simply by adding different meats or vegetables before serving, but it was also cheap to produce and provided enough of a profit margin to pay better wages.

Of course, not all Indian kitchen staff worked in Indian restaurants, just as not all Indians by any means worked in the restaurant trade. Many worked in hotel kitchens and in Italian, Greek and Egyptian restaurants and, later, in Wimpy bars and Lyons' Corner Houses. Outside catering, unskilled jobs were also found in docking and manufacturing.

The outbreak of war in 1939 meant that the docking business was moved, pretty much wholesale, from London to Glasgow in order to avoid disruption from bombing, although other ports around Britain also saw their business increase. And as the war also saw an increase in merchant shipping, there was naturally an increase in the number of Indian sailors entering British ports other than London, some of whom stayed put and entered the restaurant trade. One of the bizarre corollaries of Hitler's invasion of Poland, then, was that it indirectly spurred on the British acquiescence to curry!

Although there were almost certainly places in the docks in Glasgow where seamen could get a curry as early as 1920, the first dedicated curry house in Scotland was in business by 1938. We know this from an advertisement for the Taj Mahal in the 1938 Empire Exhibition guide, and a year later a Dr Deb from the Punjab opened another curry house in Glasgow.[12] Then, in 1945, Birmingham got its first Indian restaurant in Steelhouse Lane which later became the Darjeeling. Back in London, the main meeting place for the Sylheti community became Abdul Mannan's basement café at 36 Percy Street, along with the

[12] Y Chowdhury, *The Roots And Tales of The Bangladeshi Settlers*, 1993.

Green Mask on Brompton Road where you could also find Mosharaf Ali and Israel Miah's Anglo-Asia restaurant.

When you start talking to the men who started these establishments, you begin to understand the importance of them. These weren't just places to eat, they were community centres, job centres and welfare offices. These cafés were where you went when you needed immigration advice, money or to meet up with friends and family. Working in these restaurants was extremely sociable, and despite the long hours and meagre wages, fairly enjoyable. Curry, to these early restaurateurs, meant a lot more than either food or profit.

The passion required to run these establishments becomes all the more evident when you realise the risks these entrepreneurs were taking. In almost every case, entire life savings were invested or large loans taken out to fund these ventures. Such financial pressure forced restaurateurs to work long hours for small margins: many of the people I've spoken to said they had no choice but to work for themselves as no one would employ them, and no choice but to make a profit, however small, as the consequences of failure – poverty, shame, possible repatriation – were too painful. Of course, it is entirely possible that the records that survive are only of successful ventures. Who knows how many folded without trace? One failure that is recorded was the demise of the Dilkush in Windmill Street, which was flattened by a German bomb during the blitz of 1940, only two years after it had opened.

Although it's clear to me from this evidence that there was a vibrant interest in Indian cookery in Britain prior to the Second World War, it was small and localised compared to the boom in curry houses that happened in the years after the war. There were many reasons behind that explosion in Indian restaurants.

The first was Britain's last and most brutal act of Empire: the partition of India into two states, the primarily Hindu India and the primarily

Muslim Pakistan, prior to granting independence in 1947. The horrors of Partition are recorded elsewhere but, in short, millions of people were forced to move their lives across borders according to their faith. About 8 million Hindus and Sikhs were transported from Pakistan to India, while 6 million Muslims were forced to make the reverse journey into the newly created state of Pakistan which was split into two regions, East Pakistan and West Pakistan (later, in 1971, West Pakistan would attain independence from Pakistan and become Bangladesh). This policy was enforced by rival factions with brutality and cruelty and was followed by the first war between the two nations over the disputed territory of Kashmir. Understandably, there were many people who felt that the subcontinent was not the best place to raise their families at that time.

This coincided with an unprecedented economic boom in Britain that saw 100 per cent employment, leaving many job vacancies unfilled and creating opportunities for overseas workers. That in turn spurred on one of the biggest transcontinental waves of migration the world has ever seen, as workers left the subcontinent (and the West Indies) for new lives and careers in Britain. Many of these new arrivals from India and Pakistan found themselves in the catering business as the economic upturn had led directly to a new fashion for eating out. As the 1950s got underway, the conditions were ripe for a curry boom.

CLOVES

Cloves are the sun-dried unopened buds of a tropical evergreen tree that is native to the Moluccas or Spice Islands. The legend goes that the natives discovered these buds when branches were brought to the ground during the monsoon. Left to open they produce deep red flowers. Dried cloves are very hard, which explains why the Romans called them clavus (from which we get clove), which means 'nail'. The Chinese called cloves 'the chicken-tongue spice'.

Cloves were not known in Europe until the first century. Pliny's Natural History gives the first European account: 'they resemble a grain of pepper, but larger and more fragile. They grow on the Indian lotus tree.' Nearly a thousand years later, the Arabic writer Ibrâhîm ibn Wâsif-Shâh wrote even more romantically about their origins: 'Somewhere near India is the island containing the Valley of the Cloves. No merchants or sailors have ever been to the valley or have ever seen the kind of tree that produces cloves: its fruit, they say, is sold by genies. The sailors arrive at the island, place their items of merchandise on the shore, and return to their ship. Next morning, they find, beside each item, a quantity of cloves.'[1]

When the Dutch commandeered the clove trade the VOC increased the value of cloves by limiting the supply: they decreed that cloves could only be grown on the island of Amboina and destroyed trees on all the other islands. This caused great distress to the Moluccans who had long planted a clove tree when a child was born and believed that if the tree died, then so would the child. This brutal monopoly was broken in 1770 when the fabulously named Frenchman Pierre Poivre (the Peter who picked a peck of pickled peppers!) smuggled clove saplings to Mauritius.

Cloves are highly aromatic and so are used sparingly so as not to overpower a dish. When used whole they are not actually eaten and either removed prior to serving or pushed to the side of the plate. They will be most familiar to fans of pilau rice. When they are ground, cloves make up another vital ingredient of the garam masala blend.

Medicinally, they are used to relieve indigestion (they are often chewed after a heavy meal in some areas of Indonesia) and to alleviate toothache. One of the essential oils in cloves is eugenol, still used in the manufacture of toothpastes and mouthwashes. The fifth-century medical writer Paul of Aegina

---

[1] Ibrâhîm ibn Wâsif-Shâh, *Summary of Marvels.*

was more interested in their pharmaceutical properties but offered this description: 'Cloves are excellent in relishes as well as prescriptions, they are aromatic, sour, bitterish, hot and dry in the third degree.'

In the West, cloves are mostly used to flavour deserts like apple pie, and also to flavour wines, but in their native Indonesia they are used to make kretek cigarettes which are 60 per cent tobacco, 40 per cent cloves. Consequently, Indonesia is not just the world's largest producer of this spice, it is also its biggest consumer.

CHAPTER FIVE

The Pioneers

The Post-war Curry

'**M**y father came here in 1957 with £3 in his pocket and slept on a bench in Trafalgar Square for four nights before he got his first job,' recalls second-generation restaurateur Abdul Miah. Within three years, his dad had opened his first restaurant – the Star of Pakistan in Soho – and unknowingly started a small restaurant dynasty. Such heart-warming rags-to-riches-via-bloody-hard-work stories are plentiful among the curry house pioneers of the 50s and 60s. Like many of the other Asian immigrants arriving in Britain at that time, Mr Miah was a young, single man in search of opportunity. While few ever anticipated they'd make their living – and in some cases fortune – from catering, it was this generation of immigrants that made curry a phenomenon.

Men arrived on boats and planes, some students, some sailors, hoping to make a bit of money for a couple of years before returning to the subcontinent. However, curry and politics got in the way of their plans and many stayed for life: the politics made Bangladesh (or East Pakistan as it was at the time) a good place to leave, while the curry made Britain a lucrative place to stay.

Bazlur Chowdhury, who arrived in Britain in 1960 aged 20, has a theory as to why so many of Bangladesh's brightest students forfeited careers in the civil service, banking or insurance for the hard slog of catering on the other side of the world. 'In the mid 50s,' he tells me, 'there were a lot of students coming to Britain because of the political situation in Bangladesh and there was a lot of pressure on us to leave. Unlike India that sustained its political institutions after Partition, unfortunately that wasn't true in Pakistan/Bangladesh, and in 1958 the army had taken power and students had started a movement against military power. At this time lots of political organisations were banned and driven underground.

'My father,' he continues, 'who was a civil servant with the education department, got a lot of pressure at work about my activities, as did the families of all the politically active students. Sometimes they would get a warning that they would their lose their jobs. So my father, who had ten children and needed his job, told me that if I couldn't help him could I at least not be there,' he recalls.

'At that time there were no restrictions on coming to Britain, I don't think there were immigration controls until 1962 or thereabouts,[2] so I and lots of other people in my situation came to Britain. And in addition

[2] The Commonwealth Immigration Act was introduced in 1962. It limited the numbers allowed to enter Britain by issuing 'employment vouchers' without which you could not work. Later, in 1968, a second act restricted entry to those who had either a British parent or grandparent.

to the relatively rich students, there were also a lot of seamen from the merchant navy who managed to escape from the port. Once you were out of the port, you see, the ship owners couldn't find you and the police wouldn't touch you unless you did something illegal.' After two years of evading arrest, any hold the shipping company had over a seaman was waived and they were free to stay.[3]

Once in Britain, there was a fairly well established support system for the new arrivals, as Bazlur recalls. 'I had the address of a relative of mine who owned a house in the East End near Brick Lane. I remember I got a coach from Heathrow to Victoria for five shillings, and then took a taxi to this house in Brick Lane. There were half a dozen or so houses owned by Bangladeshis at that time, they were very run down, used as lodging houses. Even if you didn't know anyone, if you were from Bangladesh you could stay until you found a job.'

The Curry Community

Although these lodging houses provided camaraderie as well as accommodation, they weren't necessarily everyone's first choice – but they frequently proved to be the only option. 'I went to lots of lodging houses looking for a room,' one restaurateur recalls, 'and in many ways I would have preferred to stay with an English family and learn the language better and integrate more rapidly. But there were many signs that said "No coloureds" and the landladies always asked me if I would be cooking – they called it "foreign muck" – and when I said that I

[3] Chowdhury, *Bangladeshi Settlers*.

would like to they told me to go away. They said it would stink the place out and the other guests would complain.'

Despite the crowded conditions in the Bangladeshi-run houses, Bazlur Chowdhury remembers that these were good places to live. 'The landlord didn't ask you for rent until you could afford it, and he shared his food with you and even gave you two or three shillings pocket money if you didn't have any cash. Then, once you were earning you repaid him. People were very generous because everybody had encountered the difficulties of starting life in a new country.'

Each night in these lodging houses, the men cooked for each other and ate together and swapped information about where to find jobs. Unsurprisingly, then, if one got a job in a restaurant, several would also follow. These men couldn't be choosy about the jobs they took because, as one restaurateur told me, while East Pakistan was under martial law it was illegal to take any currency out of the country, which meant most arrived in Britain with only a few pounds to their name.

Most also arrived without their wives. The 1961 census records that ratio of men and women among the Pakistani community was 40 : 1. This was because few believed they would stay in Britain – their main aim was to make enough money in a couple of years to provide a better lifestyle back in the subcontinent before returning home. The reason why so many changed their plans may well have been changes to UK immigration law. If the employment voucher scheme had not been introduced in 1962, recent immigrants would have been free to come and go as they pleased. But once re-entry, and re-employment, became harder, many found that the toeholds they had sought in the British economy became knee-deep commitments and the search for employment became frenzied.

Jobs as kitchen porters and cleaners were easy to pick up and easy to leave if something better came up. Generally these jobs weren't in

Indian restaurants, but in Italian, Greek and Chinese establishments, and in hotels and coffee shops. Over the next decade or so, a generation of caterers learnt the skills that would catapult curry to dominance.

Bazlur Chowdhury was one of several Indians who found work with the J Lyons' Company. 'They owned a chain of coffee shops,' he recalls, 'and in London they had some very big establishments called Corner Houses. There was one in Trafalgar Square, and another Leicester Square I think, and I earnt £2 6s. a week!' Unsurprisingly, it wasn't long before he thought that if he was going to stay in catering he wanted to earn a profit, not just a wage.

There wasn't a great deal of competition in the Indian restaurant sector at that time as there were so few establishments in London. 'I knew of maybe half a dozen restaurants, mostly in posh places like the West End and some in the Earls Court and Kensington area. I ate in two or three of these places as I had friends who worked there. I remember my cousin worked for a Mr Ali at the New Asia restaurant in Frith Street. Now that Mr Ali, who was one of the pioneers in the restaurant sector, is very rich: he moved back to Bangladesh and is now connected with banks and insurance companies.'

Shamsuddin Khan, who came to London in 1955, remembers that London curry houses were mostly very simple at that time. 'The places in Soho were fairly plain and the menu was very simple, serving things like chicken curry or meat curry served just on the plate: there was no balti in those days. And I remember these restaurants were quite expensive, maybe charging half a crown a plate. There were also a few cafés in East London that sold rice and curry for much less.'

The smaller establishments were popular among a certain type of Londoner: usually, young, hip teddy boys and arty students who saw hanging out in the Formica-tabled curry houses as a statement of their avant-garde stance and their liberal, modern world view. In today's marketing speak they'd be called 'early adopters', 'mavens' or 'connectors', terms coined to identify trendsetters with influence. They were exactly the right kind of customer any new industry wants to attract, and their endorsement of Indian food would play a crucial part in curry's success.

Return to the Veeraswamy

Of course there was still the Veeraswamy, which was still catering for the upper classes and where prices, if not wages, were a little higher. AH Chowdhury, who came to Britain in 1957 to study was lucky enough to get a job in the capital's elite curry university: a job that would serve him well in his future career in the restaurant trade.

'At the time Veeraswamy's was owned by Sir Charles Stewart who was always visiting Ceylon and India to recruit the best staff and train them in the UK, so jobs were very scarce there. I was looking for work for three months before they took me on,' he recalls.

Just as it had been when it opened in 1927, by the time AH Chowdhury had started working there in 1958, Veeraswamy's was still one of the swankiest joints in town. 'It was very classy,' he remembers, 'the food and service was top, very top.' Which was just as well, because he also remembers that it wasn't that uncommon for dinner bills to run to £60 (that's about £600 in today's money!). 'The clients were mostly business people, and there were also a lot of actors and actresses, and overseas visitors who didn't care what they spent as long as they were getting good service.' The famous names who ate at Veeraswamy's in those days included Laurence Olivier, Vivien Leigh and Marlon Brando – it was clearly not your run-of-the-mill curry house! Apparently the demand among his American celebrity guests for Veeraswamy's cooking was so great that Charles Stewart started exporting pastes to America under the brand King's Curry (you can still buy Veeraswamy pastes today, although Charles Stewart sold the business in the 60s).

'The food was very good,' remembers AH, 'not that different from some of the dishes you get today, just more professional than the meals you get in most suburban curry houses.' But it was the service that was really remarkable. 'Some customers used to come by car and they gave their key to the doorman who wore a big turban and a moustache – it was a guy from Pakistan while I was there – and he took the car and parked it and gave the key to the lift man who escorted the customers up to the first floor. Once they were upstairs the service manager welcomed them and took them to the lounge, which had small chairs in the shape of elephants, and bells you could ring for service.

'When you rang one of the bells one of the Indian girls in sarees and sandals would come and take your drinks order, and then the restaurant manager would approach with the menu and take your food order. The menu was different every day, depending on what ingredients were available, so the menu always needed explaining. And then finally you were taken to your table where the meal would be served.'

Unfortunately for AH, the wealth of the customers didn't trickle down to his level. 'A lot of the staff used to share a massive house in Croydon,' he remembers, 'where there was a training school for the people who had just arrived from India and Ceylon. But the wages were very poor, however it was considered a classy job and we knew that we were learning the trade.' It wasn't long before AH, like hundreds of other Asians working in catering in the 50s and 60s, decided he'd be better off working for himself. It was at this time that several men started countless businesses without much in the way of experience, funding, business plans or a regular supply of ingredients. The accidental nature of curry's accession to dominance in Britain, you could say, was the reverse of Britain's accidental foray into Empire in India.

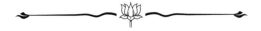

A Leap into the Suburbs

Shamsuddin Khan's leap in the dark took him to Clapham, a south London suburb he'd never been to before, when an old Italian restaurant came up for sale. He'd been looking for premises to lease for a few months before a friend told him about a restaurant on Clapham High Street that was closing down. Today, sitting in the same restaurant he took over in 1958, which is now adorned with pictures of the tea plantation he has bought in Bangladesh on the profits of curry, he starts to tell me how he got the Maharani off the ground.

'After my friend told me about this place I came here after 6 p.m. for four or five weeks to see who the clients were. I soon realised that it was absolutely dead in the evening.' Anyone who knows Clapham High Street now will be amazed, but in 1958 there were no bars and late night convenience stores, so once the shops shut at 5 p.m. there wasn't much chance of passing trade. 'I realised that in the evening it would be dead, but at lunch time the Italian guy seemed to be getting fourteen or fifteen people through the door, and I thought that I had to be able to do better. So I had a word with him and finalised the deal.'

Like practically all of his contemporaries, Shamsuddin didn't go into business alone. Typically, most Indian restaurants were started by three or four men who had clubbed their money together in order to be able to afford a lease. Not only did this enable men like Shamsuddin to make an early start in the curry game, it also meant that with four owners working full time, you could seriously cut down on your wage bill.

Shamsuddin and his three partners' business planning was negligible. 'We never think of making a plan, or think about marketing, or even think if there was a business in it or not,' he laughs now, 'I just thought it was a busy high street and therefore it must have a future. But we didn't know anything about Italian food!'

For the first three months, the new owners kept the same menu as the Italian owners. Unsurprisingly, none of them had any experience cooking spaghetti bolognese, so they hired a Cypriot chef who at least had some knowledge of European cookery. It's hard not to laugh at the image of four Bangladeshi immigrants and their Cypriot chef making pasta for the burghers of Clapham; it sounds like a pitch for a bad sitcom. During the first six months, the new owners started to make subtle changes to the menu, slowly introducing the food they cooked for themselves.

'We learnt that the customers we attracted had been to India, either in the military or civil service. Some had spent the First World War there. As we were the first restaurant in the area they were incredibly supportive and encouraging and asked us to keep making more Indian food. There was one Major, I don't remember his name, but he told me that if I served more Indian food I would be successful because everyone he knew who'd been in India loved curry! Once he organised a party and brought twenty or thirty people to our restaurant just so they could taste again the dishes they remembered from the old days. He was very good to us,' he recalls.

But there weren't enough customers like the Major to support a solely Indian menu, and for quite a while the Maharani continued to serve Italian as well as English dishes. 'The food was very different then,' remembers Shamsuddin, 'We couldn't afford rice, it was very expensive, so everything was served with chapati or paratha bread, and there was no naan then because there was no tandoor oven.'

There was, however, one other carbohydrate they used to serve curry with: for quite a few months the speciality of this particular house was curry – with spaghetti! 'Rice was so expensive, the economic conditions weren't good,' Shamsuddin explains, 'and our customers were used to eating spaghetti, so yes, we served curry and spaghetti!' Surely another one for the sitcom.

Today the Maharani is opulently decorated in deep reds and velvets, but in 1958 the décor was very simple. 'It was just wooden floors, and wooden tables and chairs, it was more of a coffee shop than a restaurant.' It was also half the size it is now – it wasn't until the 90s that Shamsuddin expanded into the premises next door. 'It was a small place that we ran ourselves. Two of us worked in the kitchen, and two of us did front of house.'

Despite enthusiastic customers and a low wage bill, the Maharani was not a big earner in the early years. 'I think we were taking about twenty pounds a week in the beginning, then maybe thirty. Maybe after a year or two it was £44 or £45 a week.' Between four that wasn't very much, and after a year one of the partners left. After three years a second partner asked to be bought out. 'It was not really profitable, we just broke even and just about balanced the takings and the bills.'

For men like Shamsuddin Khan, however, this was enough. The restaurant was paying its way, if only just, and keeping a roof over his head. Elsewhere in London, hundreds more Bangladeshi restaurateurs were living in rooms above the shop, working long hours because they couldn't afford the wage bills and learning the best way to make steak and chips to keep their less adventurous clients happy. This might have been too demoralising for someone with options, but these men had no choice but to slowly make a success of their enterprises – the alternatives were far worse. Anyway, it seems that many of them already had an inkling that curry would eventually be a big business. Mr Khan explains how he knew this without any market research, management consultancy or business planning: 'When I worked in a kitchen before I opened this restaurant I used to make curries for myself. My co-workers would smell the food and ask to taste it, and when they tried it, they loved it and asked for more. This is how I knew that curry would be big in Britain.'

Bazlur Chowdhury opened his first restaurant in Ealing in 1964, and like every other curry restaurant outside the West End of London needed to sell English dishes to attract enough customers. 'We also sold Chinese dishes,' he tells me with a smile, 'because Chinese restaurants were already quite well established. So we offered chow mein and chop suey.' Not that he'd ever really eaten Chinese food beforehand. 'Thankfully I remember we didn't get many requests for the Chinese dishes, but the English dishes were quite popular.'

The main reason why Indian restaurants offered incongruous omelettes, steaks and roast chicken was that without these tame English offerings it was very difficult to get party bookings. 'There was always someone in a party who thought that they didn't like curry and if we didn't serve them an English dish none of their friends would come into our restaurant to eat Indian food,' says Bazlur.

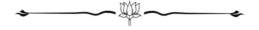

Curry Conquers Britain

Outside London, there was an even greater battle to persuade the Brits to give up their reputation as connoisseurs of bland food. AH Chowdhury opened his Bombay Restaurant in Sheffield in the very early 1960s. He had never seen Sheffield before he bought the premises, just as Sheffield had never seen a curry house before AH arrived. 'I had been studying in Manchester but I couldn't afford to continue with studies and work part-time, so I decided to stop doing both those things and use my savings to start a business. A friend told me about a restaurant in Sheffield that was for sale and I thought "Why not?".' I guess if you've already moved from Sylhet to Manchester via London, upping sticks again to Sheffield doesn't seem quite as much of an upheaval.

'Previously it had been a Chinese restaurant,' AH recalls, 'so we had to change the menu and the décor and make some changes to the kitchen too because it was not right for Indian food. To be honest, I had no idea if people would come, but I knew from my time at Veeraswamy's that if we made good food, English people would like it.'

Although there were other Asians in Sheffield in the early 60s they worked in steel or in the factories, not catering, so unless AH's customers had ventured into an Indian restaurant elsewhere in Britain, their only experience of eating curry would have been at home, made, no doubt, with the traditional mix of curry powder, apples and raisins as a base: not exactly the best advertisement for AH's more skilful fare. 'Nobody knew about curry,' he says now. 'I talked to a lot of people who hadn't even been to London, so you can imagine what sort of clients I had.

'Consequently we had great difficulty selling Indian food,' he says. 'We didn't have any Asian customers, only English ones, and everybody was asking for English food. We served steak and chips, mixed grill, sausage and eggs, chicken and chips, but we couldn't sell any other stuff. We still made curries though, hoping that someone would order one, but at the end of the day we had to throw it all away.'

This was not only heartbreaking for AH, but it didn't exactly make good business sense either. So he had an idea that, again, wasn't exactly textbook business practice: he decided to give his curries away for free. 'I gave customers a bowl of curry sauce with their chicken and chips for two or three weeks, so my regulars all got to taste it once or twice. And then when we stopped they started to ask for the curry sauce. So I said "all right, but it will cost you". They said "how much?" and I said "how about a shilling?". They thought about it for a second and said "all right", and that is how we encouraged people to try our curries.'

'Later on I suggested to these customers that maybe they should try a proper Indian curry made in the proper way – after all, they liked curry and they liked chicken,' AH recalls. 'One of my customers even said to me "Do you think we will still live after having chicken curry?" So I said to him "We have been living with curries first so I don't see why not!".' Eventually, AH discovered that customers who had once only asked for omelette and chips were starting to order his curries – and bringing their friends to try them too. AH Chowdhury's experience was in no way unique: it wasn't just the skill of the chef that ensured curry's success – it was also due to the skill and charm of the waiter.

Clearly, there was a lot of hard work involved in getting an Indian restaurant off the ground in the 60s, but AH's success involved a little bit of luck: the Bombay was in the student part of town. In the early 60s, students did for the curry what the teddy boys and Soho hep cats had done in the 50s: AH couldn't have bought a restaurant in a more adventurous location even if he'd known Sheffield as well a cab driver. Students who were missing home cooking and appalled by campus fodder proved to be vital early adopters of curry.

However, although students in search of cheap, filling food that made them feel like they were living in the modern world would in time have evangelised about curry to their peers, there just weren't enough of them to account for the boom in curry that started in the late 60s. But Bazlur Chowdhury knows who did play that crucial role in taking curry to the masses: Harold Wilson! 'If it wasn't for him I would have had hardly any customers,' he says.

When Harold Wilson led Labour to victory in the 1964 election it was the start, Bazlur reckons, of the boom years for the working classes. 'In the early 60s the only people going for Indian food were the rich people and the middle classes. But when Harold Wilson became Prime Minister there was an explosion in union activity and working class people started earning quite a bit. And once they had good wages they could afford to eat out and try a few places. And of course, once they tried Indian food they loved it!' In the 60s the number of Indian restaurants in Britain more than quadrupled from roughly 300 in 1960 to over 1,200 by the end of the decade.

For Abdul Miah, a second generation curry man, the endeavours of his father's generation are very humbling. 'I have so much respect for those guys,' he says with evident conviction. 'I take my hat off to them because they had no catering experience, they didn't know how to cook, or how to serve: many of them had been farmers in Bangladesh. But I know this for sure, I wouldn't have a business without them and chicken tikka masala wouldn't be the national dish. They were pioneers.'

Curry Grows Up

A major reason why curry became more popular over time was because it got better over time. As Abdul discovered when he started running restaurants in the 1980s, he found a lot of customers were reluctant to try curry after eating it for the first time in the 50s or 60s. 'They said to me, "Bring me egg and chips because I've tried curry and I didn't like it". I saw it as my job to explain to them that curry had improved.

'In the early days,' he explains from one of his eight restaurants in the Home Counties, 'curry was not good. It was made with curry powder by untrained chefs who probably put too much chilli in because phall and vindaloo were the most popular dishes. So when someone who didn't like really hot food visited an Indian restaurant they said "This is effing hot, take it back!" So someone would take it back to the kitchen and stir in a little Coronation milk, or add a bit of sugar. Gradually dishes started to appear that were completely tailored to British tastes.'

There were other differences too that made Indian restaurants a more mainstream choice: restaurateurs started to have wine lists, the serving staff spoke better English and also learnt how to explain some of the dishes to their customers, which became necessary as menus became more varied. And part of the reason that the cooking got more complex was because more and more diverse ingredients began to become available in Britain. So instead of making curry with English vegetables and dried spices as cooks in the nineteenth and early twentieth centuries had done, by the end of the 1960s Indian chefs were finding that a greater range of fresh herbs and vegetables, together with imported pickles and spices, were available to them.

The arrival of Indian grocery stores not only changed the food that was prepared, but also serves as an indicator of the size and prosperity of the Indian community in Britain. The first such grocer in London was the Bombay Emporium which was founded in 1931 by DS Chattwell, a former Indian Army officer. The shop, in Grafton Street just off Tottenham Court Road in the West End, stocked a range of imported spices, hot pickles, mango chutneys, rice, dhals, nuts, oils, tea and coffee. There was also a small warehouse in Portobello Road where freshly imported spices were blended into the shop's own brand of curry powder. Later, a second branch opened at 3 Leicester Place to cater for the Chinese restaurant community. By all accounts the Bombay Emporium was a successful operation and although the shop closed in the 1960s, the business continued to be run by Mr Chattwell's sons until the late twentieth century as BE International Foods Ltd, which among other things imports and packages spices under the Rajah label. It is now part of the HP Foods group.

Elsewhere in London in the 1930s there was Suleiman Jetha's store in New Cavendish Street selling dried goods and imported pickles, and in 1936 the East End got its first Indian grocers called Taj Stores, a shop that is still in operation in Brick Lane today. Outside London, there is a record of Scotland's first Indian grocers, opened in Glasgow as early as 1932 by Sher Qadir and his Scottish wife Mary, and by 1935 it was reported that the Qadirs' shop had at least two rivals.[4]

Away from these few outlets, obtaining ingredients was difficult, time consuming and expensive. 'Long before the Second World War,' records Yousuf Chowdhury, 'a number of Bangladeshis had owned coffee houses in Scotland and Wales. Often they wanted to sell Indian food, but rice and spices could not be found.'[5] While native British vegetables could be substituted for Indian vegetables, there were no substitutes for Indian spices. Consequently, the Indian community went to great lengths to get hold of spices. I've heard dozens of stories about people bringing suitcases packed with cardamom, chillies, coriander seeds, cumin seeds and turmeric roots into Britain. Where possible, members of the immigrant community also grew their own herbs on windowsills, balconies and allotments.

There were other dietary needs that were hard to meet in Britain. For instance, Bangladeshis were used to eating freshly killed chickens, and there were no Halal butchers around. Yousuf Chowdhury recalls that in Birmingham in the 1950s 'on Sunday mornings live chickens were available on Varna Road in Balsall Heath. The people used to bring

---

[4] Visram, *Asians In Britain*, p. 279.
[5] Chowdhury, *Bangladeshi Settlers*, p. 74.

chickens in a locked up van or in a car boot and sell them in the street for 60 or 70 pence. The traders were always keeping an eye out for the police in case they were taken to court.

'Not only the chicken sellers would stand and wait for customers,' he continues, 'but prostitutes in the alleyways too. If the police came they ran away and blamed each other for making the police come. I do not know who was to blame, but one thing I would say is that they helped each other to get customers.'[6] Another unusual symbiotic arrangement was found with the long-established Jewish community. Muslims in search of Halal meat found that the kosher meat at Jewish butchers was the closest they could find as instructions on the slaughter of animals are so similar in both faiths.

Nevertheless, there were still many, many ingredients that could not be found in Britain. But by the late 50s that was slowly starting to change thanks to the efforts of one man: Lakshmishankar Pathak.

Pataks (Spices) Ltd

Lakshmishankar, also known as Lakhubhai or LG, was born in the state of Gujarat in 1925 into a poor family of subsistence farmers. At the age of ten, following the death of his father, his eldest brother decided to take the British government's financial incentives and move to Kenya in a bid to get the family out of poverty. So the entire family boarded a boat and emigrated to East Africa where they discovered there was already a sizeable community of people of Indian descent, a corollary of the British

[6] Ibid.

Empire's indentured labour policies that had seen tens of thousands of Indians shipped to Kenya to help build the railways in the mid-1800s. So when the Pathaks opened a shop selling Indian sweets, it wasn't long before customers were queueing round the corner.

LG grew up, married, had children and continued to work in the family business: life was prosperous but his wife Shantagaury was getting restless living with her in-laws. When Kenya was destabilised in the 1950s by the nationalist Mau Mau uprisings, she started to put pressure on LG to find an alternative. Having heard from relatives and associates that Britain offered a certain charm and the chance of prosperity, LG visited the Mother Country in 1953 to see what opportunities he could find before returning to Kenya.

It wasn't until 1956 that LG finally moved his family to Britain, setting sail on the SS *Uganda* with eight children aged between three and eleven. In his pockets he carried some cash borrowed from his in-laws and a life insurance policy that he hoped to be able to turn into cash: apart from that and a few possessions, the Pathaks would be starting over from scratch. When the SS *Uganda* docked in Marseilles in the South of France, LG decided to make the rest of the journey overland: that way he could get to London ahead of his family and arrange accommodation and, hopefully, some employment. The journey through France was a little more expensive than he'd reckoned, and so it was that LG Pathak arrived in Britain in November 1956 with just £5 to his name. Sometimes £5 is all it takes.

Somehow, LG – armed with a character reference from a Kenyan branch of a UK bank – managed to persuade a bank to lend him enough money to rent a house he'd found in Kentish Town, north London, before greeting his family off the boat at Tilbury docks. But finding a job was more problematic: with little English, LG was considered illiterate and after several days of knocking on doors, the only job he was offered was cleaning the sewers. His wife Shanta knew the family could do better, so while LG was at work she sold some jewellery, bought some second-hand pots and pans and set about making the sweets and snacks that had sold so well in Kenya. The Pathaks then invited many of the Indian students living in the area round to their house so they could taste the home-cooked food that they missed so much. Word spread and soon there was enough demand to start a takeaway service.

The entire family helped out, whether they were preparing the samosas, bhajis, jellabies or gathias, or delivering them to addresses all over London; this was a family business right from the start. LG's son Kirit recalls that as one of the younger children it was his job to run errands. 'In the 60s my brother and I used to go round with parcels of hot samosas and jellabies to deliver because travel on the Underground was free for children under 11. Because we didn't speak much English we went out with two sheets of paper: on one was the address of where we were going and on the other was the address to get back so we could show people the piece of paper and they would point us in the right direction. Pretty soon we got to know every Tube station in London!'

All the kids joined the business – it was the only way they got to spend time with their parents – and all chipped in, either making samosas or running errands. They weren't given any pocket money for their efforts and so Kirit, displaying the entrepreneurial flair that would make their business a household name, started making Bombay mix to sell at school. 'I let them have some for free, and then if they wanted more I charged them a shilling. Each day I had my targets to sell, and each day I reached them.'

As well as serving individual customers, the Pathaks – who were still making everything in their tiny 5′ × 6′ kitchen in Kentish Town – also started catering for functions at India House and in 1958 even supplied Buckingham Palace with food for a garden party. The family was now making enough money to buy the children the kind of education LG had never had, and four of the kids were sent to a Roman Catholic boarding school in Ireland. During his time at boarding school, Kirit says he decided he wanted to be the first Hindu to become Pope! Perhaps more significantly, there was also an incident that signalled to the young Kirit the scale of the appetite for curry. 'I'll never forget the scene,' he muses. 'It was in the convent in a huge dining hall and there were rows of us kids all in our uniform waiting for the awful food. Every so often my mum and dad used to send us a parcel of goodies containing Bombay mix and other snacks that the school used to keep in a cupboard. But one time, the oil had got to the bottom and the greaseproof bag burst and the snacks spilt out on to the floor. Suddenly, half of that dining hall were like [he makes a whizzing sound]. They were like rats! It was as if they'd never been fed, and I tell you, afterwards you didn't find a single crumb. That is when I said "this is going to be a big business".'

Back in London, the neighbours in Kentish Town were starting to complain about the constant kitchen smells and ceaseless activity, so LG looked around for premises to acquire and soon found a small shop in Drummond Street behind Euston Station. Despite being called Pathaks (Spices) Ltd (soon to be changed to Pataks without the 'h' to make their name easier for the Brits to pronounce), the tiny premises at 134 Drummond Street sold everything for the Indian home from spices to joss sticks, from Bombay duck to decorations for religious festivals. Over time it became an unofficial Indian embassy, acting as a staging post for the immigrant community.

'Whatever you needed in an Indian home, we had it,' recalls LG's son Kirit. 'My father was like a godfather to the Indians coming over. People used to say "if you've got any problems, go to Mr Pathak."'

Kirit's wife Meena adds: 'He was there to hold their hand, to teach them how to live in England. He taught them stupid things like how to use an English loo, how to use toilet roll, how to eat with a fork and knife – things that they were not used to. My father-in-law was the friendliest person and people thronged to his shop and looked up to him as a godfather.' The Drummond Street shop was so successful that Kirit reckons: 'For a particular generation of Indians in Britain there is no way they could not have been to our shop.'

The Pathaks' grocery store was the catalyst that turned Drummond Street into 'Little Bombay'. By the end of the 60s, the street was home to a collection of Indian sweet shops, London's first Halal restaurant (with a mosque in the basement!), a collection of vegetarian restaurants, saree shops and snack bars. It was a street where the cultural and religious distinctions that had caused so much pain in the recent past were forgotten: the Shahs who opened the famous Diwana Bhelpuri house were from Bombay, the Alis who ran the Ambala sweet shop were from Pakistan, and the Pathaks, of course, were from East Africa.

'There was an incredible atmosphere,' recalls Meena Pathak. 'It was always heaving with people all bargaining for the best price. It was very much how Ealing Road is today, with goods out on the street and people talking in every doorway. It was very sociable.'

The diversity of customers meant LG was asked for a vast range of products: southern Indians wanted mustard leaves and fresh coconut, while Punjabis wanted chapati flour. 'My father never refused anyone,' Kirit remembers. 'If we didn't have something in stock he would try and find it even if it took a few weeks to get hold of it.'

LG's philosophy was quite straightforward: he thought about what he wanted to feed his family and assumed that others would want the same ingredients for their kitchens. So he set about importing goods to Britain, the like of which had never been seen in the Western hemisphere before. 'My father was the first person to airfreight vegetables into this country,' says Kirit with evident pride. LG imported vegetables from East Africa, spices from India and herbs from Europe in a spectacularly complex operation for such a small shop. 'There wasn't a lot of money in it,' Kirit confirms, 'but my father wanted to make his customers happy.'

Kirit and his siblings were made to work hard. If they weren't needed in the shop they were dispatched to Heathrow to pick up the daily deliveries of fruit and veg, or sent off to nearby Euston and King's Cross stations to arrange for parcels to be sent to customers as far north as Aberdeen. 'We used to be at the airport at 4 a.m. waiting for the flights to come,' says Kirit, 'and when they were offloaded and had cleared customs, the herbs and vegetables went in our van and straight to our shop, it was there by 7 a.m.'

Getting hold of fresh coriander proved difficult as it has a very short shelf life and would not survive the journey from India. 'So my father asked around at embassies and at Covent Garden [the vegetable market] and found out that Cyprus produces a lot of coriander: my father had not known it was used in Middle Eastern cookery too.' LG then found a supplier in Cyprus and, slowly but surely, his customers in Drummond Street were getting many more of the ingredients they needed for making curries.

Some ingredients remained problematic for a long time, however. 'Rice was expensive,' says Kirit, echoing Clapham restaurateur Shamsuddin Khan. 'There were no machines to clean the rice, it was all hand done, so there was the added labour cost as well as the premium for importing everything: there were a lot of duties and levies you had to apply. But you had to import it because it was a staple. Then there was the added problem of open shipping, it was not packaged like it is today, so calculating volume was a problem. Each shipment always seemed to have lost something to contamination or spillage.'

LG was very particular about the quality of his merchandise. It wasn't just enough to source and import bitter gourds or turmeric or drumsticks, he insisted that his products be of the highest quality. 'He used to go to India himself to buy the spices,' Kirit tells me from his office in the north of England. 'For the spices he flew to India and went to a specific street in Bombay where all the traders are: you can buy absolutely anything there. You had to employ a commission broker because the market is controlled by secret handshakes and favours. So you tell the broker what you want and he takes you to the best stalls where you select the merchandise you want, but he haggles for the best price and then they get it ready for shipment. But as there wasn't containerisation in those days, if you ordered thirty bags you just hoped that you got thirty bags by the time the boat got to London. You were usually short,' he adds philosophically.

Despite the meagre profits for his endeavours, the effort was worth it. 'There was incredible excitement when we got something new,' says Meena Pathak. 'When we first got hold of the baby aubergines, no one had sold them in Britain before and it caused a lot of excitement. And when we got curry leaves too. I remember that they weren't in the best condition, but thankfully with curry leaves they can be used dry, so our customers were still very thrilled.'

But today, of course, the Pathaks are not known as a sellers of fresh vegetables and herbs. They are famous for their pickles, pastes and sauces. Yet again, it is LG who gets the credit for the introduction of the ranges that would change not just the fortunes of his family, but also the fortunes of the entire Indian restaurant sector.

'My father was an artisan,' insists Kirit. 'It was he who first made a spice paste.' This assertion clearly contradicts the evidence of earlier products like Selim's Curry Paste, but Kirit is sure that it was his father who first preserved a mix of spices in oil (it is possible that earlier pastes were water-based ones). 'The paste concept was invented by my dad, it came from my dad's inherent artisan skills. He wanted to make spices taste better and last longer because he said English people did not know how to cook good Indian food. He thought this was because they were using awful curry powder that loses its flavour profiles within 30 days. So he started experimenting with better flavours and the preservation of that taste. That is how he came to roast, grind and blend spices and encapsulate their flavour in oil.'

LG's attempts to cater to the indigenous English market started to pay off and more and more of his Drummond Street customers were white, and an increasing number of them had no previous relationship with the subcontinent. 'In those days,' Kirit remembers, 'our customers were 85 per cent Indians, maybe 5 per cent British and about 10 per cent would have been restaurants. Those figures aren't based on turnover, just on my memory of who came into the shop. Over time, we had more and more English people come in.'

Not only did LG's pastes make curry easier for the hapless Brits to make at home, but – obviously – they must have been a useful purchase for many a restaurateur. Kirit's next claim for his father's roll call of successes is controversial: asked if Patak's pastes helped to propel the fledgling restaurant sector he tells me, 'it was the start of what you have today.'

While we all know that for an untrained chef the ready-made paste option must have made much sense – it would have tasted good, reduced the hours spent in the kitchen or shopping, it would have been reliable – I've found there are few restaurateurs who own up to keeping jars of Patak's pastes on their shelves. 'I think,' said one confidentially, 'that most restaurants probably kept a few jars in case things got busy on a Friday or Saturday night. That way if you ran out, you could still serve customers who wouldn't be regulars, just drinkers, and who wouldn't be familiar with your usual dishes.' Some restaurateurs have even expressed hostility towards the Pathaks for 'making money the easy way', that is, not dealing with the closing-time drunks and the hassle of running a restaurant (these restaurateurs can't have known about LG and Shantagaury's long hours in the kitchen and behind the shop counter). I've even heard some restaurateurs moan that the Pathaks aren't even Indian, but their reference to Kirit's childhood in Kenya ignores Meena's in Bombay. Despite this hostility, Patak's Foods estimates that it has sold its products to 90 per cent of the Indian restaurant sector – and personal recollection of eating the same lime pickle in countless curry houses would, anecdotally at least, back this claim up.

Whether or not restaurants were using Patak's sauces, once they had developed the method of sauce-based cooking it led to an explosion in curry houses. One sauce – be it korma, rogan josh or vindaloo – could be used with any meat or vegetable and could be prepared in advance. Sauces were cheaper, easier, quicker and therefore enabled restaurants to serve more customers per night and make more money. They had other benefits for the restaurateur: they reduced the need for large kitchens or highly trained chefs, both of which were expensive. It wasn't, therefore, a coincidence that so many restaurants ended up with the same menu from one end of the country to the other.

With the ingredients, staff, appetite and methods of production now firmly established, the stage was set for Britain to go curry crazy.

NUTMEG

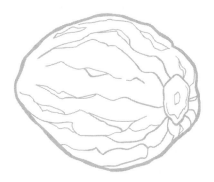

The spice commonly called nutmeg is actually the kernel of the nutmeg fruit, which looks like a white-fleshed peach, and was once native to the exotic Bandas islands. The Portuguese physician and writer Garcia de Orta published a book in 1534 on the medicinal uses for Indian spices. In his Colloquies dos Simples Drogas e Consas Medicinais da India *he recorded the following tribute to the nutmeg tree: 'It is the loveliest sight in the world to see the nutmeg trees laden with their ripe golden fruit, which splits to reveal the red mace and dark nut within. The outer fruit is very good conserved with sugar and is believed to be very good for the brain, for the nerves and for disorders of the womb. It comes to us here in Goa from Banda in jars of vinegar.' In modern times the fruit is less commonly eaten than the mace – the red slimy casing of the nut that dries to delicate pinky-red fronds and develops a pungent aroma – and the kernel which has a hard shell that is removed after drying. Both are usually ground for cooking.*

Nutmeg's culinary uses are extremely varied outside Indian cooking: in medieval times it was used for flavouring ale and in modern times it is most frequently used in apple pies and rice puddings. In Indian cooking, nutmeg is most commonly used in the popular garam masala blend but it also flavours meat. Its medicinal properties are said to include treating insomnia, curing indigestion and rheumatism. In sufficient quantities it is also considered hallucinogenic and there are medieval reports of Chinese hermits who consumed large quantities to produce visions and sensations of the eternal. In 1580 Dutch traveller Jan Huyghen van Linschoten recorded that nutmeg was the chosen narcotic of the poor. It is also a powerful aromatic and was used by the ancient Romans to scent the streets before the Emperor left his palace to remove the chance that he might smell the plebs. No wonder it was so coveted by successive European powers.

It is the lust for nutmeg that makes it one of the most remarkable spices. As discussed in the chapter on the spice trade, the love of nutmeg induced some of the most barbaric acts ever committed in the name of commerce, culminating in the genocide of the people of the Bandas islands at the hands of the Dutch. The vice-like grip of the Dutch over the nutmeg supply allowed them to precisely control its market value, and at times it was worth more than its weight in gold. In Britain in the fourteenth century, a pound of mace was considered to be worth the price of three sheep! When the British finally broke the Dutch monopoly of the nutmeg trade in 1796, they started the cultivation of the trees in Penang and Singapore and eventually in their colonies in the West Indies. Consequently the price dropped dramatically and it was said the restaurants in Paris started serving 'nutmeg with everything'.

CHAPTER SIX

The Vindaloo Years

The Curry House

In the 1970s, curry houses started to appear in every town in Britain. The vast majority were Bangladeshi-owned and most of them sported uncanny similarities. The menus were virtually identical, the names were interchangeable, the wallpaper was universal (some might say universally awful) and they only had customers at two times in the day – 3 p.m. and 11 p.m., the old closing times for pubs. Yet somehow, without a grand plan or central office, 'the curry' became a national brand.

Curry's brand values, to use marketing speak, weren't great. The restaurants were considered downmarket, the food was thought to be cheap and the clientele were depicted as drunken yobs mopping up their beer before staggering home. It was in the 70s and 80s that curry went from being an Indian dish to becoming a British institution, the values and attractions of which had little to do with the lure of spice, the pomp of Empire or the novelty of new cuisines. Curry became an emblem of change in Britain, telling on one hand of cultural diversity and on the other of an economic boom. Sadly, however, the Brits' new passion for spicy food was not matched by a commensurate interest in the food's heritage.

The curry cliché of the 70s and 80s went something like this: a group of lads tip out of the pub at closing time and fancy carrying on drinking; the curry house (called A Passage To India, the Taj Mahal, Last Days of the Raj or something along those lines) is still open so they sit down to the hottest thing on the laminated menu (thereby asserting their machismo) and carry on drinking until they feel as sick as the wallpaper looks – typically five shades of green or purple in either swirls, stripes or fleurs-de-lis. To finish the meal off they racially abuse the restaurant staff and/or run off without paying.

Abdul Miah came to Britain from Bangladesh in the 1970s and lived in the flat above his father's restaurant in Wimbledon, south west London, and knows that the curry-house cliché was based on fact. 'We used to be frightened on Fridays and Saturdays because we knew that there would be a fight. Even though we were upstairs we could hear what my father had to put up with.'

Abdul now runs several restaurants of his own, none of which fit the old cliché, and he certainly doesn't serve yobs. 'I admire men like my father because they saw that the only way to make a living was to stay open late. You could get a licence till midnight or 1 a.m. if you served food, and it was in these hours after the pubs shut that you made your money. People didn't come for the food, they came for the drink.'

Understandably, these were not the most discerning of customers. With no incentive to produce fine cuisine, the food in many of these restaurants was sauce-based, unremarkable fare and curry started to get a reputation as a 'dodgy' meal. It didn't help that after ten pints and a spicy vindaloo, customers were likely to throw up. And naturally they'd rather blame the food than the drink for an uncomfortable morning after.

Identical Menus

Whether you were ordering your meal in Glasgow or Guildford, if you were a regular curry-goer you could probably order without looking at the menu. There was a time when it seemed that every curry house in Britain had exactly the same menu, and I don't mean they were all printed on pink card (although I think you'll find they were). There are a number of reasons behind this apparent regimentation.

The first is that 80 per cent of restaurants were operated by immigrants from one part of Bangladesh, the province of Sylhet, which means these entrepreneurs grew up eating similar meals with similar ingredients. If they had been taught to cook by their mothers, they would have been taught similar techniques using identical utensils.

The next factor in curry's uniform menu was that many of these restaurateurs had worked with each other. As Abdul Miah explains: 'I saw my father give my cousins and uncles jobs, but after about four years they all left to start their own restaurants.' Understandably, if you've been encouraged to branch out on your own because you've witnessed another man's success, you're likely to want to replicate his formula. The third factor was Patak's, Sharwood's, Veeraswamy's and the other paste and sauce manufacturers who delivered uniformity in large jars to the industry.

'One thing is common among our people,' says Bangladeshi restaurateur Bazlur Chowdhury, 'is that when they see someone doing something they are very quick to follow.' So if one restaurant puts something called rogan josh on its menu, it's likely the neighbouring restaurants would spot it and try to copy it. But just because something is called rogan josh, it doesn't mean it bears any culinary resemblance to another restaurant's rogan josh. 'To be honest, I wouldn't have known what rogan josh was,' one restaurateur told me. 'I think it's a Kashmiri name, and it meant as much to me as if it was written in Japanese. So we just tried to recreate dishes by sight.' Even if people were familiar with dishes – either linguistically or culinarily – their limited kitchen skills prevented authentic reproductions. And of course, like Chinese whispers, several reproductions down the line one restaurant's interpretation of a rogan josh has virtually nothing in common with that of another.

Flock Wallpaper and Other Clichés

This keeping-up-with-the-Khans mentality also explains the rapid and blanket coverage of Indian restaurants in the most incredibly tasteless and florid wallpaper. The choice of wallcovering has two probable antecedents. The first was the desire to recreate the luxurious surroundings of Raj-era clubhouses which had themselves tried to emulate English country houses with their opulent wall coverings. The other source of inspiration was Veeraswamy's, where several of the 70s and 80s generation of restaurateurs had worked. The Regent Street restaurant was still considered upmarket and any attempt to match

Veeraswamy's opulence was no doubt an attempt to convey a rich aesthetic to potential customers.

Wallpaper historian Humphrey Boyle has another theory: that many of the fleur-de-lis designs used in curry house wallpaper were reminiscent of traditional Muslim designs. As imagery of Allah is banned in Islam, geometric patterns are often used to pay homage and show devotion. Boyle has wondered if there is not a relationship between the faith of the predominantly Muslim restaurateurs and their choice of wallpaper. Iqbal Wahhab, proprietor of London's upmarket Cinnamon Club agrees: 'I've always thought the curry house was part social club, part mosque and the wallpaper went part way to create that feeling.'

As this florid, flocked wallpaper was rarely seen in domestic houses, I'd myself wondered if it had perhaps been imported at great expense. My assumption proved wrong. Although the original flocked wallpaper was incredibly expensive, mass-produced imitations abounded. 'It was probably so popular because it was cheap,' one restaurateur thought. 'Most of us used the same builders and decorators to renovate our restaurants, so it's possible that the decorators got a good deal buying in bulk and we all ended up with the same wallpaper!'

As the interiors of curry houses became more flamboyant, so did the names. Indian restaurants of the 50s and 60s tended to be named after places – they were several Bombay and Delhi restaurants – but in the 70s and 80s, in a bid to sound more opulent, restaurants sprang up with literary names like A Passage to India or The Jewel in the Crown. This coincided with the broadcasting of the *Jewel in the Crown* mini-series on TV and the release of David Lean's adaptation of EM Forster's *A Passage to India* in cinemas. 'Basically,' says Abdul Miah, 'people called their restaurant either after the place they were from or after something the British would have heard of.'

Likewise, most restaurateurs opted to call their restaurants 'Indian' even though they themselves were from places like Sylhet in

Bangladesh. 'In Britain people did not know much about Pakistan and Bangladesh,' says Abdul, 'and if they did they probably thought about Partition or independence. India was much more familiar to them, much more appealing, so it made sense to call the food 'Indian' because, before Partition, Bangladesh had been part of India.'

Guildford v. Goa

When hippies discovered Goa in the 60s and 70s and tasted southern Indian cuisine for the first time, they returned to Britain to declare that meals served in traditional curry houses weren't authentically Indian. This added fuel to the discussion that all curry houses did was add one of a number of sauces to one of a number of meats. So not only was curry house food inauthentic, it wasn't much cop either: with a reputation like that it was hard to convince people to pay more than a few pounds for a dish. What few people realised at that time was that curry house food was authentically Bengali and as different from Goan cuisine as pizza was from fish and chips. It would be several years still before the average British restaurant goer would have both the choice of either Keralan, Punjabi or Bengali cuisine, and the ability and sophistication to know the difference.

It is for this reason that some restaurateurs feel the contribution of the Bangladeshi pioneers of the restaurant trade have been overlooked. 'This is why we started the Guild of Bangladeshi Restaurateurs,' explains Abdul Miah, 'so we can be proud of what the Bangladeshi people have done. It was the Bangladeshis who took the risks and made chicken tikka masala the national dish.' And since the curry-eating public has wised up to the regional differences in Indian cuisine, more and more restaurants are using either Bengal or Bangladesh in their titles.

Throughout the 70s and 80s the numbers of curry houses exploded. According to Menu2Menu.com, a website dedicated to ethnic cuisine in Britain, there were 1,200 Indian restaurants in 1970. By 1980 that figure had risen to 3,000, and by 1990 it had become 5,100. 'When I opened my restaurant in Hemel Hempstead in the 1960s I was the first Indian restaurant,' says one entrepreneur, 'then in the 70s I think there were two more. Now there are at least fifteen, and in that time I don't suppose the population had increased by the same amount.'

In Clapham, Shamsuddin Khan, who opened the first curry house on the High Street in 1958, had three or four years before he had his first rival a couple of miles away in Balham. Now there are seven or eight curry houses on the same high street. 'For a time it did not affect business,' he says, 'because we couldn't meet the demand. But now I think it is tough for anyone else opening a restaurant because there is just so much competition.'

The Arrival of the Tandoor

The battle for customers led to a number of innovations in the 70s and 80s, the most significant being the arrival of balti and the tandoor oven. 'In those days we used to reprint our menus every six months,' says Bazlur Chowdhury. 'This was for two reasons. The first was that we could put our prices up a little and the second was that we observed our customers and our rivals and we made changes. Eventually our entire menu was tailored to British tastes.' So when balti or tandoors took off in one restaurant, a rival could very quickly adopt them.

The tandoor taste proved very popular in the UK, and tandoori cooking – it has been argued by some – soon became as authentically British as it was Bangladeshi or Indian. The tandoor is actually a Middle Eastern oven and as a consequence of both geography and history is therefore found more often in northern provinces of the subcontinent – but not often. In fact, it's thought that the first time a tandoor was used as far south as Delhi was as late as 1948 in the Moti Mahal restaurant. Unsurprisingly, then, the tandoor is about as common in Indian as French cooking according to Camellia Panjabi, proprietor of Masala Zone, Veeraswamy and Chutney Mary. 'Ninety-nine per cent of Indians do not have a tandoor and so neither tandoori chicken nor naan are part of India's middle-class cuisine. This is even so in the Punjab, although some villages have communal tandoors where rotis can be baked.' She adds: 'Ninety-five per cent of Indians don't know what a vindaloo, jhal farezi or, for that matter, a Madras curry is'.[1]

The first restaurant to use a tandoor in Britain was, unsurprisingly, Veeraswamy's. Records show a tandoor was in operation there as early as 1959. In the 60s the Gaylord in Mortimer Street acquired one but it would be another decade before the smell of the tandoor filled restaurants up and down the country. So, what are tandoors? They are clay ovens fired by charcoal and although they can take several hours to get hot enough to cook, once they are at the right temperature food cooks extremely quickly, which makes them ideal to use in a busy restaurant kitchen.

Not all tandoors produce the same tastes. Often a chef will coat the inside of a tandoor with an individual mix of herbs and spices that sear themselves into the clay to give each oven a unique profile. The other

[1] Grove, *Curry and Spice*.

factor that has a major effect on flavour is the charcoal: both the kind of wood the charcoal is made from and the method used to make it affect the flavour. Many chefs will tell you that using the right utensils can make as much difference to the flavour of the final dish as the ingredients. It is especially crucial with tandoors. Most restaurants these days use gas-fired tandoors because they're cleaner and easier to use even though they don't create the same tastes. Of course, you never need to ask if the restaurant you're eating in uses charcoal or not – because you'll be able to smell it if they do. Tandoors are used for producing dry foods, usually naans and rotis that are cooked against the tandoor's walls, and marinated meats and kebabs that are cooked on long skewers, and which may then later be added to a sauce (the meat juices dripping on to the charcoal add to the flavour but may make a tandoori dish less attractive to vegetarians). Tandoors were such a success that new restaurants opening in the 80s frequently used the word 'tandoor' or 'tandoori' in their name.

The Truth about Chicken Tikka Masala

Of course, the tandoor's greatest contribution to Britain was chicken tikka masala, a dish that is as English as steak and kidney pudding. It is now reckoned by some to be Britain's national dish, replacing fish and chips sometime in the early 90s. While many consider it to be the archetypal curry, it is certainly not an Indian, Pakistani or Bangladeshi dish. Legend has it that one day a patron of a restaurant – in either Glasgow, Manchester or London, and in either the 50s or 60s, depending on which story you believe – sent his chicken tandoori kebab back to the kitchen for a gravy to be added. An enterprising chef then looked around for something to make a sauce from and found a tin of Campbell's condensed tomato soup. Hey presto! A legend had been born.

The problem with this story is that – despite its status as a curry legend – it is completely invented. Cinnamon Club founder Iqbal Wahhab holds his hands up. He claims to have originated the story to entertain journalists in the days when he handled the marketing for several restaurants. 'That thing about the Cambell's soup was completely made up,' he confessed to me. 'The funny thing was that people then starting saying "that was me", "that happened in my restaurant"!' Another peculiarity of this story is that chicken tikka masala is so similar to a Delhi dish known as murgh makhani, or butter chicken, that there really wasn't that much to invent: they both feature pieces of tandoor chicken in a creamy tomato sauce. What this really shows is that few of the early curry house chefs knew very much about the history and variety of Indian cuisine.

Nevertheless, chicken tikka masala is the classic British curry dish. It uses Indian techniques and ingredients but is completely tailored to the British palate – it isn't dry, it isn't hot and spicy and it's made with chicken, a British favourite. Chicken tikka masala is both exotic and safe at the same time and is often held up as an emblem of Britain's multiculturalism. The former Foreign Secretary Robin Cook famously made a speech in April 2001 to the Social Market Foundation in London in which he called it 'a true British national dish':

Chicken tikka masala is now a true British national dish, not only because it is the most popular, but because it is a perfect illustration of the way Britain absorbs and adapts external influences. Chicken tikka is an Indian dish. The masala sauce was added to satisfy the desire of British people to have their meat served in gravy.

Chicken tikka masala's disputed origins means that there is no set recipe for the dish – indeed one survey of recipes in 1998 for the *Real Curry Restaurant Guide* found the only common ingredient in 48 different chicken tikka masalas was chicken – and no chef these days admits to using condensed soup. And not only does chicken tikka masala taste different from restaurant to restaurant, but it looks different. I've known restaurants that serve a green chicken tikka masala while others dress theirs in bright vermilion. In 2004 this difference in colour brought the industry under the media's scrutiny when a survey from Surrey County Council in south-east Britain found that 57 per cent of Indian restaurants in the county used illegal levels of food colourings in their chicken tikka masalas.

While it is undoubtedly a British institution, can we really be sure that it is the national dish? The founder of the Curry Club, Pat Chapman, is often said to be the man who first labelled chicken tikka masala the national dish, but his claim was taken out of context: it is just the most popular dish ordered in Indian restaurants (some research reckons it accounts for one in seven meals in Indian restaurants). Many pundits, who have since made similar claims about chicken tikka masala's dominance, cite a piece of research by Food Service Intelligence. So I contacted Food Service Intelligence, a subsidiary brand of Horizons, a consultancy to the restaurant and eating-out sector, in the hope of seeing this research for myself.

'I have no idea where that story came from,' Managing Director Peter Backman told me. 'As far as we're concerned it was a story without foundation.' Aware that the company had been erroneously attributed with producing this information, Horizons subsequently conducted their own research. In 1998 they surveyed 800 establishments in all sectors and asked them what their top three bestselling dishes were. The results were then weighted accordingly, and the company was able to reveal that the nation's favourite dish was in fact ... fish and chips. Chicken tikka masala wasn't even the nation's second favourite dish, in fact curry only made it to number six on the list behind steak and chips, chicken, lasagne and roast dinner.

What is perhaps most interesting about this story – and in many ways it is the crux of this entire book – is the willingness of Britons to celebrate the fact that their national dish was of Indian origin. We liked to believe the chicken tikka masala myth because it made us seem open-minded, adventurous and modern. As a nation we found it cool in the same way the 50s hep cats and Hollywood stars at Veeraswamy's found it cool. If our choice of meal was an indication of our character, we liked what curry said about us. And we liked it so much that we never checked to see if it the story we had swallowed along with our curry was actually true.

It was in fact a true *urban* myth in the sense that in multicultural cities where the ethnic population is often 40 per cent of the total, it seems natural that curry is so popular. But when you leave the urban centres – the places where press releases are concocted and regurgitated by the media – you find that chicken tikka masala is harder to find than a black cab. Despite the arrival of curry houses in small Lake District villages and Welsh outposts, British villages still have more pubs than Indian restaurants and diners are far more likely to order steak and chips than curry with their pint.

Balti Barmy

After the tandoor, the next big sensation was balti. In the 80s, the ever-increasing competition between the multiplying restaurants led to more new dishes and cooking styles being offered. The most famous, and most revolutionary, was most definitely balti. Prior to the balti craze of the 80s Indian meals had been served on plates, as is common in most cuisines. But with balti, meals are brought to the table from the kitchen in small metal bowls – now known as balti dishes – allowing each diner to serve themselves.

Depending on who you believe, Balti cuisine either originated high in the Pakistani Himalayas in a province called – wait for it – Baltistan or, conversely, in the Sparkhill area of Birmingham where cheap food was served in bowls so big they were called buckets; *balti* means bucket, you see. However, both stories have flaws. Travellers who have been to Baltistan report that the food there bears no resemblance whatsoever to the food they recognise as balti. And the idea that a cook in Birmingham named his new cuisine balti after the shape of the dish is preposterous as balti only means bucket in Hindi (in Baltistan the language is an archaic dialect of Tibetan). It's actually far more plausible that 'balti' was originally coined by a Hindi speaker to be derogatory about the dishes, and that the Baltistan story was conveniently created later to give this disparaged cuisine unwarranted authority.

It seems most plausible that this new way of serving started among the north Pakistani and Kashmiri communities of the Sparkhill area of Birmingham – a place that's now been renamed in restaurant guides as the Balti Triangle – who opened a few cafes for the immigrant community and served cheap food in big bowls that could be mopped up with naan bread. However, the indigenous white population cottoned on to how cheap these cafes were and started a demand for balti-style cooking elsewhere.

There are several restaurants that claim to have been the first to serve balti dishes in Britain, just as there are many who claim to have first added tomato soup to Punjabi chicken kebabs. But the speedy expansion of balti makes investigating such claims impossible: by the mid 1980s restaurants around Britain had ditched meals served on plates in favour of balti dishes. The style of cooking, which was originally Pakistani, was adopted with alacrity by Bangladeshi and Indian chefs. Pretty soon it became the predominant method of serving Indian food in Britain.

Balti dishes are also known as *karhais* (one of the possible origins of the word 'curry') and are made from either steel or iron. They resemble flat-bottomed woks and are used for both cooking and serving. If you ever get a chance to eat in a balti restaurant where you can see the kitchen, you might get a shock: balti chefs often cook on flames several feet high, but this heat adds to the flavour. Another characteristic of balti cooking is that much of the food preparation can be done in advance. Almost all dishes start with a pulp of onion and garlic and the other ingredients are typically cut very small so as to cook quicker. These two characteristics make balti ideal for a busy restaurant kitchen.

From a restaurateur's point of view, balti has two other advantages over plated meals: first, presentation is less of a problem and is always dramatic – seeing several bowls of steaming curries coming straight from the kitchen looks, smells and even sounds exciting; and secondly, and no doubt more importantly, it encouraged patrons to order more than one dish.

Balti's success lies partly in its theatre. Scorching hot bowls of multi-coloured dishes, each promising a different flavour, each stimulating different taste buds, each feeding the eyes as well as the belly: suddenly, with balti, diners started to reassess their view of curry. It could no longer be considered a cheap option prepared by chefs with little skill, as customers were overwhelmed by the variety. Balti also made curry an incredibly sociable option: diners could share each other's dishes, which encouraged people to order more adventurously, and the sheer practicality of 'can you pass me that' encouraged conversation about the meal itself. It was with balti that Brits really started to understand and appreciate the complexity of pan-Indian cookery. And it also marked the start of curry's acquisition of a clientele who weren't young, male and drunk.

The Takeaway

The final invention that changed curry in these crucial decades was the takeaway. From a business point of view, takeaway had advantages and disadvantages: on the plus side you could make do with fewer waiting staff and save on wages, but on the downside you made more profit on drinks than you did on food. Nevertheless, with the demise of the traditional housewife and the rise in divorce and single living, convenience food was in demand.

'Takeaway was a big surprise to me,' says AH Chowdhury who first got requests to take food home in the late 70s. 'People would say to me "my wife must taste this, she'll never believe what your food is like unless I take some to her"! The problem with this,' he says, 'is that no one had invented takeaway cartons yet; we used to get some of the boxes that the vegetables had been delivered in and lined them with plastic bags! I don't know if they got them home all right without it spilling everywhere, but that's how we started to do takeaways.' In London, Shamsuddin Khan of the Maharani recalls washing up mango tins to reuse them as takeaway containers.

Preparing dishes to be eaten off the premises also had another advantage – families that couldn't agree what to eat could now collect meals from the chippie, the curry house and the Chinese restaurant, all eat what they wanted yet still eat together. 'There used to be this one guy who always came in to our restaurant on a Friday night,' recalls a restaurateur from Berkshire. 'Our place was on a busy high street and I used to see him go to the Chinese and pick up one dish, then to the fish and chip shop to pick up another, and then he would come to us. I asked him why he did this and he explained that no one else in his family liked Indian food. So I asked him what his wife liked, and he told me she liked chicken, so one week I prepared a special chicken curry for his wife. I didn't charge him, but I wanted to educate his wife about how good our food was. The next week he came and ordered meals from us for the whole family!'

Curry's path to dominance wasn't so much a bumpy one as one bedevilled by potholes, bad signposting and the odd yawning crevasse. Scare stories in the press about food additives and colourants combined with personal testimonies about food poisoning and 'Delhi belly' meant it would be another decade or so before some people would consider curry anything other than a cheap, and slightly dodgy, night out.

Lager, Lads and Loutism

It didn't help that curry houses tended to be in poorer locations where rent was cheaper. They were still not the kind of establishments you wanted to take the family to. Nor did it help that the clientele were still often lagered-up lads who would treat kids and staff alike to a barrage of bad language. 'I remember going to see a friend of mine who worked in a restaurant in Glasgow,' recalls curry entrepreneur Charan Gill. 'It was on the first floor above a cinema that screened blue movies. It even shared toilet facilities with the cinema, so when you went to the loo you could see a bit of the film too.' Elsewhere, the early restaurants were often in red-light districts, near docks or close to industrial areas: areas where women and families wouldn't often find themselves. It's no wonder that curry got itself a reputation with the lads.

The machismo associated with curry meant that ordering usually went in two stages: the first was 'bring me the hottest thing on the menu', and the second was 'bring me lots of it'. Waiters who suggested that maybe their guests had over-ordered were berated for affronting the customer's manliness in front of his mates. Some restaurateurs got their revenge by making vindaloos and phalls that were so hot they inflicted pain, while others made a virtue out of the heat of their curries with a 'if you can't educate them, entertain them' philosophy.

Famously, the Bangladeshi proprietor of Newcastle's Rupali restaurant offers to feed people for free if they can finish all of his hottest curry which is made almost entirely of dried chillies. Abdul Latif has turned the curry's reputation as the lager louts' favourite to his advantage by running an annual 'Curry Hell' competition in which Britain's bravest and barmiest curry fans line up to cause considerable pain to their digestive tracts: it is apparently a rare occasion for anyone to get a bill made entirely of zeros.

Bored of being plain old Abdul Latif, he bought the title Lord of Harpole for £5,500 and now enjoys a prominent media profile – he has even been featured in the lads' comic *Viz*. He is so proud of his association with *Viz* that he took down the sign outside his restaurant that quoted reviews from the local press and replaced it with one that simply said 'As seen in *Viz*'. While hot curries have been a boon for Lord Harpole, his profile has not helped those who were fighting to change curry's image. One of his stranger ideas was to accept that from time to time people would try and run off without paying: his menus clearly state that he will accept goods in exchange for payment.

He claims he'll take anything with a resale value and has been known to take shirts off errant customers' backs – not to mention watches and shoes – to recoup the cost of meals.

The machismo of eating curry also involved, from time to time, trying to get away without paying. It was part of the entertainment for some diners – usually young and male – who often devised elaborate plans to slip out the door without being noticed. Each diner would leave on his own, making an excuse that he needed to find a phone box or get a cheque book from his car – until the last man had to make a run for it while the waiters were dealing with other tables.

'It didn't happen often,' Charan Gill remembers from his time as a waiter in the 80s in Glasgow, 'but I used to chase people down the street and usually they paid up. They just wanted to see if they could get away with it, they were doing it for a dare with their mates. Over time you got a bit smart about it and didn't put groups of lads at tables near the door, or even groups of girls because they were just as bad, but a couple was usually a safe bet.'

Obviously, some of this bad behaviour was motivated by racism. 'I have been insulted in ways you cannot imagine,' one restaurateur says, although his words are echoed by many. 'My mother has been called a whore, I've been told that my skin is the colour of shit, that I smell, that I have no right to be here and I have been told that if I don't do as I'm told my children will be harmed. I think, though, only twice have I been reduced to tears.'

Of course it was the unappealing macho connotations that made 'Vindaloo' such an apt title for a football song. 'Vindaloo' was released by three drinking buddies – Alex James from Blur, the actor Keith Allen and the artist Damien Hirst – under the name Fat Les with the intention of creating a new anthem for the terraces during the 1998 World Cup. It wasn't so much a song as a chant and displayed the same kind of skill in musicianship that many a chef displayed in making a vindaloo. It was coarse, almost vulgar, but it was also cheeky – a bit like the bloke who calls a waiter 'Gunga Din' then adds that he was 'only joking' and didn't mean any insult. 'Vindaloo' captured the menace and humour of a lads night out, yet also highlighted how British culture can take something exotic and complex and reduce it to the lowest common denominator. Suddenly, the Brits' love of curry wasn't being celebrated, it was being lamented.

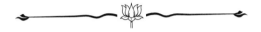

The Waiters' Revenge

Of course smart people know that the one person you should never insult is your waiter, as he is a man with considerable power. If you misbehave you may find your meal arrives with a few unexpected extras. A few of the people I'd interviewed for this book have confessed to knowing 'someone' in 'some other restaurant' who added something unsavoury to an unsavoury customer's dish. 'These people are fools to talk to us that way. Do they really think we won't mind?' asks one incredulously. 'Many times I saw people spit into drinks or add crumbs from the floor to the food. And many times when people were so drunk they were deliberately overcharged.' Such behaviour did not breed contrition or understanding, only a sense of conflict. Nor did it help the reputation of either the food or the establishments.

'When I started to work in my father's restaurants when I was 18, I saw that this kind of behaviour was really harming the business,' says Abdul Miah. 'My father's generation had made their money from serving these kinds of customers but I could see that now there were other people who also liked curry but wouldn't come and eat in a restaurant where they could witness such foul language.' So, to his father's dismay, Abdul started to make some changes.

'I used to shut the door at eleven o'clock and when the pubs shut and the drunks used to come to the door I would tell them we were closed. My father thought I was mad. "Why are you turning away customers?" he wanted to know, and I told him to be patient.

'Over the next year I made a lot of changes. I looked at other restaurants and saw that they had candles on the tables, that they had good wine lists and more tables just for two people. I also improved the menu and created milder dishes with more subtle flavours and after a year we were as busy at 7.30 p.m. as we had used to be at 11.30 p.m. It hurt financially for a time, but it was worth it.'

It was Abdul's generation of restaurateur, the generation that inherited customers with the appetite and willingness to try curry, the generation that benefited from established import businesses and an abundance of year-round fresh produce, that became the generation that took curry from the post-pub cliché to the pre-theatre choice of a different kind of clientele. The curry was about to move upmarket.

FENNEL

Technically, fennel isn't a spice, and technically its seeds aren't really seeds at all but tiny dried fruit. However, as it is added to cooking as a flavour rather than a main ingredient, it is frequently classified and sold as a spice.

As you might expect, fennel – like every other spice – has many medicinal properties, however, the range of ailments it is said to aid is really quite unexpected. Writing in the first century, Pliny the Elder reckoned fennel could ease no fewer than 22 medical conditions. They include coughs, earaches, toothaches, rheumatism, asthma and black eyes. Fresh fennel sap can also be used as an eye wash (try it at your own risk!)

and Pliny also noticed that snakes that rubbed themselves against fennel plants seemed to have better eyesight. Since Pliny's day medical practitioners have added other attributes – in India it is said to stimulate lactation in breastfeeding mothers and in China it has been used to cure snakebites! It is still used as an ingredient in gripe water to relieve colic and a tea made from the seeds is said to aid a restful night's sleep. Perhaps one of fennel's most sought-after qualities is that it helps the body digest fatty foods and therefore has a reputation for aiding weight loss.

Fennel also has associations with magic and witchcraft. In medieval Britain it was apparently hung above doorways to ward off the evil eye and – preposterously – cow's udders were smeared with it so their milk would not troubled by evil spirits. The Saxons considered it to be sacred.

Fennel seeds are rich in an oil infused with the plant's aniseed taste. The oil is therefore used as a flavouring and aromatic in everything from liqueurs to cough drops and soaps to perfumes. The aroma and taste of the seeds change dramatically after roasting, turning from something noticeably sweet to something distinctly savoury.

In cooking fennel also has several uses, as all parts of the plant – the stalk, leaves, flower, seeds and even pollen – can be added to recipes and work particularly well in rich meat and fish dishes. The leaves also make a nice addition to salads.

In Indian cookery it is the seeds that are most prized and are often added to fish curries. They are also frequently used in the making of sweets: malpuri are crispy golden sweets covered in sugar flavoured with fennel, and gaja are deep-fried pastries covered in crushed fennel seeds. The seeds themselves are sometimes sugar coated and used as breath fresheners. It is also used in Bengali cookery to flavour dhals and in Gujarat it is *added to muthiyas, a kind of dumpling that is steamed before being pan-fried. It is also used in the Hindu cookery of Kashmir, but rarely by Kashmiri Muslims.*

The best fennel seeds are said to come from Lucknow and are sold whole or ground. As with all spices, it is better to buy them whole and grind them yourself at home just before cooking. Look out for evenly coloured seeds that are still bright green – and avoid bags that still have bits of stalk and leaves left in.

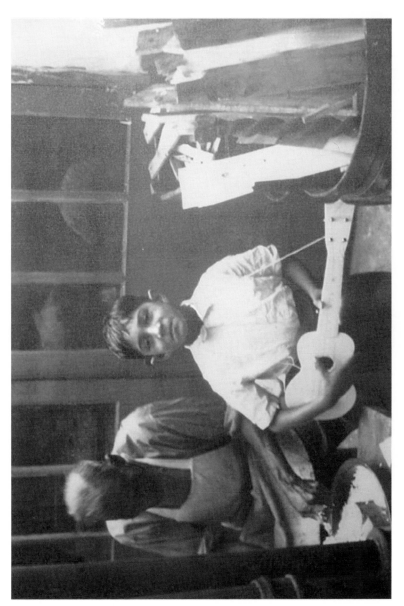

Kirit Pathak, aged 6, at the family home in Kentish Town. Photograph courtesy of the Pathak family

Lakshmishankar Pathak (far right) at the Pathaks' shop in Drummond Street, 1960s. Photograph courtesy of the Pathak family

Yorkshire farmer Robert Barraclough in his field of coriander. Photograph courtesy of National Farmers Union

Ashoka's Ruby Murray Club
Share in our success

Each time you visit one of our premises for dinner in the evening, we will stamp a box. Various concessions are available along the way with the final box allowing you a complimentary meal for 2 persons. Once this card is complete we will issue you with another one. Please leave the completed card with a member of staff and it will be entered into our prize draw. These offers can not be used in conjunction with any other promotion and may be withdrawn at any time without prior notice or warning.

1 Complimentary Drink	2 Lucky Dip	3 Complimentary Wine	4 Gift Voucher return visit
5 Complimentary Starter	6 Complimentary Maharani frozen curry	7 25% Food Discount (excludes Sat.)	8 Lucky Dip
9 2 curries for the price of 1, main meals only (excludes Sat.)	10 Complimentary Wine	11 25% Food discount (excludes Sat.)	12 Complimentary meal for two, food only (valid Mon. & Tues.)

You may bring along non-members as guests who will also benefit from your card. If your guests are also members, one concession card only, will apply for your party.

Member's Name.......

Address.......

Ruby Murray's signature on an Ashoka restaurant loyalty card. Courtesy of Harlequin Group Ltd

Shantagaury Pathak in front of the family's delivery van, 1960s. Photograph courtesy of the Pathak family

Preparing food in the Pathaks' Kentish Town kitchen, 1960s. Photograph courtesy of the Pathak family

A selection of Asian vegetables grown in the heart of London at Spitalfields City Farm

Advertisement for Vesta Chicken Curry that appeared in *Woman* magazine in the mid-60s

Advertisement for Vesta Beef Curry from *Woman* magazine from the 1960s

CHAPTER SEVEN

The British Response

Remembering your First Curry

So far, this history has concentrated on the people, events and forces among the immigrant community that fostered the rise of curry. In this chapter, though, I want to look at the curry's rise from the other side of the fence and see how changes in circumstance and attitudes within the white indigenous population of Britain also contributed to the story of curry. For as remarkable as it was for a young man to emigrate to the other side of the world, to start a business and find implausible ingredients from unexpected places, I recognise that it also took a different kind of courage to walk through the doors of a 'curry house' when you knew nothing about either the food or the culture that produced it.

I must confess that I am not particularly interested in the nabobs and early customers of upmarket restaurants like Veeraswamy's and the Mysore. This is probably because I think we know how these venues found their customers – they were men (mostly) with a connection to India through either their work or their family. What interests me more is how the more humble establishments grew their businesses beyond the ghetto of their own community. I wanted to know who the pioneer customers had been, why they had ventured to unwelcoming rooms above porn cinemas for a meal, and what they had thought of that meal once they'd eaten it. Could it be that they had gone for the porn and found the curry by accident? Was it in fact the seediness of the establishments that gave them their lure? Was curry dangerous, and therefore exciting? I hope that so far I have explained how curry was delivered, what I'd like to do now is go back in time to analyse how it was received.

During the course of researching this book I have – predictably – asked practically everyone I've met for their memories of eating their first curry. The responses are marked by a clear generational divide. For those born after 1980, the question has been difficult to answer as curry to that generation has been as plentiful and acceptable as fish and chips, or milk or even air; in consequence no one has a specific memory about their first curry – it's like asking them if they can remember when they first watched TV.

For children of the 1960s and 1970s, memories of curry were largely domestic. It was not an era when families ate out and so people recalled Vesta chicken curries or home-cooked fare made with the now seemingly ridiculous combination of apple, sultanas and curry powder. Among those who were teenagers and young adults in the 50s and 60s, I found a few who could remember going out for a curry, and below I have recorded their memories. What intrigued me was that before those dates I found only a handful of people who were even aware of curry or the arrival of a generation of immigrants. Anecdotally it would seem that curry existed primarily in a ghetto that people weren't either wary of or opposed to; they were simply ignorant of it.

'I Don't do Curry'

What has been of most interest to me however, has been the responses of people born before 1930, because with only a very few exceptions, it would seem a huge percentage of white Britons over the age of 75 have never had a curry – that is, if my anecdotal research were to prove representational. When I invited older relatives and friends to join me for a meal and try their very first curry, all but one refused – they simply didn't *do* curry. They just knew it wasn't for them! And when I did take an 85-year-old gent out to dinner – we went to the curry mile in Rusholme, Manchester where he could have had his pick of menus – he changed his mind and refused to even leave the car. My first task in telling the customers' side of the curry story was to unearth the reasons for this hostility.

'I've got nothing against the people,' Norman, my car-bound companion insisted. 'They fought in the war, they raise their families like everyone else, but I just don't want to eat their bloody food.'

For Norman, and others of his generation, the smell of curry is associated with unsavoury parts of town, with poverty and with changes in their cities that were unsettling and coincided with job losses and recessions. 'If the smell of it makes me feel unwell, lord knows what eating it would do to me,' Edna, 92, summed it up for me this way. 'There are some people who don't look good in pink and should never wear it.

Well I look fabulous in pink but I'm one of them people that should never eat curry and never wear brown: I just know it's not for me.'

Even so, I wondered how they had never not been curious to try a cuisine that has received so much attention in the media and was so visible in every supermarket and town centre. 'Why would I be curious to go into a restaurant where I don't know anyone, where I couldn't understand the menu and where I'd burn my mouth off?' Edna explained. 'Why would I be so curious to make a fool of myself? Ask yourself that.'

It also became apparent that people like Edna and Norman had actually had remarkably few opportunities to sample Indian cooking. If you didn't live in a big city, curry was quite easy to remain ignorant of until the 1970s, and even then there wasn't the dining-out culture in Britain as there is today. Takeaway was a phenomenon that was still a decade off, ready meals were comparatively expensive and pretty tasteless, and so unless you cooked curry at home, it was actually surprisingly easy to evade. By the time that Edna and Norman would have encountered curry without making a deliberate effort to make its acquaintance, they were already retired, relatively set in their ways and happier to stick with what they knew. It wouldn't have helped of course, that they would have also heard reports from braver friends of meals cooked by chefs more skilled at maintaining a ship's engine than preparing chicken or grinding spices.

Against a backdrop of such indifference and hostility, I found the occasional story of early encounters with curry all the more fascinating. Surely it must have taken either an exceptional person, or exceptional circumstances then for a white Briton with no connection to India to sample Indian cookery on British soil. Just such a man was Herbert Thomas who told his encounter with curry to his daughter, Joyce.

'My father had been a waiter at the Savoy in London in the 1920s and he told me that there were quite a few Indians working in the kitchen. He said that one night the Indian kitchen hands took a few of the white waiters to a restaurant in Holborn somewhere. I got the impression it wasn't the most successful evening ever as no one spoke English to my father and his friends and I don't think they stayed long,' says Joyce. 'The reason I remember this is because whenever my mother made a curry from leftovers with curry powder, my father always used to say how it wasn't like the real Indian curry he'd had in London. Judging from the way he told the story, I got the impression that he had liked the meal he'd that night, but got more pleasure from the fact that he'd been adventurous enough to try it. I think he considered himself to have been quite ahead of his time.'

Post-war

In the 1950s and 60s, personal recollections of curry eating become more numerous. Jenny remembers going out for a meal with friends in Liverpool in the late 50s and trying curry by mistake. 'My brother had just finished his National Service and had a bit of money to throw around and wanted to show off,' she recalls, 'so he took us to what he said was his favourite Chinese restaurant, only when we got there it had been taken over by this lovely guy from the Punjab who said he could do us Chop Suey if we wanted, but he was better at cooking curry.

'Looking back it was probably one of the strangest meals I've ever had. My brother ordered Chinese, a couple of other people had omelettes and boiled potatoes and me and a boyfriend tried the chicken curry. I think we definitely got the best deal,' she recalls. 'I remember it was a very small restaurant, probably only ten or twelve tables, and it was all kitted out like a Chinese restaurant with red paper lanterns and oriental dolls all over the place. I can't remember what the menu was like, but I don't think we got much choice – it would probably have either been a chicken curry or a lamb curry. I'm pretty sure there wasn't anything with a specific name like rogan josh or biryani.'

In London, Terry Jones remembers hanging out in a curry house in Soho in the 50s. 'I'm fairly sure it was Frith Street, but it could have been Greek Street, and we first went in there when we were trying to hide from a bloke we owed money to and we knew he'd never dare go into – you're going to have to excuse my language here, but that's what we called them – a "Paki place". There was a small gang of us that used to go to this one restaurant, I think it had the word Asia in its name, and we could spend all afternoon there and not get caught by the bookie,' he recalls.

'When you spend a bit of time in a place, you get talking to people and you get persuaded to try a few things that you might not otherwise. Abdul, the guy who ran the place always used to say to us "If you don't like it you don't have to pay". So of course, being the kind of lads we were, we always said we didn't like it so we could eat for free! Eventually he called our bluff and said "If you don't like it why do you keep coming back?" but even when we were paying it didn't cost much.'

In the 50s and early 60s going to Indian restaurants was the domain of a young and adventurous urban tribe, and at home curry had a slightly more sedate profile. But it was actually to be the growing acceptance of the ready meal that helped the rise of curry as it introduced it to a different generation, a different social class and helped it climb out of its ghetto.

A Brief History of the Ready Meal

The ready meal was as much the result of innovations in food technology as it was changes in society. In a slightly bizarre twist of fortune, it could be said that the success of curry in the twentieth century owes much to both the development of the domestic freezer and the feminist movement. If you wanted to push the cause and consequence argument further, you could also argue that the space race had something to do with it. But more of that later.

The technology that would lead to millions of frozen curries being sold each week was originally discovered by accident when a certain Clarence Birdseye (yes, that is where the brand name comes from) made an unusual discovery on a fishing trip in 1917. Lying on the ice in Labrador he noticed a number of fish that had been discarded on an earlier trip but that when cooked, still tasted as good as the fresh fish. It would appear he hatched a cunning plan and a few decades later Birds Eye was a household name. However, launching frozen food onto the market had one huge hurdle to overcome: nobody had freezers.

David Mounfield worked for Findus in the 1950s and remembers that some people didn't even realise they needed a freezer. 'I had one woman complain that her food was mouldy. So I went round there with a few bags of frozen peas and fish fingers and a bunch of flowers to apologise, and then I saw her go into the garden and put them in the outside loo. She said it was the coldest place in the house and she used it as a larder!'

Another problem David and his frozen food rivals faced was that not even that many shops had freezers. 'You've got to remember that in those days it was all corner shops and little local stores and they just didn't have the space to put in a big freezer. It wasn't until the advent of big supermarkets that anyone had the room to sell a lot of frozen foods.' And for that to happen, more households needed to own a car.

Of course, curry wasn't the first dish Findus and Birds Eye produced. Frozen fish, fruit and vegetables were sold decades before anyone thought to actually put together an entire meal in one packet – and part of the reason no one thought to do that sooner is that it required improvements in the packaging industries: so many things had to happen in sequence before mass market frozen curry could be developed.

The first so-called 'TV Dinner' – that is an entire frozen meal, as opposed to an individual component of a meal – was launched in the States in 1952. And, as has happened quite a lot in the story of curry, it was a bit of a happy accident. Apparently C.A. Swanson & Sons of Omaha, Nebraska had ordered too much turkey and it was costing them a fortune to keep all the birds in cold storage. So the cry went round the company for a suggestion as to how they could sell more turkey, and fast. It is a certain Gerry Thomas whom posterity has credited with the accolade of being the guy with the big idea. He even apparently sketched out a plate with different compartments for sliced turkey, corn bread, gravy, sweet potato and buttered peas. After a year the line up was changed to include white bread dressing and mashed potato and in 1960 an extra compartment was added for a racy serving of cranberry sauce. In 1953, 10 million of these TV turkey dinners sold in the states.

In Britain the take-up of ready meals was severely hampered by the lack of domestic freezers: as a percentage of take home salary they were more expensive than in America, and the moodier British weather meant more people could survive with just a larder. This explains why Britain's first ready meal wasn't frozen – it was dehydrated. It was Vesta's chicken curry, a meal with a kitsch reputation akin to Pan's People's dance routines and end-of-the-pier revues.

Worshipping the Goddess Vesta

Vesta's launch in 1962 coincided with great interest in the Space Race and much was made of its reputation as food fit for an astronaut. Stewart Marshall, who was eight when he tried his first Vesta, shares the following memory: 'There was something so exciting about a Vesta curry. I think it was great for kids because you somehow felt that you were cooking, rather than being presented with the mysterious result of your mum's labour. If you could boil water, you could cook, and that made you feel really grown up. Of course it also helped that you felt you were eating the most modern food imaginable. You know, if it was good enough for NASA it had to be all right for High Wycombe!'

Angie Sutton has a different memory of Vesta's appeal: 'There was something really naughty about a Vesta. You knew somehow it wasn't right, it was a bit like having a fag behind the bike sheds or kissing the hardest boy in school. It was dangerous, and of course that only added to the thrill.'

John Clarke's father had been a pilot for British Airways and used to come home from trips to India with exotic descriptions of improbable meals. 'He really wanted my mum to cook them at home but of course she had never been to India and couldn't imagine what he was talking about. One day he decided that he would do the shopping himself so he could show us what he was on about. He came home with a Vesta and very proudly put it in front us – and garnished it with a boiled egg! He told us it wasn't quite like the food he'd had in India, and he wasn't half wrong.'

Vesta's chicken curry was soon joined on the shelves by Vesta's beef curry, made with soya pieces shaped to look like beef. Although there was some real meat in Vesta's curries as well, they never enjoyed an upmarket reputation, either nutritionally or taste-wise. Vesta's appeal lay in a combination of convenience and kitsch – there was even a drag queen called Vesta Curry doing the rounds in Birmingham at one time.

As the 60s progressed, however, a convergence of cultural forces encouraged a younger generation to find out more about Eastern cultures and cuisines. By the end of the decade the hippy counterculture that had drawn so much from Eastern religions started to embrace Indian food. The Beatles' much publicised forays into Hinduism and India then popularised all things Indian – and curry in particular – in many people's eyes. This also encouraged many people to visit India where they found out just how far removed Vesta's products were. Then there were TV shows like Graham Kerr's *Galloping Gourmet* in which he travelled the world and created dishes from the country of the week. Of course, he wasn't the only person travelling abroad: as cheaper foreign travel opened up the world for more people, so their tastebuds were opened up to the possibilities of new tastes.

The other force that brought the ready meal, and hence curry, to a wider domestic audience was the decline of the nuclear family. As women went out to work in greater numbers and had neither the time to shop nor to cook, the demand for ready meals increased. The rise in the divorce rate led inevitably to a greater number of 'single person households' – to use census-speak – in which there was less incentive to cook a meal just for one.

There were other changes too, like the increase in car use and out-of-town supermarkets where shops tripled and quintupled their floor space. Suddenly supermarkets had space for aisles and aisles of frozen and chilled food – and consumers could get them home quickly and store them in ever-bigger and ever-cheaper freezers. By the mid 1980s, most weekly shops would have included at least one ready meal.

Although classic dishes like shepherd's pie and Italian lasagne were instantly popular in ready meal form, curries held a particular appeal not just for consumers, but also for the manufacturers. The preparation of curries for a mass market can successfully and relatively cheaply be automated. Curries – whether biryanis or kormas or chicken tikka masalas – could be assembled in large vats and then poured out into individual containers. This made them relatively cheap, which naturally added to their popularity.

Another factor that contributed to curry's ascent was the rise in vegetarianism. Unwittingly many Indian-style ready meals were often the only vegetarian option among shelves and shelves of cannelloni, moussaka, lasagne and hot pots. The same was also true in restaurants, of course, and as vegetarianism moved from the fringes into the main-stream throughout the 60s and 70s, Indian cuisine became the only eating-out option for more and more people. If a group of people wanted to go out for a meal together, the chances were that at least one person would be vegetarian, which made Indian cuisine a more inclusive choice.

Together these random advances in food technology and women's emancipation led to curry finding a bigger audience and greater acceptance. 'There can be no doubt that the rise in the ready meal educated the palates of many people who might not have otherwise tried Indian food,' Iqbal Wahhab of London's Cinnamon Club told me. And food historian Frances Short confirmed the affect domestic eating has on restaurant eating: 'People are much more adventurous in the food they eat at home. The availability of new cuisines on supermarket shelves leads to greater experimentation on the high street.'

Worshipping the Goddess Madhur

But there is one last factor that really propelled the indigenous Brits' take up of curry in the 1970s and 80s: Madhur Jaffrey.

'The entire industry owes a debt to her,' is how one restaurateur summed up her impact. Madhur Jaffrey's books and TV shows did more for curry's visibility, reputation and consumption than anything else. Virtually single-handedly, Madhur Jaffrey changed Brits' perceptions of curry and made them understand that there was more to it than ready-made meals and dodgy takeaways.

Her first book, *An Invitation to Indian Cooking*, was launched in 1973 and a TV series followed in the 80s on the BBC – the first Indian cookery show on British television. Shown wearing sarees and featured in beautiful locations as well as in the kitchen, Madhur Jaffrey seemed at once exotic and accessible: qualities she then lent to the food she prepared. But despite her aptitude and success in the kitchen, her career as a TV chef was accidental. To start with, as a child she hardly ever went in the kitchen, let alone cooked.

'I very much doubt that I would have had a full-blown cooking career in India, because the way I was raised, we had cooks in our house, and the cooks cooked. My mother would go in occasionally to supervise the food, but that was it,' she has said.[1] Perhaps surprisingly, it is just this childhood ignorance of food that she claims led to her later success: she is often quoted as saying that because she came to cookery late in life, she understands how daunting it can be to cook a complicated dish for the first time. It's no surprise, then, that Madhur Jaffrey has a reputation for writing recipes which are easy to follow.

Her step-by-step guides mirrored the recipes sent to her by relatives from her native Delhi when she was a student at the Royal Academy of Dramatic Arts in London where she trained to be an actress. 'That's what my first book is – it's pretty much all the recipes from my relatives, from my friends, in my city, the recipes I grew up with and that my

[1] Taken from an interview given to the BBC World Service.

mother sent to me in little airmail letters when I was a student at RADA,' she has said.

On graduating from RADA, Madhur developed a career in films and won awards, but in her 20s the acting offers ran dry and she had to look for an alternative source of income. So she started submitting articles to various magazines and found it was her cookery features – based on her relatives' recipes – that got the most positive response. One thing led to another and before she knew it she was much better known in the UK as a chef than an actress. She now describes herself as 'a trained actress and an accidental cook'.

Despite the unplanned nature of her career, there can be no doubt that Madhur Jaffrey had a talent for cookery shows. 'I think my dad had quite a crush on her,' says Vesta fan Stewart Marshall. 'She was very sophisticated and ever so slightly prescriptive. You got the feeling that if she told you to do something you wouldn't have the choice to refuse. I think it's fair to say that my dad found her very *persuasive!*'

In John Clarke's house the memories of Madhur Jaffrey were of her clothes. 'My mum always wanted to know why she cooked in flowing sarees. I remember a few discussions about what a fire hazard they were and how you should always wear an apron which, of course, she never did.'

Although many people remember watching Madhur's programmes both in awe of the incredibly beautiful woman and the incredibly edible food she prepared, few can remember ever trying to cook one of her recipes. 'I thought about it,' one woman told me, 'but I had a young family at the time and I knew they'd turn their noses up at anything that wasn't served with chips!'

Her impact, then, wasn't round the dining tables of middle England, but in the general consciousness of the nation. As one interviewee put it to me: 'She was the first person to bring a curry into my house, only we never ate one of hers.' Madhur Jaffrey's gift to Britain was one of education, and it was armed with the knowledge she imparted and the understanding she engendered that Britain really began to be a nation of curryholics.

Meet Ruby

Perhaps the clearest indication that Britain had taken the curry to its heart was the development of the peculiarly British pet name for Indian food – Ruby. Coming from the bizarre and time-honoured tradition of cockney rhyming slang, someone appropriated the name of Ruby Murray, the 50s' pop starlet famous for her hoarse singing voice. According to fans of the singer, the man who gets the credit for renaming the curry was Billy Connolly. Ruby herself was apparently quite amused at the use of her name and even agreed to take part in a publicity stunt for a Glasgow restaurant's 'Ruby Murray loyalty card'. No one knows when Ruby first lent her name to curry, or whether the way she sang made people think of the way your throat feels after a vindaloo, but by the dawn of the 80s if you had said you were 'going out for a Ruby', no one would have thought you were going to the jewellers.

By the time curry became known as Ruby, it's fair to say that it was well on its way to becoming a distinctive *British* cuisine. It wasn't just a type of food, it had become a type of culture and the experience of eating a Ruby on a Friday night with your mates was an event that couldn't be replicated anywhere else on earth. Somewhere around the dawn of the 1980s, the imported and adapted food of the subcontinent became a uniquely British category of dining.

CHILLIES

There are several varieties of chilli pepper, all of which are native to the Americas but most of which are grown enthusiastically across the Indian subcontinent. The ancient races of America were very familiar with both the culinary and medicinal purposes of the various chillies (the Mayans apparently thought they relieved stomach upsets, not caused them). In addition, the Aztecs are thought to have regarded chillies as sacred; they were also burnt to fumigate rooms and discourage germs and insects. The science behind some of these uses is now understood: chillies induce sweating, which reduces body temperature and so helps to control a fever. We also now know that chillies have more vitamin C, gram for gram, than oranges and also contain traces of magnesium, zinc, calcium and potassium. Eating chillies does make you feel better; they act as an appetite stimulator, and so ancient medics observed that chillies had the power to restore the sick to health. Eating a chilli of sufficient heat is also said to induce feelings of euphoria.

The word chilli comes from the Aztec name for the fruit of the Capsicum annuum plant, a mild variety from which paprika is produced. As a general rule, large chillies are milder than small ones and the most intense heat comes from the seeds. Recipes often don't specify which chilli is to be used even though each has a distinctive taste. Kashmiri chillies are large, dark red and quite short; sannan chillies are vivid red and long, slim and smooth; tinnevelley chillies are round like cherry tomatoes, and then there are the stubby Goan chillies, the matchstick-like green chillies from Bangladesh, the lantern-shaped scotch bonnets and the heart-shaped dundicut chillies from Pakistan – to name a handful. The Franciscan missionary Bernadino de Sahagun recorded a great deal more. In his General History of the Things of New Spain, he recorded that there were 'red chillies, broad chillies, hot green chillies, yellow chillies, water chillies, tree chillies, early season chillies, late season chillies, pointed red chillies' and so on. He also mentions that there were also 'stinking chillies, sour chillies, foul chillies and chillies without heat'. Presumably no one bothered to export the latter, but many of the former will now be well known across Asia.

Chillies are used in a variety of ways. When added whole to dishes they release their heat more gently, infusing flavour slowly into a dish (for a little extra heat, simply make an incision in the chilli to let the flavour of the seeds out). When used chopped, the same chilli can produce a far hotter dish. Often, though, chillies are sold dried as the drying process intensifies their flavour. Once dried they may be crushed to reveal their seeds, or the entire pepper maybe be ground into a fine powder.

Chillies are not just used for flavour: they also add colour and for this reason paprika has become a ubiquitous ingredient in the cuisine of the Conquistadores in their native Spain. It is also, less explicably, incredibly popular in Hungarian cookery.

CHAPTER EIGHT

The Unexpected Consequences of Curry

A Search for Ingredients

Britain's adoption of curry as one of its own has had far-reaching consequences not just for the restaurant and ready-meals sector, but also for the ancillary supply businesses. To put it simply, when more people started eating curry in Britain, more people needed to be importing ingredients, which meant more people needed to be growing them. The clearest illustration of how the agricultural and import businesses jumped on the curry bandwagon was the arrival of the coriander garnish. At some point in the late 80s or early 90s it seemed that every single curry house in Britain started serving every single dish with a sprig of coriander. Before that time coriander had been as familiar on British tables as kangaroo meat or Peruvian quinoa. This sudden influx of coriander could only have come about because increases in demand created opportunities for importers who in turn encouraged farmers to switch to this new crop. In this chapter I want to take a quick look at how the curry business has had the most unexpected impact on people around the world, from allotment owners in Bradford to farmers in Kenya.

As reported earlier, the groundbreakers in the Indian grocery import field were the Pathaks' shop in Euston and the Bombay Emporium off Tottenham Court Road. It is no coincidence that both these shops spawned businesses that today are worth tens of millions of pounds. The Bombay Emporium shut its doors in the 1960s but carried on trading as BE International Foods Ltd and is now part of the HP Foods group. Although the BE name might not be familiar, it has many high street brands in its portfolio – Rajah spices, Amoy, Lotus and Green Dragon. The Pathaks, famously, have dropped the 'h' from their trading name and transformed a small shop into an international business employing hundreds of people in several countries.

But as the Asian community in Britain swelled, these London-based businesses could not satisfy the demand. And as the supermarkets weren't yet inhabiting large out-of-town warehouses, they simply didn't have enough space to stock specialist Asian ingredients. For a time, if you wanted fresh coriander or mooli or bitter gourd, you had to grow it yourself.

Growing your Own

Aliya Rasheed grew up on the outskirts of Newcastle as the daughter of first generation immigrants. She has very vivid memories of the lengths her parents went to to obtain ingredients. 'We lived on the seventh floor of a council block and had a balcony about the size of a single bed. I swear, from that tiny piece of outside space my mum could feed us for weeks. She had hanging baskets of radishes instead of petunias, she had window boxes of coriander instead of daffodils and where other people would be quite happy with geraniums she planted aubergines and chillies!'

Not everything grew well in the British climate and getting hold of familiar varieties of beans and vegetables was sometimes impossible. 'This was the 60s,' remembers Aliya, 'so unless you had someone bring over the seeds for valor beans, you made do with runner beans. But that didn't seem to stop my parents who created elaborate trellises to support gourds and squashes.'

Naturally, the Rasheeds' balcony attracted a lot of attention. 'The neighbours used to complain, saying it was making the neighbourhood smell bad or look untidy, but the other Bengalis in the area wanted to know tips for making the most of the British weather and the British soil, which to this day my dad still complains about!'

As most recent immigrants tended to be cash-strapped, they rarely lived in houses with big gardens. So if someone wanted to grow more than a few herbs and vegetables to supplement their weekly shop, they needed to get an allotment. Parmjit Dhillon moved to Yorkshire from the Punjab in 1974. He had previously been a farmer but found himself working in factories and missed working on the land. 'I used to travel to work on the bus and see these tiny little farms and wondered how anyone could make a business from a patch of land so small. Then a colleague told me that they were allotments and that people treated them like a back garden that was just a long way away from their house. Anyway, I put my name down with the council and eventually they gave me my plot.'

When Parmjit first started planting his exotic selection of herbs and vegetables he found the other allotment owners were very curious.

'The other guys had never heard of any of the vegetables I was planting, except for the spinach, which grew very well. They hadn't even heard of an aubergine, which seems funny today because a lot of the other allotments now grow them.' Such tales reveal just how isolated parts of Britain were from a varied selection of ingredients – and how staid indigenous British tastes were. 'But as the crops started growing and I started to get a few harvests the guys became a lot more interested,' he remembers. 'They wanted to taste the herbs and see what the vegetables looked like when I cut them open. So I gave them bits and pieces so that in return they would tell me about the soil and the weather.'

When Parmjit's cousin moved to Bradford he opened a restaurant and was interested in buying whatever crops Parmjit could grow. 'But I couldn't grow enough. I had no time and no space to grow any more than I already did, so he got his own allotment.' By the time Parmjit retired from the gardening in 1998, he reckons that a quarter of the plots at his allotment gardens were used by Asians.

The community aspect that arose from such an unexpected area of life eventually became a bigger attraction than the harvest. Lutfun Hussein runs the Coriander Club at Spitalfields City Farm in East London; twice a week women from the local Bangladeshi community come together to tend their produce that ranges from mooli to scotch bonnets, and from snake gourds to beetroot. 'These days you can buy most of these vegetables from the local shop so these women don't have to come for the food. But keeping the allotment has become a big part of the community.

'You have to remember,' she says, 'that most of the women who come here grew up growing vegetables in their gardens or on their families' farms. They have a lot of knowledge and they know what these vegetables should taste like. When something has been flown in from half way round the world and kept in refrigerators for two or three days it loses its flavour. Here they get to pick something in the afternoon and eat it that evening. This allotment helps us feel closer to home.'

Farming on a Bigger Scale

Sometimes, though, allotments just weren't big enough to produce a sizeable crop. So in 2003 the Punjabi community in South Yorkshire approached local farmer Robert Barraclough to see if he could grow coriander, fenugreek and some other crops for them. In an initiative by the Grassroots Food Network, Robert started producing a commercial crop for local consumers. 'Punjabi families were growing coriander in their allotments,' says Robert. 'They came up and asked if I could grow it more extensively on my farm.' At the time wholesalers for the massive ethnic food market in South Yorkshire – there are hundreds of take-aways within ten miles of Robert's farm alone – had to travel south to get ingredients like fresh coriander. 'I thought, there's the demand here, why don't we try and grow to meet it?' remembers Robert. 'So I said "you supply the seeds, I'll put them in ground and you harvest it".'

On a small patch of land Robert planted a pilot batch of coriander, along with spinach and fenugreek. The first yield of coriander wasn't too successful and the fenugreek failed altogether. 'But the spinach grew like hell!' he laughs. The second crop of coriander was much more successful. 'That's because I learnt from them,' says Robert, 'they knew more about growing the crop than me and knew when to water, when to plant out, things like that.'

Although Robert grows these crops with the aid of a grant to support local farming for local communities, he is just one of many farmers who have changed their roster of crops to accommodate the nation's changing taste in food, most of whom work – as you'd expect – for profit. If you look at the labels on the potted coriander in most supermarkets you'll see that a herb that was once native to the Mediterranean and transplanted successfully to Asia now has a third home in the market gardens of the UK.

Supermarkets Cash In

To give you some idea of how supermarkets have had to respond to changing consumer demand over the past few decades, Sainsbury's reckons the number of products it stocked in 1980 was 7,000: by 1993 that figure had swollen to 17,000![1] Clearly such rapid change on the shelves requires mammoth change in the agriculture and freight businesses. Tristan Kitchener is the herb buyer for Sainsbury's, one of the UK's biggest supermarket chains, and directs his efforts to satisfying his customers' whims. One of his most recent tasks was to secure a supply of curry leaves following their inclusion in a recipe by influential TV chef Jamie Oliver.

'When we've identified the demand for a certain line, we'll talk to our suppliers and ask them to source the product for us. In the case of curry leaves, our supplier asked some family-run farms in Kenya and Gambia to grow the herb for us,' he says. Once the crop is established, Sainsbury's then despatches a food technologist to ensure that the farms' labour laws comply with Sainsbury's requirements (for example,

---

[1] Figures from the Food Standards Agency.

no child labour, proper worker representation) and that health and safety and quality thresholds are met and maintained. It's a huge undertaking for such a specialist product.

'At the moment [the end of 2003] we sell 500 or 600 units of curry leaves a week,' reveals Tristan. 'That compares with 60,000 or 70,000 units of parsley or coriander, so if I was talking in purely financial terms I would say that it wasn't worth our while.' What makes it worth the effort is that by selling such a varied range of herbs, Sainsbury's attracts a more upmarket customer. 'The problem with products like curry leaves is that they are so specialist people won't buy them unless they have a recipe in mind. They're not an impulse purchase, so we notice an uplift in sales when they get a bit of media exposure.' Tristan also notices that curry leaves have a marked sales curve throughout the week. 'They're a Saturday purchase, which indicates people are buying them for specific recipes that they're making time for. We sell nearly three times as many cases on Saturdays as we do on Mondays.' This purchase pattern is a small window on to the domestic curry scene where there would appear to be a pioneering handful of home cooks experimenting with this exotic newcomer in the way others must have done with coriander a generation previously.

By the early 90s, the supply business had evolved considerably since the days of Kirit Pathak waiting at Heathrow for bespoke imports of herbs and vegetables. London restaurateur Das Sreedharan recalls that when he opened his first restaurant in 1994, most of what he needed was already available in London. I found this surprising, as Rasa was the capital's first specialist Keralan restaurant, and had anticipated that he might have found it difficult to obtain specialist Keralan ingredients like the right kind of dosa flour, or curry leaves of course.

'I would say that in Britain you now have a better supply of Indian ingredients than we do in India!' he reveals. 'There are so many specialist Indian grocery shops in places like Southall, Wembley, Birmingham and all over the country that there are very well established supply chains now. This means that nothing is ever out of season. If one area's harvest is over, the suppliers will simply get produce from the area where it is in season. In India it's not like that, we simply wait for the harvest.'

Despite this bounty in Britain I found one restaurateur who found that the breadth of the supply of Indian ingredients in Britain was actually a problem for his chefs. Iqbal Wahhab owns The Cinnamon Club, one of London's most exclusive restaurants and, possibly, the most upmarket Indian restaurant anywhere in the world. In its marketing literature, the Cinnamon Club boasts that its spices are flown in once a fortnight from India. A little suspicious that such a claim might just be good PR (after all, Iqbal was a PR pro before he opened his restaurant) I asked him if such endeavours were really necessary.

'Although it's true that you can buy almost any ingredient in London, the spices and vegetables that are imported are done so for the mass market,' he says. 'If you want a chilli that's been harvested from a particular farm at a particular time to achieve a distinctive taste, you have to import things yourself. My chefs are very highly trained and they know the difference between a vegetable that's been picked at its peak and one which has been harvested a week past its best. If you want the best food, you have to start with the best ingredients,' he insists. Consequently, Iqbal employs a dedicated spice buyer to secure ingredients of a quality that is regarded as unnecessary by most grocery shops and most supermarkets. But then he does charge rather more for his fare.

Obtaining the perfect spice is a major undertaking for an organisation like Patak's Foods, which produces such a large quantity of products that they cannot rely on the availability of a certain crop in the Indian spice markets or at the whim of the monsoon. Meena Pathak, the company's director of food, explains the lengths they go to to get the flavour she requires. 'Spice exports from India have never been higher and the demand for spices for the international and domestic market is so great that people are trying to grow spices in different regions. This can have mixed results so we give the farmer the seeds of the crops we want him to grow on a specific farm to get the taste we want. This is necessary if we are to deliver a certain flavour.'

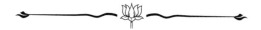

Never had it so Good

As the story of curry evolves to include countries such as France and America where Indian food represents an ever-growing sector of the market, its easy to see why some people are worried that the individuality of certain flavours will be lost under the jackboot of globalisation. In fact the further you look into the abundance on UK shelves, the more a pattern of scarcity emerges back in India. As Das Sreedharan laments: 'When I was a child I could eat one of over 300 hundred varieties of banana in Kerala. Now there are only a handful of varieties as the farmers have to cater to the needs of the big export companies,' he says. 'I remember there used to be so many different kinds of mango that you would eat in different seasons in different dishes. Now in my village they probably only grow two or three varieties. So much taste is being lost, so much knowledge too.'

Just as the Western palate – and the Western tourist dollar – starts to embrace the idiosyncrasies and delicate variation of Eastern spices, it seems there is a real danger that specialist varieties and uneconomic crops will be consigned to books, memories and – if we're lucky –

agricultural and food museums. Each year thousands of European and American tourists go on holiday to places like Zanzibar and Tamil Nadu to follow knowledgeable leaders through spice plantations and impossibly busy markets with the hope of gaining some knowledge of the exotic harvest. Sadly, this has coincided with many in the growing regions opting for jobs outside agriculture, leaving a once-diverse business subject to economic forces.

It is for this reason that Das is opening a farm close to the village where he grew up so that generations of knowledge are not lost. 'It is my dream,' he says, 'for people to understand the food they eat and to love the food they eat. You cannot love a vegetable, you cannot cook it with love, if you do not understand how it grows.' His farm will also serve as a training school for chefs who might one day work in one of his London restaurants. 'I want to find people who can be passionate about the food. I don't care if they've got this qualification or that certificate in health and safety. I want to find people who are fascinated by food.' Part of the problem, he identifies, is that India has been subject to the same social change that's been seen in the West. 'Mothers work, so children do not grow up in the kitchen as they used to do,' he says, 'and these days there are so many new industries in India, lots of technology companies and call centres. Working in the restaurant business is not to the only way to see the world any more, so people do not even know that they are losing knowledge when they are so busy with other things.'

A key strategy for Das's mission is to include as many older people from his community to instruct the students. 'Our elders are so wise,' he says, 'and we must honour that wisdom. In respecting them, and respecting the land and our culture, we honour ourselves.' What he seems to be saying is that if India loses touch with its cuisine, it loses some of its identity. 'India wants to be another America at the moment. I want it to be proud of being India.'

The other hidden message in this look at the curry house's colossal impact on the hinterland of businesses is that specialist skills, whether at the farming level or the preparation level, are being squandered. In five years' time it seems quite plausible that the ingredients of your meal will have been grown by less knowledgeable farmers and your meal prepared by a less passionate chef. To put it simply, right now could be the best time ever to eat a curry, as right now throughout Britain and across the world the availability of ingredients is matched by the skill of the chefs. As there are indications that the quality of ingredients will decline and good chefs – as we shall see in the chapter on curry's future – will be harder to come by, history may well prove that these are curry's golden years. Eat it while you can!

CORIANDER

Originally native to the Mediterranean, coriander was used by the Greeks, Persians and Egyptians (it was found in Tutankhamen's tomb) long before it was introduced to Asia where it has become a vital ingredient of many eastern cuisines. There is some evidence to suggest that its use may stretch back to the seventh century BCE, which would make it one of the first spices used by man. In the Jewish tradition coriander is one of the bitter herbs eaten at Passover to commemorate the exodus from Egypt (c. 1250 BCE). According to spice historian Andrew Dalby it was probably introduced to Asia during the dominance of the Persian Empire and slowly made its way further east

along the Silk Road to China where people once thought the seeds held the promise of immortality. Following the European colonisation of the Americas it also became a vital constituent of Mexican cooking. In Britain it is actually not that uncommon to find it growing wild (especially in East Anglia, apparently) after its introduction by the Romans.

The same plant produces two separate ingredients: the leaf, known as cilantro in America, and the seed (in Thailand, the roots, which have an even more intense bite, are also used). The two have completely different tastes. The seeds are sold whole, crushed or in powdered form and the leaf is used fresh or occasionally dried. Before grinding, the seeds are roasted to produce a more intense and aromatic ingredient of many popular masalas (spice mixes).

The seeds are thought to possess several medicinal characteristics. Teas made from crushed seeds and boiling water are said to reduce fevers, aid digestion, cure flatulence and ease headaches. If stewed into a paste and then chewed, coriander seeds are supposed to be an effective breath freshener. Some people believe that the seeds have a slightly intoxicating effect and in the seventeenth century the French made the most of this reputation by making a liqueur from coriander seeds known as Eau de Carnes that also doubled as a perfume.

In Britain, Russia and Scandinavia coriander is still grown for the liquor market as it is used to flavour certain varieties of gin. There are also those who say vets have used a concoction made from the seeds to drug cattle and horses.

Coriander leaves, on the other hand, are most commonly used to garnish spicy dishes as they are said to have a cooling effect on the mouth. They are also widely used in chutneys, raitas and pickles. In some parts of Europe the herb was apparently once known as 'dizzycorn' after farmers noted that livestock that had eaten it started to behave as though they'd had a glass too many of wine.

There are people who find the aroma of coriander unappetising, while others inhale it as some do roses. We can only assume that the person who gave coriander its name was not a fan: the word comes from the Greek koris, which means 'bug'. It seems that some of the ancients thought its aroma was reminiscent of bed bugs!

CHAPTER NINE

The Curry Conquerors

Money, Money, Money

Curry isn't just very popular, it can be hugely profitable. Many people haven't just made a living out of curry, they have made a fortune, and in this chapter I'd like to take a closer look at some of those entrepreneurs who have turned piles of curry into piles of money.

In recent business history there has been a trend towards worshipping the brand over the product or the business. Making a name for yourself has been deemed more praiseworthy than turning a profit. Never was this more clear than in the dotcom boom at the turn of the century when companies with huge debts, that were years away from turning a profit, were thought to be more successful than their competitors if more people on the street had heard of them. Since that time, popular books like *No Logo* and *Fast Food Nation* have raised public understanding of brands, branding and ownership and the homogenisation of the high street, especially in relation to the fast food industry.

From the outside it appears that the Indian food industry flies in the face of that thinking. Each restaurant has a different name and, apart from Patak's Foods, there are no other nationally or internationally known Indian-owned food brands. Yet a little investigation of the ownership of the Indian food business throws up the same names again and again. The Gaylord Group, Taj Hotels, S&A Foods, Noon Products, the Harlequin Group and the Chutney Mary group are just a handful of names of companies that own a much larger stake of the Indian food sector than a first glance would suggest: you may not be familiar with the names, but you have almost certainly eaten their food. Just like the Bahadur brothers in the 1930s, there is still a strong tradition of family ownership and diversification in this industry. And behind each of these holding companies there lies an entrepreneur, or two, and a spectacular story.

Perveen Warsi

S&A Foods supplies many supermarket chains with chilled Indian dishes from samosas and onion bhajis to curries and biryanis. The company is worth over £50 million pounds and enjoys the kind of success associated with MBA graduates, tome-like business plans and corporate governance. But S&A is one of those companies that almost never happened; a series of coincidences and flukes were as significant in its development as opportunity and acumen. It is a rather spectacular happy accident.

Perween Warsi arrived in Britain in 1975 as the wife of a student doctor. With two young children to look after she was quite happy to play a domestic role for a few years, although she says she always harboured professional ambitions. From time to time she would entertain her husband's colleagues at home and prepare fabulous Indian meals. Encouraged by their reaction – many suggested she take up cooking professionally – and the increased popularity of Indian food in Britain in general, Perween hit upon the idea of supplying supermarkets with her food.

She started the business incrementally. Her first client was the local fish and chop shop in Derby: she prepared a small batch of samosas that sold out on the first night. Before too long she was supplying a number of local takeaways, which meant she needed staff to meet her orders. She hired two Punjabi housewives who worked long hours chopping, cleaning and cooking. But as the business started to grow, two helpers and one kitchen was not enough, so Perween hired three more helpers and took over her house's conservatory, apparently moving her husband's precious plant collection into the garage in doing so.

Although the business was pretty successful for a home-working operation, Perween still had ambitions to supply supermarkets. She phoned most of the major chains only to be confronted with impersonal forms and quotas – no one would actually taste her food.

In 1986 she had a breakthrough with Asda, one of the UK's major supermarket chains. Having observed the increase in the number of restaurants on the high street, Asda had decided to overhaul its ethnic food ranges. So when Perween called up and told them their food was bland and she could do better, they invited her to send some products for a blind tasting session they were conducting.

When her food was accepted she was invited to meet executives at Asda who told her they wanted to put a bulk order her way – the first of many regular orders. Perween's conservatory simply wasn't big enough and she would need more than five staff. She had no option but to reveal the true size of her operation and was then advised to find a factory – and some staff – very quickly.

Excited and determined, this is exactly what Perween did: if she hadn't accepted the challenge she would have lost the contract. She found a disused industrial unit that had previously been used for car valeting. With only a couple of days before the Asda inspection of her premises, the factory was overhauled, virtually overnight. New sinks were installed, walls were half-tiled and the whole place was cleaned. Twenty-four hours before the premises were due for their inspection, Perween asked a friend and director of a local laboratory for his opinion. What he told her would have sealed the fate of a lesser entrepreneur.

More familiar with health and safety legislation than Perween, he advised her that the factory would not get the necessary certificates unless it was fully tiled and all working surfaces were made of stainless steel. Not one to be deterred easily, Perween immediately sought out a tiler and a supplier of stainless steel catering equipment. Fortunately one of her husband's patients was a tiler. Unfortunately he had booked to go on holiday the very next day! After some skilful pleading and negotiating, he agreed to cancel his holiday and duly turned up with five colleagues to retile the factory overnight. Later that day the catering equipment arrived, thankfully before the Asda inspector who gave it the necessary thumbs up.

By the end of 1987, S&A Foods (the initials are those of Perween's sons) had a contract to supply Safeway as well as Asda and throughout the 90s the business expanded steadily. By the end of the century, S&A was also making food under the home-brand labels of the Co-op and Budgens as well as preparing catering for hotels, pubs and airlines. And, not satisfied with the Indian market, S&A diversified into Chinese food supplying meals for TV chef Ken Hom's label. By the time of S&A's tenth birthday in 1997, Perween employed over 600 people, some of whom came directly from India, Malaysia and Thailand to ensure that recipes remained authentic.

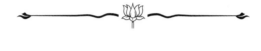

Sir Gulam Noon

S&A's major rival for supermarket contracts is another huge company with a name few outside the industry have heard of: Noon Products. Sir Gulam Noon started his business in 1988 after sampling some of the Indian ready meals already available in British supermarkets. They were so poor – and so poorly resembled real Indian food – that he figured he could do better.

Gulam Noon was born into a catering family of sorts: his father ran a sweet shop in Bombay's Crawford Market. He was just eight when his family was struck by the tragic deaths of both his eldest brother and his father. With no obvious breadwinner around, the entire family started working in the shop whenever they could (although Gulam still found time for his beloved cricket: he told his mother school started three hours earlier than it really did so he could play before classes!).

Although he had ambitions outside the sweet business, the young entrepreneur realised he could learn much about business in general from a close observation of the sweet trade: he even got up early to take accountancy lessons from the shop's book-keeper. Motivated by a desire to provide financial security for his mother, Gulam was determined to make a success of the business his grandfather had started in 1898.

In 1962 he made some changes to the shop – like installing air-conditioning and modern shop fittings (both considered an extraordinary luxury) – and saw a marked upturn in trade. Buoyed by this success, Gulam ventured into different industries such as printing and construction and soon set his sights on an international business; by 1973 he had opened his first sweet shop in London, and pretty soon after that he had opened several branches and a factory.

Never one to rest on his laurels, Gulam Noon went in search of a new challenge on a new continent. In 1979 he headed for New York and into a joint venture with the Taj Hotels Group, another of the giants of the Indian food industry, to produce chilled and frozen ready meals. Although America was ahead of Europe in its love of TV dinners and more homes had freezers and microwaves, few Americans had developed a taste for Indian food. The business foundered, and Gulam returned to Britain where he knew the appetite for Indian food was growing.

Armed with the necessary knowledge about the technology required to mass-produce Indian foods, and a belief that the current supermarket offerings would be easy to trump, he set about acquiring premises and securing orders. Gulam Noon knew he didn't want to build a piecemeal business hawking small quantities to small retailers: he wanted big contracts with big businesses where the unit cost savings made more financial sense. So he approached Birds Eye, one of the biggest players in the frozen food market.

He was confident of a contract and expected an order to come through for between £20,000 and £200,000 – he was a little shocked when the first order came in at over £2 million! Encouraged by this success, Gulam started approaching supermarkets directly and now Noon Products can count Sainsbury's, Waitrose and Somerfield among its supermarket clients. Outside the retail market, Noon also supplies airlines and motorway service stations with Indian meals. And outside Britain, Noon has clients in France, Switzerland and Germany. The combined output of Noon's various factories is around 100,000 meals a day.

The business went from strength to strength as its leader built rewarding relationships with his staff, his suppliers and his customers. These were to stand him in good stead when disaster struck Noon Products in 1994: one night in November Gulam took a phone call telling him his factory was on fire. He drove straight to the scene in Southall, West London, where he knew 150 shift workers were labouring through the night. He arrived to find that all his staff had survived, but that millions of pounds of machinery, supplies and finished products were going up in flames.

Some of the staff who had worked for him since the beginning were crying openly, and Gulam resolved to reward their loyalty by reopening the factory as soon as possible, thereby safeguarding their jobs. Such was the warmth people felt for Gulam that he was swamped by offers of help. The chairman of Sainsbury's – Noon supplied 70 per cent of their Indian ready meals – offered to employ several of Gulam's staff at its nearby depots in Hayes and Wembley. Gulam also received offers of cash from friends to help rebuild the factory. Less than eight months later, he proudly opened a new factory in Southall and re-employed his former staff.

The Pathaks

Unlike Noon and S&A, Patak's is a familiar supermarket brand. When the Pathaks' grocery shop in Drummond Street was purchased by British Rail under a Compulsory Purchase Order in the early 70s (there were plans to redevelop Euston Station that never came to fruition – the Pathaks' old shop is still standing, although no longer in business), Kirit Pathak saw it as an opportunity to take the business in a new direction. He saw that the appetite for Indian food had grown so much since his father's arrival in Britain that he had an opportunity to become a supplier rather than a retailer.

Having already built up a reputation for supplying the Indian market – both the restaurant and domestic sector – Patak's-branded pickles and pastes were well set to capture the same customers when they were sold through an ever-growing number of Indian grocery stores throughout the country. The Pathaks' new business was a success, but a modest one. Two events were to change a small business into a global one, the first of which was Kirit Pathak's marriage to Meena.

Their wedding had been engineered by their families and they had only met a few times before they married. Although Meena recalls telling Kirit that she had studied food technology before their engagement, Kirit does not remember this. He only found out how much Meena knew about food when he asked his new wife if she would like to see his factory. Bored with being a newly-married housewife with not much to do, Meena leapt at the opportunity. When she started asking extremely pertinent questions and offering extremely sound suggestions, Kirit realised there was a lot about his wife he didn't yet know. When she revealed – for the second time – that she had studied food technology, Kirit's response was to hire her.

One of Meena's first and most significant contributions to the business was to improve the recipes of some of the Patak's range. This led directly to the next event that changed the Pathaks' fortune: an article in the *Daily Telegraph* that described Patak's products as superior to others in the fledgling ethnic food sector. This unsolicited article had an immediate effect as the next day a distributor called and offered to put the Patak's range in over 150 stores nationwide.

The business grew fairly rapidly after that but Kirit was still dismayed that his sauces and pickles weren't getting the same distribution as brands like Sharwood's which he considered inferior. 'I wanted to know why they were so much more successful than us,' recalls Kirit. 'They were an English company importing curry powder and making sauces. After some thought I realised the reason they had a better market position than us – it was marketing.' But what Kirit realised was that he didn't need to invest in his own brand, he needed to boost the appeal of the Indian food sector in general. 'My worry was that Indian food would never really get off the ground unless people were exposed to good enough food. So I decided to do what no one else would do: I went to my competitor and said to Mr Sharwood 'We have some pretty nice [products], so why don't we make some sauces for you?' It was a good deal for us because we already had most of the restaurant sector, now we had the supermarket business too.'

Crazy as it seems, that's what happened. Patak's Foods produced sauces under the Sharwood's label and in doing so started to educate supermarket shoppers about more authentic flavours of Indian cooking. As sales took off, supermarkets started to realise the commercial potential of the ethnic food sector and conducted some market research. When several focus groups mentioned Patak's favourably – either because people had used their sauces in their restaurants or at home – the company was approached to put their own-brand sauces on the shelves. As soon as that happened Sharwood's cancelled the contract and although it cost Kirit £1 million in the short term, he more than made that up in the long term by selling sauces under his own brand.

Despite better distribution, there was still a huge marketing task ahead. And for the Pathaks, marketing meant education. It was Meena's task to take the product into shops and encourage customers to try something new. 'We were lucky in those days because we could have in-store tastings,' she remembers. 'That's not possible now because of environmental health, but in those days whenever we got stocked in a new supermarket, I would go and do hot tastings. We would actually cook on site and the aroma drew people to our aisle.

'It was then that people realised that each dish had a different flavour to it and that curry wasn't just one taste. The biggest challenge of any new cuisine is to get the first mouthful into the mouth,' she says. If people like the first mouthful, the second mouthful takes care of itself. With the British market now fully educated in the ways of Indian cookery, the Pathaks are continuing their campaign of education around the world and Meena now undertakes similar tasting sessions everywhere from France to the US.

Cobra Beer

The pattern of a single entrepreneur attacking a particular niche of the Indian food market and coming up trumps was repeated in the 90s when Karan Bilimoria had a notion to capitalise on the association between curry and beer to produce the Cobra brand. As a student at Cambridge University he noticed that most people's beverage of choice when eating curry was beer. But Karan felt that the European beers sold in restaurants didn't complement Indian food. Calling them 'Eurofizz', he thought that they were too gassy and filled you up too much: he reasoned that if a less fizzy beer was available you'd have room for more food – as well as more beer, of course.

It wasn't till after graduation that he began to make the contacts that would turn his idea into a business. While meeting with a seafood importer he discovered his potential business partner also owned a brewery, and in the course of their conversation gave up on the seafood deal to embark on his plan to develop a beer for the British curry market. That brewery was the Mysore Brewery, where the ingenious Dr Cariapa concocted a beer to Karan's specifications.

Once he was happy with the recipe, Karan faced a new obstacle: the Mysore Brewery only produced large bottles (as this is more convenient in a society where most bottles are recycled) and weren't convinced enough of Karan's business to produce smaller bottles for the British market. So Karan had to find a way of turning the bottle size to his advantage and hit upon the idea that it made Cobra more authentically Indian.

His next problem was his debt and lack of staff. Hamstrung by loans of £20,000 acquired as a student and lacking the investment to take on staff, Karan had to sell the beer himself. So in the early 1990s this Cambridge law graduate, who could have been earning a vast salary with a city firm, was driving round London in a Citroën 2CV that was so dilapidated that you could see the road through the hole in the floor. His car – called Albert – could only hold fifteen boxes of Cobra at a time and Karan realised that getting a toehold in the market would be very time consuming. In a bid to appear more professional when cold-calling on cash-and-carries and restaurants, Albert was always parked round the corner so that potential customers were not put off by the state of the delivery vehicle!

The next hurdle to overcome was the fact that few restaurateurs could sample Cobra as they didn't drink alcohol for religious reasons. Karan persuaded them to take a few bottles anyway and let their customers decide. Like many other products designed for the restaurant market, Cobra's success was enabled by humble waiters who had no financial stake in the business. For this reason, you will find many restaurateurs who resent the success of companies like Cobra as they appear to have made profits the 'easy way'.

Easy or not, there certainly were profits in Cobra and to meet demand Karan started brewing his beer under licence in Bedford in the UK. Despite its marketing, Cobra is about as Indian as chicken tikka masala. It now has a turnover in excess of £150 million and is sold in most of the UK's 6,200 Indian restaurants and several supermarket chains: it is also exported to 30 countries worldwide – including India!

Behind the Scenes

Although the Cobra brand is well established in the consumer's consciousness, many Indian companies – like S&A and Noon – have been happy to have their products often passed off as someone else's. Kirit Pathak estimates that 90 per cent of Indian restaurants in Britain use a Patak's product in the kitchen. That doesn't necessarily mean that the korma you order in your local curry house is exactly the same as one you could make at home, as the Pathaks encourage chefs to experiment with their pastes, blending them to make unique flavours that a chef can call his own.

This lack of ego on behalf of the big producers can also be seen among restaurant owners. At the beginning of the twenty-first century we are starting to see branded restaurants – like the Shere Khan chain around Manchester and the Ashoka chain in Glasgow – but for the preceding forty years, a single proprietor was generally happy to own several restaurants with different names: brand ownership seemed to have little value in the Indian restaurant business.

Most of the restaurateurs interviewed for this book owned more than one restaurant, all with different names. Or to be more accurate they were *part* owners in several restaurants. Whether for investment, tax or immigration purposes, few restaurants were wholly owned by one individual, a consortium of family members was more common. These 'secret' chains exist at all levels of the industry, obscured from the limelight by the use of so many different restaurant names.

One such chain at the top end is the Gaylord Group. Mahendra Kaul opened his first restaurant in London in Whitfield Street and launched the flagship Gaylord in London's West End in the 1960s. Always considered slightly classier than your average curry house, his restaurant was one of the first to install a tandoor. Mr Kaul now has interests in two of London's more glamorous restaurants, the Chor Bizarre and Viceroy Brasserie, but also owns eateries in places as far apart as Manchester, San Francisco, Bangkok, Hong Kong and Japan.

Another major player on the global restaurant scene is the Taj Hotel group. Although their assets in Britain are limited (in number, not in style) compared to some chains, this giant of the Indian hospitality industry is responsible for training many of the staff now at the top of the profession. Chefs like Cyrus Todiwala from Café Spice Namaste and marketing executives like Camellia Panjabi of Chutney Mary learnt skills at Taj Hotels with which they transformed the restaurant business in Britain. Many of Taj's graduates pass through the group's landmark London restaurant, the Bombay Brasserie, before starting out on their own.

Camellia, who founded the Bombay Brasserie, now works with her sister and brother-in-law who operate London's high-class Chutney Mary as well as the legendary Veeraswamy. They are also rolling out a series of Masala Zone restaurants that are bringing a stylish option to the affordable end of the market.

If you take a look at most of the high-profile Indian restaurants in Britain, you'll see the names cropping up again and again. For instance, the Red Fort – one of the capital's first luxury curry destinations – is owned by Enam Ali, who also launched Soho Spice. The Bombay Palace turns out to be part of the Bombay Palace Group that opened its first New York restaurant in 1979. Even less well-known restaurants, like the Malabar Junction, turn out to have the same proprietor, T Haridas, as other Keralan restaurants such as Pallavi, Radha Krishna Bhavan, Kerala Bhavan and Ragam. Then of course there are the Rasa restaurants, of which there are now six in London alone. And the proprietor of the Tandoori Nights chain turns out to be the woman behind the Organic India supermarket brand.

Around Britain there are a number of regional chains, some of which are more visible than others. Charan Gill's Harlequin group owns a number of restaurants around Glasgow under the Ashoka banner, but he also owns Mr Singh's, the Spice of Life and the Kama Sutra to name a few. Manchester's Shere Khan chain is a little more explicit about the ownership of its many outlets, as is the Birmingham-based group Shimla Pinks, while newcomers like Danny Punia's Miles From Delhi operation attempt to give individual restaurants their own name depending on just how many miles from the Indian capital they are (Nottingham, for instance is 4550 Miles From Delhi, while the planned outlet in London will be 4320 Miles From Delhi).

What all these chains illustrate (and there are many, many more) is that behind the slightly amateurish 'mom and pop' exterior of many of Britain's curry houses, there lies a huge and highly organised industry. Similarly, behind the unique and bespoke facades of many of the top end restaurants, you find extremely wealthy operations with many outlets.

FENUGREEK

Fenugreek is one of the mainstays of Indian cookery and is also one of the oldest spices used by man. Egyptian papyruses show it was used in creating perfumes and incense, as well as for embalming. Originally a European plant, it was also used as horse fodder by the Romans and ancient Greeks. In fact its name comes from foenum-graecum, which translates as Greek hay. Such was its popularity that in ancient times, there is evidence that it had started to be cultivated as far east as China. In the medieval period, there are records that Charlemagne cultivated it extensively to feed his horses.

The fenugreek plant is a legume and can grow to a height of three of four feet. The spice is made from the seeds of its slender bean-like fruit; they are dried and, usually, ground. Fenugreek seeds are sold whole, crushed and – more commonly –

powdered. The leaves are also used dried as a herb in cooking or fresh in salads as are the seeds, when sprouted. Aside from its culinary use, fenugreek has been used for many varied medicinal purposes throughout history. When soaked in water the seeds produce a jelly that is thought to aid mouth ulcers and blistered lips. Like most other spices, fenugreek is also considered useful in digestion. It's said to help cure diarrhoea and chronic coughs, and some have made claims that it can help lower blood cholesterol and blood sugar levels. Perhaps its most unusual property, if true, is that it can cure baldness. Whether this is achieved by eating copious amounts or making a paste for topical application is not clear, but we now know that fenugreek is extremely rich in folic acid which traditionally has helped in baldness cures. The folic acid levels may also account for some reports that it helps with fertility. Additionally, fenugreek has been used in some cultures to stimulate lactation (in animals as well as humans).

Fenugreek has an unmistakable smell. In fact, for many people, it is the smell of curry as it is a major constituent of most commercial curry powders. It has a flavour commensurate with its smell, which is why most recipes suggest tempering its impact by either dry roasting or frying the seeds in oil before use (be careful – burning them only increases their bitterness).

Fenugreek is used throughout India but it has a reputation for being emblematic of northern cuisines such as those of Kashmir and Bengal. Meats are often stewed with fenugreek, it is added to certain naan recipes and its fragrance is also used in vegetable dishes such as saag aloo. It is also vital to the famous Bengali masala panch phoron, used in many dishes. In the south, fenugreek is generally used more sparingly to flavour bread, batters and lentil dishes as well as being a vital component of *the Tamil masala, sambaar podi. It also works well with fish and is a common ingredient of chutneys.*

Perhaps its most surprising culinary use is as a flavouring in maple syrup substitutes!

CHAPTER TEN

The Five-star Revolution

Curry goes Upmarket

When the Cinnamon Club opened in 2001 and the food critic for the *Telegraph* told the proprietor that the English didn't want fancy curries, it highlighted the struggle restaurateurs had to drag Indian cuisine out of its post-pub pigeonhole. Throughout the 80s, but increasingly in the 90s, there were a number of entrepreneurs who tried to get Indian cooking the credit and acclaim traditionally offered to European, and particularly French, cookery. They abandoned the heavy stews of the curry house and began to use spice with greater subtlety. But such was the Brits' love of the old style curry house that this new 'food of Indian origin' had to fight to win over customers. The new breed's struggle might not be quite as epic as that of their forefathers who endured penury and racism to bring curry to our high streets, but their battles for Michelin stars and equality with European cookery were bruising nonetheless.

There were a number of factors that made the 90s ripe with opportunity for taking the curry upmarket. The first was that the restaurateurs themselves had the vision, the talent and the cash to bring a new style of restaurant to the market. The second was a growing appreciation of Indian cookery – either through travel or ready meals – from certain sectors of the public. Nevertheless, convincing even the most ardent fans of Indian food that they now had to pay £50 for a curry when they could get one for a fiver on the high street was always going to be an uphill struggle. In this chapter, then, I'd like to take a look at the factors that led to upscale restaurants like Tamarind and Zaika being awarded their Michelin stars, and the problems they encountered along the way. After that, I'll look at how the changes at the top then filtered back down to the high street.

As we have already seen, there were always upmarket Indian restaurants in Britain. London's very first, the Hindostanee Coffee House, was designed for the nabobs and gentry, and through much of the twentieth century Veeraswamy's remained a treat for the toffs. It may not seem so remarkable, then, that towards the end of the century a few restaurateurs should want to develop exclusive venues for an upmarket clientele. What made their challenge so difficult, and so remarkable, is that they were actually *hampered* by the high-street curry's success and dominance. As many a celebrity will attest, it is much easier to tarnish a good reputation than to overcome a bad one and, as any retailer will tell you, it's very easy to cut prices but almost impossible to put them up.

By the early 80s, even Veeraswamy's, the stalwart of top-end Indian dining, no longer enjoyed the profile and kudos of former years. The only other restaurant in London with pretensions to being more than a high street curry house was, arguably, Shezan in Knightsbridge, though few of that borough's residents would have even been aware of it. So when the Bombay Brasserie opened in December 1982 it had little in the way of competition, but that by no means guaranteed it any success.

It was the brainchild of Camellia Panjabi, a former Cambridge economics student whose work at the Taj Group had convinced her that the talent of a new breed of Indian chefs could be married to the increasingly well-educated British palate. Like many Indians in Britain, Camellia could see the disconnect between the British love of curry and the lack of care with which it was served. As a skilled and educated cook herself, she was frustrated and bemused that the regional vibrancy of Indian cookery was ignored and standardised by the high-street curry houses. Her ambition was to launch a restaurant that celebrated regional cooking and challenged perceptions not just of Indian food, but also of Indian restaurants. Flock wallpaper was definitely not on the menu.

The venue for the Taj Group's latest venture was to be the run-down Bailey's Hotel in Kensington. A beautiful Victorian building with ornate plasterwork, it lent itself easily to Camellia's vision of neo-colonial chic. The hotel was totally refurbished by Taj: the company imported cane chairs for the cocktail bar, ceiling fans for the dining room and the walls were adorned with paintings depicting Parsi life in Bombay. It was an 1980s take on the Raj-era clubhouse. In her review of the Bombay Brasserie the *Evening Standard*'s influential critic Fay Maschler described the new restaurant as 'a sweep of grandeur'.

Reviews were to be vital to the restaurant's early success as it opened without any advertising – an unusual move for such an expensive launch. But the reviews were favourable and attracted a curious clientele. Maschler – who was born in India and whose reviews betray a sense of romance for the sounds and smells of Indian cooking – wrote that the Bombay Brasserie 'altered preconceptions of a cuisine that had long been immured in yards of flock wallpaper and all-purpose sauces'. Among the curious were many celebrities who lent the Brasserie some of their caché. In the early days, it became a favoured hang out of the famous who – just as Marlon Brando and Vivien Leigh had done forty years previously at Veeraswamy's – got a kick out of trying something more adventurous. Some of the people spotted there included Michael Caine, Goldie Hawn, Anthony Hopkins, Charlton Heston, Mick Jagger, Paul and Linda McCartney, Stevie Wonder and Martina Navratilova.

Celebrity endorsement has secured success for many establishments over the years and it was no different in this case: within a year the Brasserie was extended by creating a conservatory that increased its capacity from 94 covers to 175. Even after this doubling of tables (it has since been extended again and now seats 265), the restaurant was still turning customers away. At the Bombay Brasserie, the combination of Camellia's vision, a team of highly trained chefs and a truly elegant dining experience was enough to change Britain's perception of a cuisine that was so familiar that many held it in contempt.

Of course it wasn't just the gossip columns and eating-out guides that marvelled at the Bombay Brasserie, it attracted a lot of attention within the Indian restaurant sector too. It was the carrot that would tempt a handful of other restaurant staff to attempt to replicate its success, although without the backing of a huge hotel group behind them. Where there are carrots, of course, there are often also sticks, so it is probable that even without the Brasserie's shining beacon, one of the more passionate restaurant workers in London at that time would have attempted something similar sooner or later.

Among the restaurateurs who would go on to open upmarket Indian restaurants, there were a number of motivations to develop a different kind of Indian restaurant, and money was not always one of them. Some, like Amin Ali, were frustrated at the way they were treated as lowly waiting staff and knew that if people were treated better they would work better. Amin went on to open the Red Fort in Soho, one of the first top-end Indian venues. Others, like Das Sreedharan, were simply appalled at the food colleagues were passing off as Indian. When he was working in someone else's restaurant he longed for customers to taste authentic Indian food, and even saw vegetarian dishes prepared with meat juices – an insult both to his faith and his customers. Das would later pioneer Keralan cuisine at Rasa.

Unlike earlier generations of restaurateurs, entrepreneurs in the 80s and 90s had the option of going into other industries. No longer was a restaurant seen as a business like any other high-street outlet, people were *choosing* catering as a profession. And where there is choice, there is usually also pride. New restaurateurs felt patronised by the clichés of flock wallpaper, waterfall pictures and laminated menus and were determined to express their own individuality through their work. Others simply looked at the prices that French, Japanese, British and Italian restaurants were charging and dreamed of similar profits.

In contrast to previous generations of restaurateurs who arrived in Britain without professional qualifications, many Asian immigrants in the 80s and 90s arrived with degrees in accountancy, law, marketing and business administration. Nevertheless, many still found work in the restaurant trade when they first arrived, often through a family connection, where they gained first-hand knowledge of the sector. For the first time, those that had the desire to improve the reputation of Indian cookery often also had the skill and contacts to make their vision become reality. There was also by then – thanks to the millions of pounds sent back to the subcontinent – a number of Asians stalking the British restaurant scene confident of making money.

For some there wasn't too much forethought involved as they saw the move upmarket was inevitable: in a crowded marketplace where a single street could have five or even fifteen Indian restaurants, it made business sense to find a way of differentiating your offering. The only way was up.

Of course, for a clutch of seriously top-end Indian restaurants to arrive within a few years of each other, other factors outside the ethnic food sector had to be at play, and in the 80s restaurants attained a caché they had never known before. Whether you were in London or New York, LA or Sydney dining out became a statement and declaration of status. This was the decade fuelled by Thatcherism, cocaine and Dynasty, and whether you were a plasterer earning substantial sums or a city broker getting a £500,000 Christmas bonus, it was important that you 'flashed your cash'. It's not surprising then that in every major city, restaurants sprang up to cater for this new crowd. In London the man behind many of the more famous ventures – including Quaglino's and Bibendum – was Sir Terence Conran, and he was fêted as one of the most influential men in Britain. This sort of accolade in turn attracted celebrities, many of whom embarked on their own high-end restaurants, the most famous of which was Michael Caine's Langham Brasserie (he would later open an Indian restaurant, Deya, not far from the site of London's very first Indian restaurant, the Hindostanee Coffee House).

This decade of the super-restaurant fuelled the interest in glamorous Indian restaurants in two ways: firstly investors were queueing up to be associated with the next big launch; and secondly, diners using their expense accounts were always looking for something different with which to impress a client. A posh curry had much more than novelty value for some customers.

Following the Brasserie's opening in 1982, the next significant Indian restaurant launch was Amin Ali's Red Fort in 1984. Amin had been instrumental in starting Britain's first Bangladeshi co-operatively owned restaurant, the Last Days of The Raj. Opened in 1979, it was an early attempt to improve the dining experience of Indian food. When he found the Red Fort premises in the centre of Soho, he had an idea that he could transform people's perceptions of the curry house.

Everything in the new restaurant indicated class. From the cocktail list to the hand soap in the stylish toilets, there was nothing in the Red Fort that would let customers think they were in a standard curry house. Perhaps Amin's most unusual move was to hire a PR agency, and the man he appointed was Iqbal Wahhab, the former journalist who would go on to open the Cinnamon Club.

Iqbal got very involved in every aspect of the Red Fort, from the menus to the hiring of staff, making sure that each element would be 'on brand' and attractive to the right kind of clientele. 'Looking back I can see how brave Amin was,' says Iqbal, 'I wasn't a big name PR by any standards, but he trusted me and we worked together to create something really special.' One of Iqbal's jobs was to make sure the right people came to the Red Fort, and sure enough the gossip columns frequently mentioned that talent like Mel Gibson, Bruce Willis and Emma Thompson had been seen there. The Red Fort also courted political support, and appropriately – given its name – Labour party leaders Neil Kinnock and Tony Blair were regulars.

Although Iqbal recalls that it was relatively easy to persuade the mainstream press to write about the Indian restaurant sector, it always helped if there was a particular story to tell. If Bombay Brasserie's story was that it celebrated authentic regional cuisines, the Red Fort's selling point was its attempt to recreate the dishes of the Mughal palaces. Another angle was a promise of a 'fat-free meal' – a significant attraction at the height of the Jane Fonda/aerobics/fitness craze of the mid-80s.

Elsewhere in London, a number of other restaurants attempted to fill the gap between the cheap and cheerful high-street curry house and the haute cuisine of the Red Fort and Bombay Brasserie. These included the Gaylord, which upped its game, and the newly renovated Star Of India and the Viceroy of India, each offering wine lists and décor that elevated both the experience of Indian restaurants, and their reputations.

It wasn't until the end of the decade that London would get its next five-star Indian restaurant. Chutney Mary – a term used both affectionately and disparagingly to describe a westernised woman during the days of the Raj – was opened in 1990 by Camellia Panjabi's sister Nameeta. Located in upmarket Chelsea, it unashamedly attempted to create an ambience that was nostalgic for the Raj. This was achieved through décor, which was suitably elaborate, but also through the menu which sported dishes like 'salmon kedgeree' and 'hill station bread and butter pudding'. Aside from tugging at the emotional ties of the past, Chutney Mary also attempted to educate future generations of Indian food fans with recipes from around India. There was a noticeable number of Goan dishes, reflecting Goa's increasing popularity as a holiday destination.

Reaching for the Michelin Stars

Despite effusive reviews and celebrity clients, the new glamorous Indian restaurants still faced two prejudices, one from the industry and the other from their customers. The industry was extremely reluctant to give these new restaurants the highest awards. Gongs of 'best Indian' or 'best ethnic' restaurants were frequently handed out, but there was a mindset that Indian food – no matter how good – wasn't equal to European cuisines. The top awards in the business, those precious Michelin stars, were not considered suitable to adorn the front doors of Indian restaurants. Even though critics loved the food, it seems that few were actually knowledgeable enough about Indian cookery to truly understand the sophistication of their meals. If this was true of the critics, it was certainly true of the customers, many of whom would look at their bill and say 'It was very nice, but do you really expect me to pay this much for a curry?' The feeling among restaurateurs is that a top-end restaurant from any other ethnic cuisine (with the exception of Chinese food, which was also hampered by years of high-street ubiquity) could charge higher prices as it wouldn't be burdened with so many preconceptions. Somehow, restaurants needed to dissociate their food from the word 'curry'.

To do this, the industry embarked on an extensive education and marketing programme that included organising Indian food festivals and dropping the offending word from all menus and promotional literature. One of the techniques used to distinguish the new breed from the high-street curry house was to assert the Indian nationality of the proprietors. There were countless column inches devoted to the 'inauthentic' Bangladeshi curry houses and the 'superior' Indian restaurants. This may have been a genuine marketing ploy or an unintentional skirmish over old racial tensions, and it caused genuine friction between the two camps. 'I used to say to some of the snootier restaurateurs, "you wouldn't be here if it wasn't for the Bangladeshi curry houses",' remembers Iqbal Wahhab. But it seems some Indians were so appalled at the food that was being sold as 'Indian' that they were determined to make a name for themselves by distancing themselves from the Bangladeshi high street and supermarket offerings.

By the early 90s the Indian restaurant scene was so big, and becoming so diverse, that it lacked the unified voice it needed to affect real change for the sector. This diversity also proved to be a bit of a problem for Cobra boss Karan Bilimoria: the only way he could sell his beer to restaurants was to visit them. With over 7,000 then in operation, he wondered if there might not be a better way of selling his product to his customers. So together with his PR man – Iqbal Wahhab, again – he hatched a plan to launch a magazine for the restaurant sector that would carry advertising for Cobra.

Despite Karan's involvement, *Tandoori Magazine* was intended to be independent and unbiased towards any chain, supplier or restaurateur. It was written in English, unlike a few previous attempts to launch a trade publication for the sector, not just so that it could be read by restaurateurs of any nationality, but also by mainstream journalists looking for stories about curry.

It was launched in 1994 and the stories it covered highlighted just how unusual restaurants like Chutney Mary and Bombay Brasserie were. Iqbal, who edited *Tandoori* when it began, remembers a huge gulf between the needs of London restaurants and those of regional ones.

'Restaurants outside London had completely different concerns,' he says. 'They still wanted to know how to deal with badly behaved customers. In the north, they wanted articles about how to use steel shutters and employ security guards. We used to subscribe to a news cuttings service and every day we were presented with stories from the regional press about these issues. There was a terrible story about a church in Bradford that was converted into an Indian restaurant and two nights before it opened it was desecrated by racist vandals. For some of us in London who were so involved in the new wave of upscale restaurants it was a shock to learn that waiters were still being called Gunga Din.'

Generally, he says, the closer restaurants were to London, the more money they were making and the more they could afford to recruit staff from India. These readers wanted advice on work permits, while London restaurateurs wanted to know how to get Fay Maschler to review them. *Tandoori*'s other role was to provide a focal point for the industry and a voice to demand full recognition from the Michelin reviewers. 'We provided a bridge between both ends of the market and between the Indian restaurant community and the restaurant community in general,' says Iqbal.

One of the trends *Tandoori* articles highlighted was the increasing number of specialist regional restaurants. Not only were a growing number of restaurateurs giving their businesses regional names highlighting their Bangladeshi, Punjabi or Indian heritage, but a few of the newcomers identified their cuisine as being either from Kerala, Goa, Bangalore or perhaps even the Himalayas. In addition, some chose to label their food as 'Parsi' or 'Brahmin' to make it known that in India too there was a culture of high-class food.

Even among the top-end restaurants there were significant divisions. Some restaurateurs, like Reza Muhammed of the Star of India, expressed dismay at the continuing use of Raj-era interiors of the type found at Chutney Mary. 'That Raj-style décor was very patronising. If you stick with it, it just paints people into a category, and I don't want to be categorised as anything,' he has said. 'But now the English palate is ready and I am able to assert my own identity through the food and by throwing away all the old stereotypes about Indian cooking and Indians in general.'[1] Reza's refurbishment of the Star of India was noteworthy for its muted colours and dearth of Indian ornaments: it was almost French in style, perhaps to indicate that Indian food was now worthy of the accolades formerly reserved for European cuisines.

The Michelin board finally anointed Indian cookery with a long-awaited star in January 2001 when Tamarind, another of the capital's exclusive dining experiences, was finally deemed good enough for the honour. Tamarind had opened in 1995 in Chelsea and was in the mould of a traditional London restaurant catering for upmarket business clients. The décor was modern, the staff were immaculate and

---

[1] Taken from C Hardyment, *Slice of Life*, BBC Books, 1995.

knowledgeable, the wine was eclectic and the food was prepared with passion, flair and attention to detail. It also added theatre to the mix: the kitchen was visible from the dining room and apparently there was a waiting list for a table with a view of the tandoors! Finally, the lobbying of organisations like *Tandoori* had paid off and the Indian restaurant sector had external proof of the diversity and quality it had long claimed.

Tamarind's award was swiftly followed by Zaika's Michelin star. Opened by chefs Vineet Bhatia and Gowdham Karinji, Zaika was another reason to visit Chelsea. With a reputation for sourcing the freshest ingredients – and the rarest – these two establishments raised the bar of Indian cookery by several feet, making it almost impossible to compare them to a traditional curry house. It would be a fairer comparison to measure them against restaurants run by well-known European chefs like Marco Pierre White, Gordon Ramsay, Heston Blumenthal, Gary Rhodes and Jamie Oliver. The choice is not between paying £5 or £50 for a curry, but between paying £50 a head for any cuisine. As one restaurateur put it: 'To compare us to a curry house is like comparing Gordon Ramsay to Brenda in your local greasy spoon.' It's a fair point, but one that many potential customers have had difficulty accepting.

It wasn't just the quality of the ingredients or the skill of the chefs that set this new breed of Indian restaurants apart from their high-street forefathers. Everything from the calibre of the waiting staff to the wine selection to the tablecloths demanded to be taken seriously. These places did not need to make Indian food seem exotic or welcoming, as earlier establishments had done: they needed to make it seem refined and elegant. To do this they employed interior designers, almost all of whom rejected wallpaper in favour of plain painted walls (often white), ditched upholstered furniture in favour of wood or metal and threw out pink tablecloths and napkins and replaced them with white linen. And the wailing sitar music was replaced with classical music to create a more sophisticated atmosphere. (In 2002 Leicester University carried out research into restaurant music and found that customers paid more in premises choosing classical music.

Even the waiting staff had a makeover. Not only were tatty black bow ties thrown out to be replaced by continental-style aprons, but some of the restaurants didn't even have Asian waiters – a shock to many customers. Instead table staff with experience in top hotels and rival restaurants were employed, regardless of ethnic origin. In these establishments you were as likely to be served by a Russian or an Australian as you were by a Bangladeshi. And of course, they all spoke very good English.

Perhaps the biggest change, however, was the menu. Gone were the predictable list of beef dishes followed by lamb and chicken, the chef's specials and vegetable side dishes. The word 'curry' was shunned and no one served a chicken tikka masala. Well, they didn't *call* it chicken tikka masala, but if you deciphered the menu you could usually find something that was pretty close. Cyrus Todiwala at Café Spice Namaste famously served kangaroo tikka masala – and even crocodile tikka masala on occasions.

Most restaurants with ambitions for awards and glowing reviews avoided putting chicken tikka masala on their menu at all costs lest they be associated with curry's downmarket past. At the Cinnamon Club, Iqbal Wahhab and his chef Vivek Singh tried to recreate butter chicken, or murgh makhani, the most famous dish from the respected Delhi restaurant Moti Mahal. 'Vivek wanted to introduce it so one day he was in the kitchen and he came up with a recipe,' remembers Iqbal. 'It was actually very good so we wanted to put it on the menu, but we had to work out how we could make what was essentially chicken tikka masala a Cinnamon Club dish. So we decided to use the best chicken available and ended up putting it on the menu as "French black leg chicken cooked old Delhi style"!'

Another item missing from the menus was poppadums. 'I have no idea how they became so popular,' one restaurateur told me. 'I have never eaten them in India. I think they may have been introduced just to give the kitchen more time to get meals ready. And of course the longer people are waiting, the more beer they will drink, so they made financial sense, but they have no place in real Indian cooking.' Others have suggested that they were simply a substitute for the packets of crisps served in pubs.

Some restaurants borrowed more heavily from European menus by offering delineated starters and main courses. And of course those who make a virtue out of their use of fresh and seasonal ingredients changed their menus everyday. Long gone are the days when you kept your menu until it either got too grubby or you needed to put your prices up.

Curry gets Sophisticated

The other major stylistic difference between curry houses and these new restaurants was that balti dishes were nowhere to be seen. Nameeta Panjabi, who took over and updated Veeraswamy's in the 1990s, says she didn't like the way people had to reach over their friends to get their food. Instead, food arrived plated and beautifully presented.

And then of course there was the wine. Lager wasn't even served in some places. As Reza Muhammed put it: 'I think that Indian food goes really badly with lager, wine is much better. I'm trying to phase out beer altogether at the Star of India, and I've got rid of all the pint glasses. Fifteen years ago you couldn't have done that, I don't think the market could have taken it.' For some, the removal – or at least demotion – of beer from their restaurants is a symbol that Indian food has moved on from the days of the laddish curry house.

To capitalise on the new vogue for eating Indian food with wine, Cobra's Karan Bilimoria developed a range of wines – under the General Bilimoria brand – especially for the Indian restaurant sector. Many establishments now choose them as their house wines, but the best restaurants employ sommeliers who select a wine list to complement every dish on the menu.

The arrival of this clutch of upmarket restaurants not only coincided with a wider trend in the hospitality sector, it was also a very visible sign of a growing confidence within the Asian community in Britain. On television, for example, Asians were no longer played by blacked-up Brits as they had been in *It Ain't Half Hot Mum* but had major parts in soap operas, while films like *Bhaji on the Beach* were successful both at the box office and with the critics. Bhangra music became mainstream and Bollywood became fashionable. Newspapers were full of stories about successful Asians in business – the Asian Rich List, published in *Eastern Eye*, made front page news – and more and more Asians became councillors, mayors and MPs.

Perhaps the most important manifestation of the community's new confidence was an ability – hitherto unexpressed to the wider world – to make fun of itself. The first (half) Asian band to get to number one in the Top 40 called themselves Cornershop (with *Brimful of Asha*), after the place where Asians had previously been most visible; and the title of the first Asian sketch show on TV – *Goodness Gracious Me* – came from the comedy record released by Peter Sellers and Sophia Loren to publicise the 1960 film *The Millionairess* in which Sellars, blacked-up, played an Indian doctor.

Arguably *Goodness Gracious Me*'s greatest sketch was called 'Going Out For An English' in which a group of Indians, tanked up on lassis, go to the Mountbatten restaurant in Bombay and insult the English waiter. They start by ordering twelve bread rolls and then ask for the blandest thing on the menu. This role reversal struck a chord with the show's predominantly white audience: even they realised it was time to move on from treating curry houses as pubs that served food. The problem was that not every restaurateur was interested in changing their business to move with the nation's mood.

A 'Miserable' Scandal

Tandoori Magazine was instrumental in trying to encourage the sector to upgrade its image. It ran editorials suggesting that restaurateurs looked at the pub sector and observed how many were being turned into wine bars with more elegant names and interiors. 'I wrote that people should be updating their names and their wallpaper, but a lot of people just didn't want to listen,' recalls Iqbal. 'There were guys who didn't see the point in changing their ways if they were still making money.' But as the 90s progressed, more and more customers had a different kind of curry experience to compare with their local high-street outlet. 'Now I think if the son is going to take the business over, then they've probably made some changes. But if the son is going into law or medicine or business, then I think we will see a lot of curry houses dying with their present owners.'

Iqbal's editorials might not have encouraged everyone to change their restaurants, but they were nevertheless very well read as he found out in 1998. In one edition of Tandoori, instead of taking issue with the food, the décor or the name, Iqbal decided to highlight another emblem of the curry house: the waiters, or as he called them, the 'miserable gits'. He wrote: 'Forget flock wallpaper and twangy sitar music; nothing typifies the Indian restaurant experience as much as the surly, miserable waiter.' He suggested that better motivated, better informed table staff could increase the proprietor's profits.

Although many customers would have known why he was making such comments, it's a brave or foolish editor who attacks his core readership. The furore that followed made it into the mainstream press and turned Iqbal into a minor celebrity. He received death threats at the office and says he knows of an attempt to raise money to pay a hit man. At the time it was very frightening, 'But the thing you find out later,' he says now, 'is that people don't threaten to kill you, they just kill you.'

Like most scandals, Iqbal and his partner Karan assumed it would blow over. However, some of their readers reportedly announced they would stop serving Cobra beer unless some action was taken. Iqbal resigned, and used the opportunity to put his money where his mouth was and in time opened the Cinnamon Club where the waiting staff are – as you'd expect – legendary for not being miserable.

Despite the fracas, Iqbal had a point: times were changing and those who updated their image were better placed to fight a renewed challenge from the supermarkets. Not only were ready meals often more imaginative and challenging than the standard curry house menu, but supermarkets started to offer a fully packaged 'Indian takeaway for two' complete with naan, rice, pickles and side dishes. These were invariably cheaper than the curry house offerings, were more convenient and many people also said that they felt more confident about the provenance of the ingredients – the restaurant sector continued to be affected by scare stories about food poisoning and derogatory comments from the top-end operators. Supermarkets then increased the pressure by offering curries from their deli counters, giving the impression that these meals were made by skilled chefs and could offer a more personal meal. And once it became known that many curry houses used ready-made sauces from the likes of Pataks, some consumers understandably wondered why they should pay restaurant prices.

There were other changes, too, that made it necessary for old-style curry houses to sharpen up their act. Customers became used to paying for everything by credit and debit cards and therefore needed to feel more secure about the company they were entering into a transaction with. Paying in cash became something you did when you were trying to avoid VAT or buying something dodgy and, generally, people don't want to feel that their food is dodgy. It was necessary for restaurants to have a more professional appearance.

The upgrading of many 'curry houses' into more appealing 'Indian restaurants' was not just reserved for London. Up and down the country, proprietors saw the opportunity to charge more for their food by improving their environment. In Birmingham restaurants like Shimla Pinks started to emerge, Bradford got the Aagrah, Edinburgh the Verandah, Milton Keynes the Jaipur and Coventry got the improbably named Country Joes.

It was a brave move for the proprietors who took the risk of alienating an established clientele by making the changes, especially when there would still be an old style Koh-i-noor down the road that would undercut their prices. In many ways it is harder to persuade a customer to upgrade from £5 a meal to £7.95 than it is to convince them into parting with £50.

But such was the gentrification of the Indian restaurant sector that by the beginning of the new millennium, it became cool to seek out a curry house with the worst wallpaper, Formica tables and a menu you could recite from memory. It turned out that the Brits hadn't just loved curry, they had loved curry houses too and there were some who resolutely remained nostalgic for the flock wallpaper and the all-you-can-eat-for-tuppence buffets!

CUMIN

Written records of humanity's love of cumin date back centuries. Tablets written in Linear B (an ancient form of Greek) show it was used in Mycenae in the fourteenth century BCE, and cuneiform tablets in Mesopotamia date its use there to around the same time. In Egypt, where it is native, it was used some 2000 years before Christ (seeds have been found in excavated tombs of pharaohs). We also know it was used in Palestine as it is mentioned in both the old and the new testaments of the Bible. Classical historians Hippocrates, Dioscorides and Pliny also catalogued it. There are even records of cumin from the Celtic communities on the west coast of France as long ago as the first century CE. Known to the Greeks as kymnion and the later Romans as cuminium, this is clearly a spice that has been appreciated for a very long time. It reached India during Alexander's conquests (c. 335 BCE) and gets it first mention in Sanskrit literature around 300 BCE. A small plant (they rarely exceed a foot in height) with delicate fennel-like leaves, cumin has adapted well to many different climates. In summer it produces tiny delicate pink flowers. In Kashmir a smaller variety of cumin is grown, and this black cumin is both sweeter and more expensive.

Like most spices, it is frequently used in medicine. It has stimulant properties but is most frequently prescribed to reduce stomach cramps and colic. In India, cumin is more commonly used to soothe colds and fevers and, when taken with honey, is reported to calm sore throats. In medieval times it was also reckoned to keep lovers faithful; quite how it achieved such a reputation is, sadly, not recorded.

Cumin seeds are light brown, tiny and sharp. They are roasted before cooking and commonly sold ground. Their flavour is distinctively sour and warm and is popular in cuisines throughout the world: Mexicans use it in spicy sausages, Moroccans use it in practically every meat dish and it is ubiquitous throughout Arabia.

In Indian cooking it is another of the constituents of the popular garam masala spice mix as well as the panch phoron masala from Bengal, but it is also used to flavour meats and fish and is popular in many tandoori marinades. In Kashmir it is often used in rich meaty dishes, while in Bengal it is mainly used with fish. In the south, cumin is frequently combined with coconut in dishes.

An incredibly versatile spice, cumin is used to flavour breads, dhals and soups. It can also be added to salads and raitas and – most peculiarly – used to make drinks. Pan jeera (literally cumin water) is made from tamarind juice, sugar, salt and plenty of dry roasted cumin before being garnished with mint and lime. Some restaurants also serve a cumin lassi (yoghurt drink).

Perhaps the most bizarre culinary use for cumin, though, comes from Europe. In parts of the Netherlands and France cumin is used to flavour certain types of cheese.

CHAPTER ELEVEN

The Future of Curry

Supermarkets Lead the Way

With curry available in every conceivable location and in every possible price bracket, it's difficult to know where it can go from here. It's certainly arguable that the curry empire is now so dominant and so vast that it must be at its apex and will therefore shortly enter – as all empires must – a decline.

I have asked many of the people I have interviewed for this book how they see the curry landscape changing in the coming decades, and this chapter is a distillation of their thoughts. As most are relentlessly optimistic, I have tried to read between their lines and plot a likely course for the future of Indian food.

The first area to look at is supermarket curries. As the big stores make a bigger and bigger percentage of their profits from ready meals, they are likely to invest more and more money in their research and development. Most of the big chains now employ people – and sometimes teams – to scour the world in search of new recipes that can be transferred to Britain. With more and more universities offering degrees and training in food sciences, there are now qualified and dedicated professionals working in food-buying positions within the supermarkets. With greater cultural awareness, a better understanding of the cuisines and the ingredients *and* a greater pressure to deliver for the customer, it seems inevitable that supermarket ranges will continue to diversify and expand.

Already we've seen restaurant brands like Tamarind and Bombay Brasserie develop products for supermarkets (Tamarind produced a range of sauces, while Bombay Brasserie devised suitably upmarket ready meals for Sainsbury's), while further down the glamour scale, chains like Shere Khan have produced stir-in sauces. From the conversations I've had with restaurateurs, I think it's a sure bet that several others will try to establish a reputation for themselves on the shelves as well as the high street. However, the lack of brand loyalty in the Indian restaurant sector could make it difficult for anyone to capitalise on high-street success.

As well as stocking other people's curries, supermarkets will no doubt continue to extend and diversify their own offerings. Upmarket retailers like Marks & Spencer and Waitrose have already produced speciality Goan, Madrassi and Gujarati dishes, and this trend is bound to spread to other retailers.

Greater Regionalisation

With greater resources behind them, the huge supermarket chains can take risks that even quite large restaurants cannot contemplate. That's largely because research also shows that shoppers are far more likely to be experimental in the supermarket than they are when they go out for a meal. Sainsbury's, for example, is likely to have far more success introducing a regional or obscure dish than a high-street curry house. In time, though, this means that people who have had their palates excited and educated by the ready meals which are available will feel let down when they eat out. It is this kind of pressure from the super-markets that some expect will force greater levels of regionalisation and sophistication onto the high street. In fact, you could even see a time when the word 'Indian' disappears from restaurant signs. We've already seen this happen in London where restaurants label themselves 'Goan' or 'Keralan', and throughout Britain there is an established trend to label food as 'Bangladeshi cuisine' or 'Punjabi'. My hunch is that during the next decade this new-found regional pride will lead to previously invisible sub-genres of Indian food asserting their identity: expect to see Tamil, Hyderabadi, Kashmiri, Rajasthani and Gujarati restaurants opening up.

For neighbourhood restaurants that build up good reputations with loyal customers, there may be opportunities to extend their relationships with them. Several individual restaurants I know of are looking at ways to effectively extend their takeaway market by offering fresh ready meals through local shops. A few of the better neighbourhood restaurants are already trialling the feasibility of selling their meals – packaged for home consumption – through corner shops and petrol stations. And as many restaurateurs have connections either through family, community or organisations like the Chamber of Commerce with retailers, this is a plausible route for those who can combine a good enough reputation with the necessary health and safety expertise.

But just as there are good restaurants, there are those that don't take such good care of their customers and it seems likely that this will lead to a certain amount of consolidation at the mass-market end of the spectrum. Modest chains like the Ashoka restaurants in Scotland, Shimla Pinks in the Midlands, Shere Khan in the North West are likely to take market share from dated curry houses that haven't invested in décor, service and – crucially – kitchen staff.

The McCurry

The big question is whether one of these chains will become a national brand. Certainly there are entrepreneurs and investors stalking the curry market looking to launch the curry equivalent of Nando's, or maybe even KFC. As one restaurateur put it to me: 'There are a handful of people who have made a lot of money from curry, but they can see that the really big money is in establishing a multiple retail outlet chain.'

Already we've seen some of the big name restaurateurs experiment with formulas with the intention of rolling them out. The Chutney Mary group, for example, runs Masala Zone – of which there are currently two outlets – specialising in Indian snack meals that are served quickly and relatively cheaply. Amin Ali, of the Red Fort, developed Soho Spice with the intention of rolling out the Indian café concept. Café Lazeez now has four restaurants and across the country there are a handful of other restaurateurs looking to work out a formula that can be successfully replicated. 'There are a number of people looking to create the Indian Pizza Express,' one interviewee revealed.

What I wanted to find, though, was the restaurateur with dreams of starting a fast food outlet to rival the big US chains. Given that curry houses had long offered the same menu, the same ambience and effectively the same brand, wasn't it conceivable that they could be united to form, effectively, a McCurry chain? Is there someone out there who wants to take curry back to the one-sauce-fits-all days and sell curry like McDonald's sells burgers?

'The problem with doing that,' one entrepreneur told me, 'is that you can't eat curry with one hand. And you need cutlery. The really successful fast foods have been burgers and hotdogs because you can eat them and drive at the same time.'

It seems that for McCurry to happen, curry itself would have to go through another metamorphosis and meals would have to be adapted, for instance chapati wraps, or dosa rolls, or tikka pieces without the sauces, and established snacks like samosas and onion bhajis could be made more substantial. There are, of course, chefs and entrepreneurs working on such a menu, but whether they will have the necessary investment and business acumen to take on the high street remains to be seen.

I spoke to a City financier with links to the curry trade and asked him if he knew of any companies seeking finance for such a launch. He was unable to name names for reasons of commercial sensitivity, but he said there was no shortage of people wanting to invest in such a project. 'Mostly it's the big hospitality chains who believe they can marry their knowledge of the market with someone else's curry expertise,' he told me.

Certainly that tallies with rumours I heard from the restaurateurs' side of the negotiations. 'I get offers all the time,' one London entrepreneur revealed. 'The big brewers and pub chains are especially interested in converting their kitchens to cook curry. From their point of view it makes perfect sense because at the moment they lose a percentage of their punters at 8 p.m. when they go off for a curry, and many of them don't come back when they've eaten.

'And as most pub food is pretty poor – it's often heated from frozen by untrained staff – they can't charge all that much for it. If they started serving curry, they could maybe charge £20 a head instead of £5 or £10.' So, just as Indian restaurateurs make a bid to divorce their food from beer, the brewers are scheming for a reunion!

These are some of the opportunities in the offing for the industry, but it's clear from my conversations with restaurateurs that the sector also faces some fairly onerous challenges. The most serious of these is finding the staff.

The Hunt for Staff

Salaries in the sector are typically low. Waiting staff in restaurants like the Cinnamon Club may make £25,000 a year, but the income for most staff in provincial restaurants is less than half that figure. Even head chefs in most curry houses will be lucky to earn £15,000. Unsurprisingly it is very difficult to attract and retain staff with earnings at that level.

'It used to be a cash business,' Charan Gill recalls. 'The customers paid cash and at the end of the night, and staff were paid the same way.' The move to credit card payments has meant that it's harder to get paid cash in hand. Staff are now usually paid through the payroll and their income is taxed at source. Although this is good for the treasury, it has proved a disincentive to what was traditionally a casual labour force. 'Now you can't get people to help out on a Friday or Saturday night because it will affect their tax code or mean they lose benefits,' one restaurateur said. Abdul Miah, from the Xenuk restaurant in Finchampstead, also feels the British benefit system is a barrier to keeping staff. 'I've had many people come to work for me from

Bangladesh. They work very hard for the first few years, but then when they've got their council house and their benefits they tell me that they don't need to work!'

The truth is that catering is a tough gig. It involves unsociable hours, often antisocial behaviour, and is physically demanding. Unless there is a family tie it can be difficult to motivate staff. Increasingly, restaurateurs from the subcontinent are looking to recruit from the indigenous white population. 'I would hire anyone if I thought they could do the job,' says Abdul Miah. 'I had a girl come in the other day asking for work, but when I told her she needed to work Friday and Saturday nights she turned me down! Asian teenagers have traditionally been more family orientated and therefore willing to work the weekends, but now even they want to be out with their friends at the weekend.'

The difficulty in finding staff is one shared by every restaurateur I spoke to, whether at the Michelin-starred London establishments or typical curry houses in the provinces. It is the single biggest problem for the sector and was so severe a few years ago that the sector lobbied government to relax the immigration procedures for skilled staff coming into the Indian restaurant sector. To ensure that there are enough people with the skills, some restaurateurs are even taking steps to train people in the subcontinent – for roles throughout the business from chefs to waiters, and in all levels of establishments. For some, starting catering colleges is a way of giving financially to the communities they left, but for others it is just sound business sense.

Despite the relaxation of controls, those wishing to move to Britain still have to meet stringent criteria and now some organisations are starting to specialise in recruitment from India. Charan Gill's Harlequin group, for example, has a department dedicated to recruitment. Specialist skills are necessary as hiring from overseas involves plenty of red tape; for instance, each position has to have been previously advertised in Britain and no suitable staff found. Many restaurants constantly advertise so that when a position becomes available they can avoid the delay of advertising. And to avoid the delay of finding staff on the subcontinent, several restaurateurs visit India regularly to interview potential staff and keep a database of suitable people. That way, when a vacancy arrives, the new recruit can be in place within weeks, rather than months. Such specialist services are now so crucial to the industry that Harlequin also arranges recruitment for other – even rival – restaurants.

Even though finding waiting staff is hard, it doesn't compare to the lengths British restaurants go to to find chefs. Unlike the first generations of curry houses where the cooks were self-taught and reliant on shop-bought sauces, these days chefs need training – not just in cooking, but in health and safety, hygiene and personnel issues. Although many British students leave catering college with the necessary paperwork, British colleges haven't yet developed courses to produce chefs who can cook proficiently in the Indian style. There simply isn't the skills base in the UK to provide the next generation of chefs. Many therefore decide to take on apprentices, like Cyrus Todiwala, who considers his Café Spice Namaste to be a finishing school for trainee chefs. Mostly though, chefs still need to be recruited from India.

A generation ago, the talk was of a 'brain drain' from India in which the brightest and best qualified students in law, medicine, engineering, etc. emigrated to Europe and America. These days the talk is of a 'chef drain' with those trained by the Taj Group or the Oberoi Group receiving several job offers upon graduation. For the really ambitious chefs, Britain is seen as the ideal destination as there they perceive they will have greater creative freedom to push back the boundaries of Indian food. In India, the fanciest restaurants tend to be in the big hotel chains where demands for uniformity limit the opportunities for invention. Despite the attractiveness of working abroad, India and

Bangladesh simply can't meet the demand for chefs fast enough and many British restaurants that would like to hire better chefs simply can't afford to pay for them.

This will probably lead to one of two things: either the price of the high-street curry will go up to pay for a higher wage bill, or the number of curry houses will dwindle as restaurants go under through lack of talent.

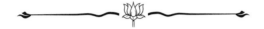

A Drop in Numbers

Several of the people I interviewed thought that the number of Indian restaurants would inevitably decline in the next few years anyway. This is because they believe that the market is saturated and there is simply not enough business for one high street to support three, or five or sometimes more Indian restaurants. 'Not only can you not get the staff,' said one, 'but you can't get the customers.'

For years Brits have pondered why so many curry houses manage to stay open when they appear to only have a few customers a night. There are a number of explanations: the first is that they cater mainly for takeaways and the second is that they still cater for the post-pub crowd and come alive at 11 p.m. Nevertheless, profits are still nerve-wrackingly slim for many who stay in business for reasons other than cash: often there are family ties that enable restaurants to limp on, and as unemployment is statistically higher among the Asian community, even having a poorly paid job is preferable – for some – than unemployment. That is especially true for those in Britain on work permits that state that they must leave the country if their jobs end.

Despite this incentive to carry on, the increased threat from supermarkets is likely to see many urban curry houses disappear from our streets. The truth is that many restaurateurs are disincentivised from investing in their businesses, or changing them to meet the new demand for better food and nicer environments, if their children show no inclination to take over when they retire. 'I didn't come to this country for my son to work as I have done,' London restaurateur Bazlur Chowdhury says. 'I am proud that he is a lawyer, that is the sort of career I wanted him to have.' Some restaurateurs have expressed sadness that their children will not follow them into the family business, but most understand why their offspring would choose not to do so. 'It is very hard work, and there are long hours, and they have plenty of options,' Abdul Miah says of the next generation. There is another reason too: even within the Asian community work in catering is seen as something you undertake out of desperation and lack of choice. To enter catering, then, is to announce to the wider community that Asians aren't progressing in the mainstream.

Not only is catering seen as a profession with long hours and limited rewards, those with parents in the trade can see that it is becoming increasingly difficult to make a success of a small curry house. This is largely because of government initiatives and red tape – something which has sporadically made the restaurant business harder. The sector only just survived the introduction of VAT on eat-in meals when fifteen per cent of all takings immediately went to the treasury. Restauranteurs were faced with the option of either putting up their prices and losing regular customers, or swallowing the cost. Other restrictions regarding working hours, health and safety, sick pay and holiday entitlement have changed what was once a fairly casual business into a mass of red tape. Even the air extraction systems used in most kitchens now have to meet higher standards as restaurants are no longer allowed to 'pollute' the air with kitchen smells (the very thing that used to draw so many people through the door). Extractor units that used to cost £4,000 are being replaced with systems that cost closer to £40,000.

A Russian Revolution?

The natural consequence of these changes is that many Indian restaurants regularly come on to the market for purchase. 'I had two types of people express an interest in buying my restaurant,' one guy told me. 'And they were Indians who had previously run corner shops and who had been put out of business by the supermarkets. The other lot were all foreigners – Nepalese, Kosovars, Poles and Russians. I couldn't bear to sell to another Indian family because I knew that the supermarkets would only put them out of business again in the future, so I sold to the Nepalese people.'

Outside of the top end where second generation entrepreneurs seek to build on the legacy left them by their forefathers, catering seems destined to remain the preserve of first generation immigrants. In Britain, where immigration from the subcontinent has slowed dramatically, that means that old curry houses are likely to become gateways to new cuisines. In the coming decade it looks likely that the adventure curry and its pioneers embarked on in the 50s and 60s will be replicated by immigrants from Poland, Slovenia, Russia, Somalia, Nigeria and the other countries now well-represented in Britain. Whether the cuisines of Eastern Europe and Africa will enrapture Brits in the same way as curry is another matter.

CARDAMOM

A relative of ginger, the cardamom plant can grow to eighteen feet tall on the lush hillsides of southern India. Each fruit produces three of the familiar cardamom pods available in supermarkets, and in turn each pod contains as many as twenty seeds. The fruits are harvested before ripening and sundried until the pods attain a pistachio-green hue.

There are several varieties of this spice: Bengal produces a large podded plant, Sri Lanka a pale green one and Mysore a slightly more delicate pod. The Alleppey variety – originally from Mysore but now grown commercially throughout southern India – is considered the most desirable by chefs.

Outside the kitchen, cardamom has many uses. In India, individual pods are chewed as a breath freshener after a meal. According to Ayurvedic principles, cardamom also has a mood-enhancing effect – try it out by chewing on a pod (it'll make your breath fresh too). Its other reported qualities include curing urinary infections and helping with weight loss. In Saudi Arabia where it is a common flavouring for coffee, it is estimated that coffee use accounts for half of all cardamom imports the fact that is also thought to have aphrodisiac qualities no doubt helps sales too. In China the fourth-century botanist Ji Han imbued it with another power – clearing wind and dissolving phlegm. Certainly its hints of camphor and eucalyptus can help clear a blocked nose. It's also said that drinking a tea made with cardamom pods can relieve headaches. The ancient Greeks and Romans found one last use for cardamom outside the kitchen – the essential oil extracted from the seeds was frequently added to perfumes.

When buying cardamom, the ancient Romans – as advised by Pliny – sought out green pods and these are still the best to buy today if you can find them (some supermarkets only stock brown pods). The seeds are available separately but they tend to be more expensive and, like ground cardamom, lose their flavour very quickly. To get the most out of cardamom buy the pods and lightly crush them before adding them whole to dishes. Some chefs also advise storing pods in the freezer to lengthen their shelf life. The brown pods can be used in savoury dishes, but tend to imbue them with a peppery and slightly medicinal taste.

The green pods are used throughout India in sweet dishes but their warm, aromatic profile also sees them added to biryanis, pilaus and some meat dishes. They are a popular flavouring in ambala (Indian sweets), milk drinks and fruit juices. Cardamom is so popular in Indian cooking that only a small percentage of the Indian crop is ever exported. Most of the pods sold commercially around the world are grown in Guatemala where almost the entire crop is sold overseas.

Cardamom is reported to be especially popular in Scandinavia where it has been put to an unusual use – pickling herring.

CHAPTER TWELVE

Curry Conquers the World

Curry in Europe

*T*his book has so far concentrated on the journey of curry from the subcontinent to Britain, but of course you can eat curry in more countries than you can eat McDonald's. Britain is definitely peculiar in having so many Indian restaurants, but most cities on Earth now have a handful – or more – of curry houses. However, without the ties of Empire, other countries have a different relationship with curry, often seeing it as something exotic and refined rather than a low cost option for a lads' nights out.

The Asian diaspora covers every continent, and almost every country. Indentured labour programmes in the nineteenth and twentieth centuries took people from India – which then included Bangladesh and Pakistan, of course – to places as far apart as Tanzania, the Caribbean and the South Pacific. Economic migration has since seen South Asians find homes in Japan, Finland, the US, Greece, Australia and pretty much everywhere in between. And wherever the Indian community has found a home, curry has been sure to follow. In this chapter, I'd like to take a quick look at how the journey and experience of curry has altered from the British model in a few illustrative countries.

I've always been curious to know if India's other imperial invaders – France, Holland, Spain and Portugal – have been left with any kind of culinary legacy from their conquests. Obviously, of those four countries only Portugal had any lasting relationship with India as Goa remained a Portuguese colony right up until the 1960s. I wasn't therefore expecting to find an equivalent to Manchester's Curry Mile or Birmingham's Balti Triangle anywhere outside Britain, but I hoped to stumble across some kind of curry culture in those countries.

The relationship between Goan food and Portugal is a complicated one as it could be said that several Goan restaurants actually serve Portuguese food. The imperial influence in Goan cuisine can be seen with the use of ingredients like egg yolks, salt cod, spicy pork, bread, vinegar and port wine, mainstays of the native Portuguese diet. Some Goan dishes are only slightly different from the original Portuguese dish. The added complication comes from the fact that there are two distinct Goan cuisines – one that is broadly Hindu, and one that is identified as Christian. In Lisbon, and no doubt in other Portuguese cities, there are a number of restaurants serving Goan food from the Christian tradition. But as far as I've been able to ascertain, most of the restaurants serving a Hindu menu only started post-independence in the 1960s. What I find most surprising is that there are more restaurants serving the food of the Indian north – that is, modelled on the British curry house. Their presence in Portugal is not a corollary of empire, but an extension of the British curry scene with several of the restaurateurs benefiting from family connections to similar operations in Britain.

Indeed, elsewhere in Europe the curry has actually followed in the wake of British expatriates. A number of the Indian restaurants in Spain, for example, are found in coastal resorts where large numbers of Brits either live or go on holiday. Most of these restaurants have menus in English and are run by families who previously ran restaurants in Britain. In Spanish cities there are a handful of Indian restaurants for the Spaniards, but even these attract a large number of Brits, either on holiday or in Spain on business.

In Amsterdam, the culinary legacy of the Dutch empire is a predominance of Indonesian restaurants, some of which have lengthy histories as – like London – Amsterdam was a major port with a sizeable Asian population centuries ago. Despite the popularity of Indonesian food, Indian curries have nevertheless found a home in the Netherlands as well. Amsterdam probably has around twenty curry houses – mostly with familiar names like the Koh-i-noor, Akbar and the Indian Cottage – with the Netherlands' smaller cities sharing a few other restaurants between them. The ones in Amsterdam are, predictably, very popular with the stag parties that descend on the city at the weekends, and some locals believe Indian curry has a worse reputation for thuggery in Amsterdam than it ever had in Britain.

France got its first Indian restaurant in 1975 when Yogen Gupta opened Indra in Paris. Apparently he was part of an Indian government delegation that was being entertained in a succession of French restaurants. The French Prime Minister reportedly enquired why they were not eating in any Indian restaurants and, on hearing that there weren't any at the time, Yogen did something about it. In style Indra is most definitely upscale – a cross between old style French hotels with a dash of the British Raj thrown in. He has since opened three other restaurants in France, as well as premises in Rome and New York.

The uptake of Indian food in France has been hampered by two factors: a well-established and revered indigenous cuisine with the best reputation in the world, and by France's later colonial conquests accounting for much of the ethnic food market (Moroccan restaurants, for example, are both plentiful and excellent). Outside Paris there are very, very few Indian restaurants although there are now some on the Côte d'Azur. The difficulties of starting an Indian restaurant in France were highlighted by Channel 4 in their 2004 series *A Place In France: An Indian Summer*. In it a British expat with no experience of catering teamed up with Reza Muhammed of the Star of India to turn a small café in a village in the Ardeche into an Indian restaurant for the summer. The locals, while impressed, didn't really understand why France would need to import another nation's cuisine and their difficulty in finding a chef highlighted how small the Indian community is in France. That's not to say that the French don't like curry: Marks & Spencer reported that chicken tikka masala was the most popular ready meal in its Paris branch. In 1999, M&S in Paris actually sold more Indian ready meals than any of their British stores.[1] And Meena Pathak confirmed to me that France is one of the countries where Patak's Foods expect to see sales soar in the coming years. It seems France is ready to embrace curry but as a domestic alternative, not an eating-out experience.

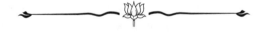

Curry in America

Another territory in which Meena Pathak expects growth in the Indian food sector is the United States. Even though the States probably has the

---

[1] S Basu, *Curry In The Crown*, Harper Collins, 1999, p. 46.

biggest Indian restaurant scene outside the subcontinent and Britain, very few Americans have ever tried Indian food.

Historically, the pattern of Indian immigration to America is drastically different from that to the UK and goes some of the way to explaining why there isn't a similar curry culture. Whereas immigration to the UK was largely unskilled and newcomers had to make a living any way they could, immigration to the States was largely professional. People either went to study or arrived armed with qualifications in areas such as law, medicine, business and IT. Not only did this mean that immigrants didn't need to rely on catering for an income, it meant that the Indian newcomers moved right across the country and no significant ghettos developed. There wasn't therefore, even much of a market in making curry for the Indian population.

This has meant that curry has developed as more of a sophisticated dining experience; the first curry restaurants in the States were incredibly glamorous. In fact, you could argue that the pattern of Indian restaurants in America is the exact opposite of Britain: it started with the top-end, chic, megabucks restaurants and only in the 90s was there a rolling out of smaller scale, smaller budget curry houses in smaller cities.

Curry really came into focus for America in the 80s and 90s when it attracted attention from diners newly educated in Asian food thanks to the fashion for 'fusion food'. While most fusion restaurants borrowed more heavily from other Asian cuisines – notably Vietnamese, Thai and Malay – Indian food was cited as an influence by many chefs, few of whom were actually Indian.

Few American chefs were sufficiently skilled in using spices to replicate the flavours of India and many culinary faux pas were made, like sprinkling untoasted mustard seeds on meals as a garnish (unless mustard seeds are toasted they are very bitter). This hindered appreciation but fuelled a determination among Indian chefs to better promote their food. New York's Tabla was the first restaurant to really make a success of Indian fusion food and its chef Floyd Cardoz became one of the US's few Indian TV chefs.

Later on, a clutch of more traditional Indian restaurants opened across the States. The Bombay Club, launched in Washington DC in 1988, made a virtue out of its menu's Ayurvedic properties. In California, Neela Paniz opened the Bombay Café after nearly 30 years in America. She finally grew so homesick for Indian food that she got her aunt to teach her old family recipes and opened her LA eaterie in the early 90s.

Pannala Sharma came to the States in 1989 after several years travelling the world as Indira Gandhi's personal chef. He grew up in the Amber Palace where his father had been the master chef, catering for the maharajas, and his father's recipes still influence his cooking at his restaurants in New Jersey: Namaskar, Bombay Bistro and Flavor of India. Although a Kashmiri by birth, Pannala's menus reflect the fact that Punjabi is the regional cuisine familiar to most of his customers. Over time, he and other chefs hope to introduce greater regionalisation into the American curry experience.

One of the more recent additions to the list of New York restaurants is the Bukhara Grill where the main attraction is the tandoor. The house specialities include sheesh kebab, mulmul kebab, tandoori chicken, malai kebab, tandoori aloo, tandoori mushrooms and tandoori raan in which the entire leg of lamb is cooked. There is also an impressive bread selection from roomali rotis, naans, parathas and their signature family naan, which is three and a half foot long and two and a half foot wide − a clear adaptation of a dish to the needs of a city not known for its portion control. The demand for tandoor chefs is now so great in America that many believe that training as a tandoor specialist is the easiest and surest way to get a green card.

There are now Indian restaurants in most sizeable cities in America, but whereas a city of 50,000 people in Britain might have 15 restaurants, in America it would be likely to have just one. Cities like Boston, for example, probably have around 30 or so curry houses, but a city of a similar size in Britain would probably have a thousand. Nevertheless, in the bigger cities, the States is starting to see a greater regionalistion in the cuisines available and the process that took fifty or sixty years in Britain has been condensed into a decade or two.

The boom in Indian restaurants has, fairly naturally, fostered a subsequent boom in Indian grocery stores, which in turn has seen a number of specialist import and spice companies make profits where previously there were none. It's estimated there are now around 9,000 Indian grocery stores in the States serving the immigrant community and the restaurant trade. Demand for Indian ingredients is increasing – basmati rice is now even being grown in Texas, the demand for it is so great – and companies like House of Spices, Deep Foods and Chirag are slowly becoming household names. Deep Food's Green Guru frozen ready meals has found that India's reputation as the birthplace of yoga, meditation, Ayurveda and spiritual wellbeing has helped recruit customers: Green Guru lines are promoted as vegetarian and vegan, additive and cholesterol free.

This kind of reputation for Indian food, married with a reasonably well-established distribution network, should make Meena Pathak's attempts to add the US to the list of countries Patak's Foods has conquered a little easier. 'There is definitely an interest in holistic therapies and a lot of things can stem from that,' she says, 'but it's a huge country, a huge percentage of which is not interested in any food other than their core food.'

Consequently, Patak's has embarked on the same kind of education programme it carried out in Britain in the 70s and 80s. It is very difficult to sell shoppers a product when they have no reference points from which they can understand the taste. Meena now makes several promotional trips to America every year to promote her recipe books on TV and in print. She's also undertaking in-store tastings, ground level market research and public speaking. Most Americans still do not have access to an Indian restaurant or grocery shop, and even if they do they have no incentive to experiment. 'They have lived on fast food for so long,' says Meena, 'and the portions are huge. However they are also quite tasteless.' This provides Indian food with an opportunity and a headache all at once: most Americans like Indian food when they try it for the first time – like the Brits – as it is so different from the fries-with-that food on offer elsewhere, but the portion sizes don't compare well for those who value quantity ahead of quality.

It is the Pathaks' belief that to really conquer America, they first need to educate Americans about the potency and dazzling delicacy of spice. But, as most Americans' experience of spice is the jalapeno pepper, familiar from Mexican food, there is an awful lot of educating to do. Launching with complex sauces and sophisticated recipes won't win over the unsure, Meena says. 'We are trying to introduce Indian food through flavours. We're not approaching the market from the high ground, but from the bottom up and educating at a very basic level about the flavours and individual tastes.'

Their quest isn't helped by the lack of the same kind of national supermarket chains that exist throughout Europe. The fragmented nature of the US market, and the relative scarcity of Indian restaurants, means the Pathaks are taking a long-term view on their plans for America. 'It's a huge education process,' Meena says, 'and it will be difficult and expensive.' But, by launching milder products and with careful explanation, the Pathaks believe there is no reason why Americans won't in time be as dedicated to curry as the Brits. And of course, where America goes, several other nations are sure to follow.

ASAFOETIDA

If you ever buy asafoetida, make sure you keep it in an airtight jar. It is one of the foullest-smelling substances in the world and is known in several countries as 'devil's dung' due to its high level of sulphur compounds. This unusual claim to fame did not prevent it being heavily in demand in the kitchens of ancient Athens and Rome where it was used as a substitute for silphium, which became extinct during the reign of Emperor Nero.

It was also in demand by physicians who used it to treat a number of conditions: wind, constipation, colic and the over-production of phlegm were all thought to have been soothed by it. Sufferers from respiratory conditions like asthma and bronchitis are said to have benefited from its consumption as well. Perhaps the most unusual medicinal benefit, however, is asafoetida's reputation for enhancing a singing voice. In the days of Mughal rule, the court singers of Agra and Delhi would apparently rise in the morning and consume a spoonful of asafoetida mixed with ghee before going to the banks of the Yamuna River to practice.

The spice is harvested from the stout stems of a plant native to Afghanistan that looks a little bit like giant parsley. The milky white sap is then collected, rather like rubber, from incisions in the stem and mixed with some kind of flour – either from wheat or beans – to produce a solid block of resin that can then be ground into a powder. Its name comes from the Persian word for gum – asa – and the Latin for stinking – foetidus. Of all the spices, it is possibly the hardest to envisage how on earth anyone ever thought of cooking with it.

However, when it is cooked, asafoetida – also known as hing and perukaya – loses its ghastly aroma and infuses food with the flavour of fried onions. This has made it particularly popular with Jains and Brahmins who do not eat root vegetables on religious grounds (eating a root vegetable means killing the entire plant). Asafoetida resin is stored in oil and the oil is then used for cooking. The ancient Romans found another way of infusing its flavour: they stored it with pine nuts which absorbed the spice's characteristics and could then be crushed and used instead of the asafoetida, which was too prohibitively expensive to be used often.

As it tastes so strongly of onions, asafoetida is never used in recipes that call for them. It works well in meat marinades and batters which benefit in taste, but not texture, from onions. It is also considered a sensible addition to dishes containing beans as it is said to help dissipate the gas from legumes, thus making them more digestible.

Asafoetida is sold in many forms, the most common – and mildest – of which is a straw-coloured powder. You can also find it in granules and as lumps of resin that vary from pink to *chocolate brown in colour. Chefs use it sparingly – a pinch is almost always enough – and those using resin tend to press a piece into the lid of their pan to let the steam transfer its flavour into the food.*

Epilogue

*O*n the surface, the Delhi restaurant sounds like hundreds of other curry houses I know. Smoked glass windows, practically empty, laminated menus printed on pink card, walls dripping with various shades of fuschia that glisten with grease and condensation. In the background amenable waiters hover and sitar music engages in an epic battle with an aged tape machine. The menu is as familiar to me as the Lord's Prayer is to Sunday worshippers – it starts with the specials, then runs through the meats in price order (beef, lamb, chicken) before advertising a predictable selection of vegetable side dishes and the usual mix of rice and naan. But despite appearances, this is possibly the most remarkable curry house in the world. And for me, this is where the story of curry ends.

Although the Delhi restaurant could be on any high street in any town in Britain it happens that it's actually in Bangladesh, one of several 'Indian' restaurants in the town of Sylhet where it seems that curry has come full circle. Like a backpacker, it left home to seek and conquer and has now returned home, changed but essentially intact.

The Delhi – like the Last Days of the Raj and the Taste of Bengal down the road – serves a menu that Brits would recognise as Bangladeshi, but that the Bangladeshis consider to be English. Those who order chicken tikka masala from the menu tend to be Londonis, a label used to identify the thousands of Sylhetis who left Bangladesh for Britain and now return to visit family or retire there. Just as once they had been nostalgic for the curries of Sylhet, now they long for the curries of Brick Lane and Rusholme and these Brit-style curry houses cater for a most surprising gap in the market. It is impossible to eat somewhere like the Delhi and not consider how peculiar curry's journey has been.

And it is difficult to look at Sylhet and ignore the bounty that curry has bestowed on those who have cooked it. As you drive round, you see glimpses of privately owned palaces proudly poking up behind the tea plantations. On the roads you become used to brand new Jeeps and Land Rovers overtaking you, and after a while you notice that the English names of streets and shops don't stem from the days of Empire, but from a much more recent association.

In amongst Sylhet's smoky sprawl, where stalls, repair shops and municipal mosques gang up on occasional Mughal palaces and East India Company outposts, there are some unexpected additions. Like a newly built shopping centre made of polished black granite that gleams in the sun like a beetle waiting to pounce. The centre is regarded with circumspection by shoppers and traders alike: none of the units on the top floor have ever been let. There's also a hospital, the kind that would be well-suited to an affluent American suburb. The locals are happy to have it, but many wards are closed as people can't afford treatment there. And everywhere there are grand villas, mock-Tudor mansions and haciendas, all crowned with enormous satellite dishes and adorned with BMWs, Mercedes and Audis in their drives. They should be garaged, of course, but they're not really for transport – you need a jeep for these roads – they're for show.

Sylhet is the town that curry built: nowhere else on earth better demonstrates that there is profit in pasanda. The Londonis who made millions in Britain, many of them from the Brits' love affair with curry, are now sharing their wealth with the people they left behind and showing off to each other in the process. This bragging is serving Sylhet well.

The ties to London are everywhere: one of the new chrome and glass shopping malls in the city is called London Mansions. Elsewhere you will find London Shoes and London Fashions; there's even a Tescco (deliberately misspelt for legal reasons) supermarket to make the Londonis feel at home. Then there are the Last Days of the Raj, the Taste of Bengal and the other Indobrit curry houses.

These unexpected restaurants and superfluous hospitals are just a couple of examples of how curry has changed the countries that created it. Curry isn't just an export; it is a force that has changed lives, fortunes and landscapes.

Almost all of the people I have met in the course of researching this book have made sure to tell me of their business ventures 'back home'. Dhaka, I gather, is gleaming with new office blocks and towers of luxury flats paid for with curry money. Such is the pride in these developments that I have had impressed upon me that this tower 'is fourteen storeys' or that one 'is sixteen storeys – the tallest for the area'.

But the development isn't just about one-upmanship and bragging. Nor it is just the cities that have benefited: one London restaurateur took me to his office to show me pictures of his tea plantation that he said provided 1,000 jobs during the harvest. 'In London I can only give eight people jobs, but in Sylhet I can do more.' It still amazes –

and humbles – me that eating a curry in south London for under a tenner can do so much for the developing world. It is one of the tenets of Islam that ten per cent of all income should go to benefit others, and in the past fifty years Londoni money has been used to build kindergartens, health centres, drug rehabilitation bureaux and fund extensive charitable work. It makes chicken tikka masala seem even more remarkable.

Unsurprisingly, the fact that so many Londonis are flash with their cash – after all, a modest figure in sterling is quite substantial in Bangladeshi taka – has led some young Bangladeshis to believe that it is impossible not to make your fortune on the streets of London. To many people in Sylhet it seems that every Londoni is a millionaire. Consequently, there are always people who want to go to London and make their own, and for some the route is still curry. A number of the schools started by curry entrepreneurs have been catering colleges and right across the subcontinent there are young people queueing up to replicate their success.

What makes these fortunes all the more remarkable is that the men and women who are now ploughing money back into Bangladesh were not allowed to leave their homeland with any money whatsoever. These are fortunes that have been made from initial investments of just a few pounds. None of the early pioneers could have imagined that they would have worked in catering, or that curry would be so popular and profitable. It feels to me that the improbability of the story of curry is a fitting bookend to the improbability of the food itself. Who knew you could get three spices out of nutmeg? And who knew you could make a hospital out of curry? It is, I hope you'll agree, the most peculiar and most wonderful food on the planet.

SAFFRON

Saffron is famously the most expensive spice in the world, and the most sought after variety of saffron comes from Kashmir. It is so precious that in many parts of Asia it is a spice associated with celebration and worship, whether as a dye for the robes of monks, or for rice used as confetti at weddings or in the select and complicated dishes prepared for such celebrations. The pigment in each strand is sufficient to tint a volume of water equivalent to 150,000 times its own.

Its expense is due to the extreme difficulties faced in harvesting it. Strands of saffron are in fact the stamens of the crocus flower, can only be picked as the flowers come into bloom and must be harvested at dawn before the sun evaporates their potency. The harvested stamens are incredibly delicate and must be handled with great care as they are taken away to be dried. It takes an incredible 140,000 crocus flowers to produce one kilo of saffron.

Typically the spice is sold in small glass jars containing only a few strands for a higher price than larger jars containing greater quantities of other spices. Although by weight saffron is far more costly than gold, only a small amount is needed to infuse an entire dish with its warm golden tones. If over-used saffron can sometimes taste quite medicinal, so there are plenty of reasons to use it sparingly. The longer saffron is steeped in a dish, the deeper the hue it will impart. It is also available ground but it is inadvisable to buy it this way as it is quite likely that the powder has been adulterated with turmeric, which is fine for colour but offers a different flavour profile (in medieval Germany, people found tampering with saffron is such a way were burnt at the stake). If you have a choice of saffron to buy, the Kashmiri variety of mogra cream is the finest, although most commercially available saffron is grown in the La Mancha district of Spain. Despite commercial operations it is still an expensive crop as the harvest cannot be automated: never be tempted to buy cheap saffron as it will almost certainly be an inferior impostor.

Medicinally saffron is reported to treat hypothermia and to stimulate both appetite and libido. Throughout history it has been associated with miracle cures; few of these have any basis in fact and appear to have been attributed to saffron merely as a consequence of its price. In 1670 the German historian Johann Hertodt wrote an entire book in praise of saffron called Crocologia in which he claimed it could cure everything from the plague to toothache. There were some in the Middle Ages who even thought it restored the dying to full health. It has *been held in such awe that it was thought some cures could be obtained without actually eating the spice: the Romans believed that sleeping on a pillow of saffron would ensure you didn't wake up with a hangover.*

APPENDIX A

A Guide to Regional Cuisine

As has been said many times, Indian cookery embraces several regional cuisines, and this is my attempt to list the defining characteristics of each. It is not an easy task as generalisations are fraught with inconsistencies. For instance, many will tell you that rice is the staple of the south and bread the staple of the north, yet Bangladeshi cuisine favours rice over bread. Others will tell you that coconut is emblematic of the south, which is true, but it is also true that just about every coastal kitchen in India – whether in Gujarat or Bengal – will also use the coconut and the fish usually associated with the south. And of course fish isn't just a southern ingredient – Bangladesh is a mesh of rivers producing fish for kitchens and Kashmir is home to what some people have labelled 'the tastiest fish in the world', the Kashmiri trout.

There are many simplifications you will hear about Indian food, perhaps that in the north people eat more meat or that in the south they use less chilli, but the variations of religion and geography throughout India make accuracy in simplification impossible. Even when you think it's quite safe to say that Brahmins are strict vegetarians, you find that the Brahmins of Orissa have long defended their fish-heavy diet. Sometimes the difference between regions can be very subtle, perhaps just being the way vegetables are cut or the shape of the chapatis, or in some cases it is just that a particular spice can dominate.

But none of these prove to be quite such an obstacle to clarity as the way regional differences within India vary from those outside India. For instance, most British curry houses have a largely Bangladeshi menu, yet most include rogan josh, which is traditionally Kashmiri. The best example of how cuisines have been co-opted once they have left India's shore is the Glasgow dosa. The dosa is traditionally a southern Indian speciality yet it is the signature of many Glaswegian restaurants, most of which are run by Punjabis. Many Glaswegians consequently consider the dosa to be a Punjabi speciality. The confusion stems from a single Punjabi chef who, after holidaying in Kerala, started serving dosas in his restaurant only to be copied by his rivals.

Taking all this into account, what follows is my attempt to simplify and identify the major distinctions between the regions and some of the religions within them. I hope it is not too confusing!

Andhra Pradesh

This is the largest state in the south and one of the most diverse, for although the state is mostly Hindu the capital Hyderabad is predominantly Muslim, and the Mughal influence of the pre-Empire rulers (the Nizams) can still be seen in the food. The Nizams had a reputation for high culture, fine food and feasts of multiple courses that could last for days. Andhra food is noted for its heat as well as its spice and each course is supposed to be hotter than the last.

Perhaps one of the richest and spiciest cuisines within India, in Andhra Pradesh you will find a mix of the heavy meat dishes of the Muslim north and the dosas of the south. Hyderabadi cuisine is considered rich and aromatic with liberal use of spices, ghee, nuts and fruit. Many consider the biryani to be the archetypal Hyderabadi dish.

Bangladesh

When most people think of Bangladeshi cuisine, they are actually imagining Sylheti cooking as virtually all Bangladeshi restaurants are run by Sylhetis. As many Sylheti-run restaurants have adopted the cuisines of other regions, there are many misconceptions about authentic Bangladeshi cuisine. Another complication in identification is that when most people say 'Bengali' they mean 'Bangladeshi' as what was once the single state of Bengal is now divided between Bangladesh and India.

The mainstays of Bangladeshi cooking are fish, rice and dhals with dhal more dominant in West Bengal (India) and a preference for river fish over sea fish in East Bengal (Bangladesh). Both East and West Bengal use mustard oil for much of their cooking. Of all the cuisines covered in this list, Bangladesh's diet relies most heavily on meat, although not pork as most Bangladeshis are Muslim. A typical Bangladeshi meal would include a curry of either fish, meat, eggs or vegetable, a spiced dhal and rice. Chapatis are also served and koftas – spicy meat kebabs – are also popular.

The old state of Bengal was host to several European colonies before the British gained supremacy and as such was introduced to several crops from the New World. This legacy can still be seen in Bangladeshi cooking which makes extensive use of potatoes, tomatoes and – of course – chillies. Another characteristic of Bangladeshi curries is that they are almost always 'wet', in a gravy or sauce. The hallmark of

Bengali cooking is the use of panch phoron, a blend of five basic spices: cumin, kalaunji (black cumin), fennel, fenugreek and mustard seeds. Bangladesh is also considered to produce the finest desserts in the subcontinent.

Delhi

Delhi has been conquered throughout history by successive dynasties, and this shows in its cuisine which borrows not just from Punjabis, Muslims, Gujaratis, Tamils, Malayalis, Bengalis and Lucknavis but also from the British, the French, the Thais, the Chinese, the Lebanese and even the Mexicans! As there is no one community that can call Delhi theirs, the same is also true for Delhi's food which is a true fusion of styles from all over India. So when a restaurant says it serves Delhi food, what can you expect? Generally it means that they consider themselves to serve fine food from the tradition of the grand hotels that boast political and business leaders among their clientele. Delhi food is meant to impress.

Goa

There are two traditions of cooking in Goa – Christian and Hindu. The Christian-influenced (Portuguese) cooking sports many familiar Iberian touches, making it one of the most distinctive of all the regional cuisines.

The Portuguese influence can be seen in the liberal use of egg yolks, salt cod, pork, bread, vinegar, port and even chorizo. The distinctive toddy vinegar gives Christian cooking an unmistakable sourness. The Hindu meals are also atypically sour for India, but in Hindu cooking the sourness comes from the kokum – a deep red fruit that gives many dishes a distinctive sharp edge. Both traditions rely heavily on fish and coconut. Goa also has a reputation for using more alcohol than other regions and the local liqueur, feni, accompanies most meals.

Goan food tends to be hot, spicy and pungent and most meals feature seafood – prawns, lobsters, crabs, and jumbo pomfrets are used in everything from soups to salads, pickles, curries, and stir-fries. Goa also has its own famously red chilli. Tamarind is another signature flavour.

The traditional Goan vindaloo – which bears no resemblance to any vindaloo on most British menus – is a spicy concoction of lots of red chillies, garlic, pork, Goa vinegar and palm jaggery (sugar) and is best enjoyed with plain boiled rice. Another Goan delicacy is sarpotel, an exotic curry featuring liver, heart, kidneys, red chillies, cinnamon and cloves all drenched in tangy local vinegar.

Holidaymakers to Goa often return home to dream of Goa's famous bebinca dessert. Made of coconut milk, flour, sugar and spices, this layered dessert must be baked one layer at a time and traditionally should have sixteen layers.

Gujarat

Gujaratis are often said to have perfected the art of vegetarian cooking, using everything from lentils and vegetables to buttermilk and yoghurt to make a mouth-watering array of dishes. Gujarati chefs have long been in demand as domestic cooks in well-off families in India, and they in turn have helped influence other regional cuisines. The most famous Gujarati dish is the thali – which literally means a meal served on a silver platter – in which the diner is treated to everything from rice to bread, from curry to pickles. Less well known is the khichdi, a simple lentil and rice mixture that is a daily staple for many. One of the many highlights of Gujarati cooking is its pickles, traditionally served in winter when fresh vegetables were not widely available. Dhals, made from dried lentils, are also popular for the same reason.

Other specialities to look out for include khaman dhokla, a salty steamed cake made from chickpea flour; doodha pak – sweet, thickened milk confectioned with nuts; and shreekhand, a dessert made of yoghurt, flavoured with saffron, cardamom, nuts and candied fruit which is eaten with hot, fluffy puris.

Karnataka

This state, previously and perhaps better known as Mysore, is famous for its strictly vegetarian Brahmin cooks. Its signature dish is definitely the dosa and the flavours of tamarind, cardamom, cloves and cinnamon ripple through many of its dishes. Karnataka also grows the best coffee in India.

Similar to Keralan food, coconut and banana feature frequently, particularly on the coast. Mysore masala dosa is another favourite from Karnataka as is the coconut chutney. The Karnataka meal is traditionally served on a patravali (a banana leaf).

Kashmir

The cuisine of the mountainous province of Kashmir is heavily meat based – usually goat or chicken – and is consequently well-liked in Britain and America. It is one of the few Indian cuisines that uses pork (though not often) which was popular in the region before the advent of Islam. Kashmiri food has other signatures too: the extensive use of prized Kashmiri chillies that release an intense red colour although only a mild taste indicates a Kashmiri dish, as does the use of dried fruit and nuts (the best-known example being Peshwari naan). Another key ingredient is yoghurt. One of the key flavours of Kashmir is the smokiness imparted from charcoal ovens.

Kashmiri dishes are on the menus of most British curry houses. The most famous is rogan josh, but others like gushtaaba (spicy meatballs), aab gosht (lamb cooked in thickened milk) and rista (delicately flavoured meatballs) are fairly common.

The mountainous landscape and milder climate make vegetable cultivation harder than in other regions. Traditionally, therefore, vegetables were often dried for use over the winter. One of the visual highlights of a trip to Kashmir is the floating vegetable beds: reeds are smothered in mud from the bottom of lakes and then – often the only flat surface for miles around – are planted with cucumbers, melons, strawberries, mint and tomatoes.

Kashmir is also famous as the home of the ultimate Indian banquet – the wazwan, which consists of an incredible thirty-six courses!

Kerala

Kerala is sometimes known as the home of hospitality, such is its reputation for entertaining and feeding guests. Over the years it has been host to communities from Portugal and Syria, as well as Christians and Jews, all of which have left influences in Keralan cookery. It has also been very receptive to ingredients imported by its visitors, and things like cashews, pineapple, tapioca and even cocoa are used in Keralan cooking. Its signature ingredients, however, are fish, coconut, curry leaves and mango. Garlic is very rarely used.

On the coast there is a wide variety of seafood available including shrimp, prawns and crab – all of which are largely unheard of in some of the regions of the north west of India. Dishes in Kerala tend to be drier ones like thorans, and both dosas and rice are eaten as accompaniments. Much of the diet is vegetarian.

Maharashtra

Maharashtra – which means great state – is in the midwest of India and is diverse in geography and climate, factors that have influenced its cuisine. Garlic and onion form the base of many dishes, most of which have a reputation for being heavily spiced. The area is also known for its stuffed vegetables that are traditionally cooked with very little oil.

On the coast, fish dominates but inland meat dishes replace the fish. Throughout the region the kokum fruit is used to lend a distinctive sourness while peanuts are a frequent addition to many curries. All dishes are traditionally eaten with boiled rice or with bhakris, soft rotis made with rice flour. Special rice puris called vada, and amboli – a pancake made of fermented rice, urad dhal, and semolina – are also favourites in Maharashtra.

Shreekhand, a thick sweet yoghurt served with spiced puris, is a favourite dessert at weddings and festivals and has made its way on to menus throughout India and Britain.

Pakistan

Pakistani food has distinct regional characteristics, with the most well known being Punjabi food (see below). In the other provinces of Pakistan the food displays Afghan, Turkish and Iranian influences. Baluchistan is famed for its sajji barbecues in which whole chickens and goats are impaled on sticks and cooked next to the flame, rather than over it. In Sind fish is more common and is often stuffed with a mixture of spices, seeds and fruit before being wrapped in cloth and baked in hot sand for several hours.

Breads made from wheat are the staple, with rice usually reserved for special meals. Meat features heavily in diets across Pakistan, as do beans and other pulses. Milky desserts are prepared everywhere, the most noted of which is barfi, a kind of fudge made with milk and thickened with ground nuts.

Punjab

The state of Punjab was divided at the time of Partition. West Punjab became part of Pakistan, and the East became part of India. On the Indian side of the border the population is predominantly Sikh, and it is Sikh cuisine that has become synonymous with Punjabi cookery.

The best known element of Punjabi food is the tandoor, a large clay oven half-buried in the ground and fired with charcoal. Long skewers of marinated meat, chicken, fish, paneer and occasionally vegetables are inserted into the oven while naans and other breads are cooked quickly on the sides of the oven. The marinades provide the key flavours in Punjabi food. Wheat is the staple in Punjab, not rice, and the area is known for its breads: as well as naans, an infinite variety of rotis, parathas, puris, kulchas and chapatis are made.

Punjab is sometimes called the 'land of milk and honey' and you can certainly see plenty of dairy products in Punjabi cooking. The first and most obvious is the liberal use of ghee and butter, but you will also see paneer (milk curd) on Punjabi menus, dahi (yoghurt) sauces and makhan (white butter), and no meal is complete without either a sweet or savoury lassi. Another speciality from this region is khoya, a thick cream used to make desserts.

Rajasthan

Much of Rajasthan is desert, and the geography is reflected in the food, as is its war-torn past. Food was prepared to nourish fighting armies that would be away from home for long periods. Recipes from this region therefore tend to have long shelf lives and need little water. Milk, which can be collected from wandering herds, features heavily. Recipes from the arid regions feature dried dhals and preserves to replace fresh vegetables and fruits. Traditionally the meats used in Rajasthan were game, either from royal hunting expeditions, or from armies eating what they could find.

Neither rice nor wheat grow well without vast amounts of irrigation so lentils, beans and millet are used instead to make pancakes and dhals. Gram flour is used throughout the state.

To balance the creaminess of using so much milk, ghee, butter and cream, Rajathani cookery is sharpened with powerful spices. Asafoetida (used as a substitute for onions and garlic), ginger, fenugreek and aniseed are frequently used.

Tamil Nadu

Known as Madras in the days of the British Empire, Tamil Nadu has a misplaced reputation for very spicy food. The 'chicken madras' of many menus simply does not exist in modern Chennai (the contemporary name for the city of Madras), as most of the population is vegetarian.

Tamil food has much in common with the food of neighbouring Kerala. Coconut features regularly, as do mustard seeds and curry leaves. Pancakes made from urad dhal and rice flour – dosas, idlis and vadas – dominate and are stuffed with curries flavoured with black pepper, red chillies, cumin, turmeric, coriander, fennel, fenugreek and ginger. Rice accompanies most meals and rice desserts are popular. Pongal, a rice pudding made with jaggery, is a speciality.

Restaurant Names

*T*here are many restaurants all over the world that have chosen the same name. Names, like wallpaper, change with fashion. In the 1930s Shah Jalal was probably the most widely used name, while in the 70s and 80s it was probably Taj Mahal. Today there is a fashion for using Hindi words like Masala and Rasa. I was intrigued to find out what they all mean, so here is a list of some of the most familiar restaurant names, and the meanings that lie behind them.

Akash Tandoori – Akash refers either to the sky, or more obliquely to a sense of space and contentment that can be obtained through an Ayurvedic diet.

Argee Bhajee – The name of the Indian restaurant in *EastEnders* which, considering the nature of many of the confrontations in that particular soap opera, would appear to be incredibly well-named!

Ashoka – The great Indian emperor, Ashoka, was born in 265 BCE. He was the most famous of the Mauryan kings and was one of the greatest rulers of India. After leading his people in battle he was so distraught at the bloodshed that he forsook his warrior ways to lead peacefully instead and encourage his followers to embark on a life of virtue.

Bengal Lancer – The Bengal Lancers were a cavalry division of the Indian army during the days of Empire. They were popularised by a book by Francis Yeats-Brown called *The Lives of a Bengal Lancer* which was made into an Oscar-nominated film in 1935.

Ellora – The Ellora caves in Maharashtra are famous for having thirty or more temples carved into their rock faces. They are one of the less well-known tourist attractions in India.

Garden of Gulab/Gulab Tandoori – Gulab is the Hindi for 'rose'.

Jamuna – Also spelt Jamina and Yamuna. Jamuna is the name of a goddess who was the consort of Krishna. It is also the name of a river in the north of India.

Jewel In The Crown – This name became popular in the 1970s and 80s. It was the title of the first book in Paul Scott's *Raj Quartet* which was made into a highly successful TV series. The phrase refers to India being the jewel in the crown of the British Empire.

Koh-i-noor – The name of a huge diamond that once belonged to Mughal emperors but became the property of the British crown during the Empire. Some say that the Koh-i-noor is actually one piece of a legendary older diamond called the Great Mughal about which there are many legends, some of which are now ascribed to the Koh-i-noor – for instance, that many of its male owners have met with misfortune and untimely deaths. Its first known owner was the Rajah of Malwa. Two centuries later it was in the hands of the Sultan Babar, the first Mughal emperor, who passed it down to successive Mughal rulers including Shah Jehan, the builder of the Taj Mahal. It gets its name from the Nadir Shah of Persia who – when he was sacking

Delhi – saw it for the first time and exclaimed 'koh-i-noor', which means mountain of light. It was sent to Britain in 1851 and Queen Victoria had it recut to add to its lustre before having it set in a crown. Legend has it that 'no man should wear it': queens, it seems, are immune to the curse. It is now kept with the Crown Jewels in the Tower of London.

Lal Qila – Also spelt Lal Quila. This is the Hindi translation of Red Fort, which is one of the most magnificent buildings in India.

The Mahabharata – The title of an epic poem (it is 220,000 lines long) written in 900 BCE about an ancient battle between ruling dynasties.

The Maharaja – This simply means 'great king' or 'great ruler' ...

The Maharani – and this is the title of the Maharaja's consort or queen.

Masala World/Masala Zone – Sometimes written as massala. This is a Hindi word for a blend of spices as in garam masala or chat masala.

Mother India – This is a phrase used to denote India's physical ability to provide for her people with sunshine and monsoon rains, and to chastise them with floods, droughts and other natural disasters. It is also a title that was often given to the country's first female Prime Minister, Indira Gandhi.

Mumtaz – Mumtaz Mahal was the wife of Shah Jehan who built the Taj Mahal in her memory when she died. She was depicted as the ideal wife who accompanied her husband everywhere and was seen as a comrade as well as a confidante. Mumtaz means 'the chosen one'.

Namaste/Café Spice Namaste – Namaste is a greeting that can either be translated as simply as 'hello' or more extravagantly as 'the Great Perfection within me honours the Great Perfection within you'. It can also mean thank you.

The Nawab – Nawab is a term of respect used to address rich and prominent people.

A Passage To India – the title of a twentieth-century novel by EM Forster. It became a popular restaurant name in the 1980s when David Lean made a film based on the book.

Posh Spice – one of the more recent additions to the list of curry house names. This is, presumably, a cheeky reference to a former member of the Spice Girls, Victoria Beckham, and no doubt an attempt to attract some publicity.

Raj Bari – Rajbari is a town in Bangladesh about 130 km from the capital Dhaka. It is a popular name for curry houses as it sounds regal and Indian, though it is in fact Bangladeshi.

Raja Balti House – Raja means 'royal' or 'kingly'.

The Rajput – This simply means 'prince'. Also spelt Rajpoot.

Rasa – This means 'taste'.

The Red Fort – One of India's most famous landmarks. Made of red sandstone in the seventeenth century, it is one of the main tourist attractions in Delhi as it's one of the finest surviving examples of Mughal architecture. Construction was started by Sultan Sikander Lodi and completed by Shah Jehan.

Ruby/Ruby Murray – This is cockney rhyming slang for curry and was a popular choice for new restaurants in the 1980s. No one knows for sure who first used the name of the famed singer from Northern Ireland in place of curry, but many Ruby Murray fans attribute its use to the Scottish comedian Billy Connolly.

The Sagar/Sagar's – Sagar means 'ocean' in Sanskrit

The Shafi – The name of one of London's first Indian restaurants, Shafi is simply a common family name. It has associations with loyalty and community.

Shah Jalal – This was a popular name for the early restaurants in the 1930s and 40s. Shah Jalal was an important Muslim saint; he is buried in Sylhet. Restaurants called Shah Jalal are almost always run by Sylhetis.

Shah Jehan – Shah Jehan was one of the great Mughal rulers and is best known for building the Taj Mahal in memory of his wife.

The Shalimar – Shalimar is a Sanskrit word which means 'surrendering your soul to your senses' or 'the purest of human pleasures'.

Shere Khan – The name of the tiger in Rudyard Kipling's *The Jungle Book*.

The Star of India – This was the name of a great sailing ship that transported people and goods between India and Britain during the days of Empire.

Surma Tandoori – The Surma is the major river flowing through Sylhet, named after an old queen of the kingdom of Kamrup.

The Taj Mahal – Made of white marble and adorned with domes and minarets, this is one of the most famous buildings in the world and it is synonymous with India. Taj means 'crown' and 'mahal' means palace.

The Viceroy – One of the many names that refer back to the Empire. The Viceroy was the representative of the Crown in India.

Veeraswamy's – Veera translates as 'hero', and swamy as 'god' or 'divine'. It is also a relatively common name in parts of India.

Xenuk – this means 'pink pearl', something that is both precious and rare

Zeera – one of the increasingly popular spice names. Zeera is an alternative spelling of Jeera, which is cumin.

Menu Mate

$\mathcal{B}$elow is a list of words found on many menus complete with explanations. As has been discussed elsewhere, there are no set rules about what goes into a lamb rogan josh or a chicken tikka masala – each restaurant has simply copied and interpreted another restaurant's menu. Sometimes the language differences have meant that the recreation of a Hindi recipe by a Bengali chef, for example, can result in two dishes with the same name that are utterly unrecognisable. It is entirely possible that your encounter with these dishes will differ from the descriptions below!

Achar – Pickle.
Aloo – Potato.
Amchur – Dried mango powder sometimes used as a souring agent.
Appam – South Indian rice snacks.

Atta – Wholewheat flour finely milled for making chapatis. Sometimes called chapati flour.

Avial – A vegetable curry from Kerala made with drumsticks, coconut and green bananas.

Baigan – Aubergine (eggplant). See also Brinjal.

Balti – The word 'balti' can be translated as bucket or may refer to a style of cooking in an area of northern Pakistan known as Baltistan. The balti pan has two small round handles on either side and is used for cooking and serving. Traditional balti meals involved several small bowls of different dishes being served. They are usually wet dishes with sauces to be mopped up with naan bread.

Barfi – A fudge-like dessert made with milk and either ground nuts or ginger, chocolate or a spice.

Basmati – Fragrant Indian rice. Basmati means 'queen of fragrance'.

Betel nuts – The small coconut-like fruits of palm trees.

Bhaji – A savoury snack or dish.

Bhelpuri – A savoury snack, not unlike Bombay mix, often mixed with salad.

Bhindi – Okra, or ladies' fingers.

Bhugia – Stir-fried vegetables.

Bhuna – Bhuna is a cooking process where spices are gently fried in oil to bring out their flavour. The bhunas that appear on most menus contain meat which has been added to the spices and then cooked in its own juices, resulting in strong flavours but very little sauce.

Biryani – The biryani is traditionally a mild dish of rice baked in the oven with meat or vegetables served at special occasions. In practice, many restaurants do not have the time to slow bake biryanis and they tend to be stir-fried. Usually served with a side dish of vegetable curry to add some sauce.

Bitter gourd – A popular vegetable from the north, this is a variety of pumpkin that looks like a cucumber crossed with a toad! It has a thick bumpy green skin and – once peeled – can be boiled, fried or mashed.

Bombay duck – Not a duck at all, but a fish called Bombil. It's a small, translucent flying fish caught off the coast of Bombay (and along much of India's west coast) and left to dry in the sun. Before eating, its head (and mass of teeth) are cut off and what's left is deep-fried. They can either be very chewy or cooked until they are brittle and then sprinkled into other dishes. They were banned for a while in the EU after traces of salmonella were found in some supplies. Even though supplies are no longer contaminated, the health scare still taints this little fish's reputation.

Bottle gourd – A fresher tasting squash, with a taste reminiscent of cucumbers – it is often cooked with dhals.

Brinjal – Aubergine, or eggplant

Chana dhal – A yellow dhal (lentil) that resembles split peas and tastes like chick peas. Often ground into a flour used primarily for making batters.

Chana masala – A vegetarian dish of onions, tomatoes and chick peas.

Chapati – A round unleavened bread made with finely milled wholemeal flour. Tear off into pieces and use to scoop up other dishes.

Chat – Usually refers to cold snacks flavoured with chat masala, which is a blend of spices familiar from Bombay mix.

Chenna – A rich curd cheese made from full cream.

Curd – Can mean either yoghurt or paneer cheese.

Dahi – Yoghurt.

Dhal – A catch-all term for lentils, peas and pulses but on menus refers to dishes made with lentils, usually spiced with garlic and chilli (for example, tarka dhal).

Dhania – Another word for coriander that refers to both the seeds and the leaf.

Dhansak – A dish of meat (usually lamb) and lentils. It is often described as 'hot, sweet and sour' with the heat coming from chillies, the sweetness from sugar and the sourness from lemon juice. Some restaurants add fruit for the sweetness, but this is not authentic.

Dopiaza – A dopiaza is any dish in which there are twice as many onions as meat – its literal translation is 'double onions'.

Dosa – A southern Indian pancake made from fermented dhal and rice flour. Usually pan-fried and filled.

Drumsticks – Long, hard, thin vegetables that could be used as drumsticks. Usually cut into finger sized portions for cooking, the skin remains too tough to eat even after cooking. Scrape away the flesh with either your cutlery or your teeth and leave the skin at the side of your plate.

Dudh – Milk.

Feni – A Goan liqueur distilled from fruit.

Ghee – Clarified butter made by heating unsalted butter until the dark sediment sinks allowing the golden ghee to be 'creamed off'. Clarified butter has two benefits: firstly, it doesn't go rancid and, secondly, it can be heated to higher temperatures before scorching.

Gobhi or **gobi** – Cauliflower.

Gobindavog – A black variety of Indian rice.

Gosht or **ghosht** – This means meat but usually refers to lamb or mutton.

Gulab jal – Rose water, used to flavour desserts and as an air freshener.

Gulab jamun – Fried balls of dried milk powder served in rose syrup.

Haldi – Turmeric.

Haleem – A dish made with minced meat and grains such as wheat and oats.

Hilsa – A popular Bengali freshwater fish.

Idli – Steamed rice cakes, often eaten at breakfast.

Jaggery – Lumps of brown sugar made from boiling sugar cane juice. Has a slight caramel flavour.

Jalebi – A sweet batter pastry resembling a pretzel filled with syrup.

Jalfrezi – A hot dish that has its origins in the days of the Raj. Originally devised as a way of incorporating the left-over meat from the Sunday roast, this features meat with plenty of green chillies in a light sauce.

Jeera – Cumin, also spelt zeera as this is closer to the correct pronunciation.

Kacha kela – A type of green, unripe banana used in South Indian kitchens.

Karhai – A wok-style pan sometimes interchangeable with a balti dish and used for stir-frying food over an intense heat. Also spelt karahi.

Kedgeree – A dish made from smoked fish, rice and lentils.

Keema – Minced meat, usually lamb.

Korma – Traditionally, a korma was a style of slow cooking meat in which the juices had cooked down to a thick sauce. In practice, the thick sauce is created by using ground almonds, coconut and/or cream in most restaurants. It is usually yellow/orange in colour – but can be green or red – and very mild.

Kulfi – Indian ice cream.

Lassi – A whipped yoghurt drink that is usually sweetened with fruit but which can also be savoury.

Luchi – A deep-fried bread, similar to Puri, but made with coarser flour.

Madhu – Honey.

Madras – Madras-style curries are an invention of the British curry house and have no precursor in traditional Indian cooking. It is just a label – no doubt devised by some waiter or chef wanting to lend credibility to a dish – for a hotter than normal curry, usually with a tomato base. The name probably comes from the use of Madras curry powder, an early Sharwood's import. A Madras curry was just a dish made with this powder.

Masala – This just means a blend of spices.

Meen – Fish.

Methi – Fenugreek, refers to both the seeds and the leaves.

Mirch – Chilli.

Mishti-doi – A Bengali dessert made from curd and jaggery.

Mooli – A long white radish, or a dish containing coconut.

Moong or **Mung** – A type of bean.

Murgh or **Murghi** – Chicken.

Muri – Puffed rice.

Muttar – Peas.

Naan – Leavened bread cooked on the walls of a tandoor oven. Its flavour comes from the charcoal and the juices of the kebab meat on skewers cooked in the oven at the same time. Naan breads are often stuffed with vegetables, meat, fruit or nuts.

Paan – A digestive served at the end of meals consisting of spices in a small parcel of leaves.

Pakora – A deep-fried patty of onions, potato and spinach.

Palak – Spinach.

Panch phoron – A mix of five spices, popular in Bengali cooking.

Paneer – A cheese made from boiling milk and an acid (usually – and hopefully – lemon juice). The whey is scraped off and pressed into a block through cloth to extract the moisture; it is then cut into cubes for cooking. It has a very mild taste.

Paratha – This bread is similar to a chapati but is cooked with butter and layered to give a flaky texture. Sometimes served stuffed with vegetables or minced meat.

Pasanda – This is a mild dish containing ground almonds, cardamom pods, puréed tomatoes and cream. In practice in many restaurants it is only distinguishable from a korma by virtue of the flaked almond garnish.

Patia – A sweet and sour fish dish cooked in a heavy vinegar sauce that some restaurants offer in chicken and lamb versions. Usually garnished with fried tomatoes.

Phall – An incredibly hot curry. Designed to be painful!

Pilau rice – Rice flavoured with spices and ghee, sometimes also dyed for added entertainment.

Poppadom – A curry-house favourite. These are deep fried wafers made of lentil flour. Served warm with pickles and chutneys, they are a way of keeping customers happy when the kitchen is busy.

Puri – Deep-fried bread served hot and puffed up.

Raita – Chopped vegetables in seasoned yoghurt.

Rogan josh – This classic Kashmiri dish translates literally as 'red meat'. The colour was traditionally derived from Kashmiri chillies, but is now usually provided by tomatoes. It should be medium hot.

Roti – A type of griddle-cooked flat bread.

Saag – Saag refers to any green-leafed vegetable, but is usually taken to mean spinach.

Samosa – Triangular deep-fried pastries filled with spiced vegetables or minced lamb.

Seekh kebab – A sausage-shaped kebab made with spicy minced lamb. Can be cooked in a tandoor or char-grilled.

Shakarkand – A sweet potato.

Shashlik – A kebab made of marinated chunks of meat (or occasionally, vegetables) on a skewer with pieces of onion, pepper and tomato. Can be cooked in a tandoor or char-grilled.

Snake bean – As the name suggests, these beans can be several feet long. They absorb flavour well and are a good addition to curries.

Surmai – Also known as kingfish, or king mackerel, this is now widely available in Indian grocery stores.

Taro – A thick-skinned tuber, it looks a little bit like a yam.

Tava – A heavy flat frying pan.

Thali – A platter (traditionally silver but now usually steel) holding several small bowls with different dishes in them. A complete meal with rice, bread, curry, pickles and chutneys.

Tiffin – Lunch.

Tikka – This just means little pieces.

Tinda – A small squash that resembles a yellow tomato. Often served stuffed with other vegetables or paneer.

Tindoori – A small cucumber. It's very pretty but lacking in much flavour of its own.

Urad – A white dhal made of split beans.

Vada – Deep-fried patties made from various dhals.

Vindaloo – Traditionally this was a Goan pork dish (its name comes from its two of its ingredients: vinho (wine or wine vinegar) and alhos (garlic). It's unlikely that any curry house serves authentic vindaloo as the chances are that a Muslim chef would be unwilling to cook pork. The vindaloos on most menus will have absolutely nothing in common with the original and it has just become a term for a very hot curry.

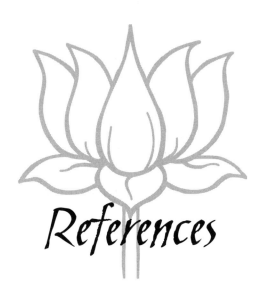

References

I have relied on many sources for some of the information used in this book. For those interested in further study in this area, I recommend the books on this informal list.

Yousuf Chowdhury, *The Roots And Tales of the Bangladeshi Settlers*, published in 1993 by the Sylheti Social History Group. A fount of detail about the lives of the Sylheti community both in Bangladesh, in transit and in Britain. This is a very personal, very moving and highly entertaining account of the realities of mass migration.

Jennifer Brennan, *Curries and Bugles*, published in 2000 by Periplus Editions (HK) Ltd. An affectionate memoir of her childhood in Raj-era India married with plenty of recipes.

Christina Hardyment, *Slice of Life*, published in 1995 by the BBC. This book accompanied a TV series about British culinary habits and has a very useful chapter about the 'currification' of our diet.

Edwina Ehrman, Hazel Forsyth, Lucy Peltz and Cathy Ross, *London Eats Out*, published in 1999 by the Museum of London. This records the restaurant business from the sixteenth to the twentieth centuries.

Rozina Visram, *Asians In Britain, 400 Years of History*, published in 2002 by Pluto Press. An extremely thorough history of Asian immigration to Britain.

K.T. Achaya, *A Historical Dictionary of Indian Food*, published in 1998 by Oxford University Press.

Linda Bladholm, *The Indian Grocery Store Demystified*, published in 2000 by Renaissance Books. Everything you ever wanted to know about the mysterious wares in Indian grocers.

Andrew Dalby, *Dangerous Tastes*, published in 2000 by the University of California Press. An incredibly detailed history of spices.

Shrabani Basu, *Curry in the Crown*, published in 1999 by Harper Collins.

Denys Forrest, *The Oriental, Life Story of a West End Club*, published in 1968 by BT Batsford Ltd.

Archie Baron, *An Indian Affair*, published in 2001 by Channel 4 Books.

Michael H Fisher (ed), *The Travels of Dean Mahomet*, published in 1997 by the University of California Press.

Peter and Colleen Grove, *Curry and Spice and All Things Nice*, published online at www.menu2menu.co.uk.

Index

Chapman, Pat 137
Chattwell, DS 113–14
chefs 90–1, 226, 228–9
  see also under names
chicken tikka masala 3, 4, 49, 112, 132, 135–8,
  213, 240
chilli 34
chilli pepper 21, 165–6
Chirag 243
Chor Bizarre 195
Chowdhury, A.H. 104, 105, 109–11, 141
Chowdhury, Bazlur 100–1, 102, 103, 109,
  111–12, 130, 133, 230
Chowdhury, Yousuf 89, 114–15
Chutney Mary 84, 184, 195, 208, 210, 211, 224
cilantro 180
cinnamon 10–11, 25, 75–7
Cinnamon Club 1, 87, 131, 136, 161, 174, 201,
  207, 213, 217, 226
Clarke, John 159, 163
Clive, Robert (Clive of India) 51
cloves 25, 95–7
Cobra 192–4, 209–10, 215
Coen, Jan Pieterszoon 24
Columbus, Christopher 3, 6, 9, 21, 22
Complete Indian Housekeeper and Cook, The 55
Connolly, Billy 164
Conran, Sir Terence 206
Cook, Robin 136
coriander 21, 25, 120, 167–8, 179–81
Coriander Club 170
Cornershop 215
Cradock, Fanny 85
Cradock, Johnny 85
Cross and Blackwell's of Soho Square 70
cumin 13, 25, 36, 219–20
Curry Club 26, 137
'Curry Hell' competition 143
curry powder 69–73

da Gama, Vasco 17, 18, 20, 21, 22
Dalby, Andrew 179
Daly, Mary 65
Deb, Dr 91
Deep Foods 243
Delhi, cuisine of 260
Deya 206
Dhillon, Parmjit 169–70
Dilkush (Windmill St) 88, 92
Dioscorides 30, 219
dizzycorn 181
Dutch East India Company 20, 23–5, 96
Dwarkadas, Nitisen 80–1

East India Company 25–6, 50–2, 59, 64–5
Eau de Carnes 180
Elizabeth I, Queen 49–50
Empire Exhibition (1938) 91
etymology of curry 25–7
Europe, curry in 237–40

false saffron *see* turmeric
farming 171–2
Fat Les 144
fennel 13, 37, 147–9
fenugreek 12, 16, 197–9
Fidle, G. 71
Findus 157, 158
Fisher, Michael 65
Food Service Intelligence 137
Forme of Cury, The 25
Forster, E.M. 131
Francatelli, Charles Elme 69
France, curry in 239–40
frankincense 13
frozen food 44, 157–8, 243

galangal 25, 29
Galloping Gourmet 160
Gandhi, Indira 242
Gaylord (Mortimer St) 134, 207
Gaylord Group 184, 195
General Bilimoria 215
George IV 67, 68
Gill, Charan 142, 144, 196, 226, 227
ginger 16, 25, 29–31
Glasse, Hannah 63–4
Goa, cuisine of 42, 132, 238–9, 260–1
Goodness Gracious Me 215–16
Goush, Nogandro 88
Grassroots Food Network 171
Green Guru frozen meals 243
Guild of Bangladeshi Restaurateurs 132
Gujarati cuisine 261–2
Gupta, K.N. Das 80
Gupta, Yogen 239

Halal meat 114–15
Hale and Fleming of the Poultry, Messrs 70
Haque, Jobbul 88
Haridas, T. 196
Harlequin Group 184, 196, 227–8
Harpatta 13
health and safety requirements 186, 230–1
Herodotus 10–11, 75
Hertodt, Johann 254
Hindostanee Coffee House 65, 66–9, 202, 206
Hippalus 16
Hippocrates 219
Hirst, Damien 144
Holzman, James M. 60
Hom, Ken 187
Hookah Club, The 67
Hooton-Smith, E. 86
Horizons 137
House of Spices 243
HP Foods group 114, 168
Hussein, Lutfun 170

Ibn Batûtâ 14, 15, 76
ibn Wâsif-Shâh, Ibrâhîm 96